The Gothic Text

THE GOTHIC TEXT

Marshall Brown

STANFORD UNIVERSITY PRESS
STANFORD, CALIFORNIA
2005

Stanford University Press
Stanford, California

Printed in the United States of America
on acid-free, archival-quality paper

Designed and typeset by Yvonne Tsang of
Wilsted & Taylor Publishing Services in 11/14 Sabon

Library of Congress Cataloging-in-Publication Data

Brown, Marshall
The Gothic text / Marshall Brown.
p. cm.
Includes bibliographical references and index.
ISBN 0-8047-3912-9 (cloth : alk. paper)
1. Horror tales—History and criticism.
2. Gothic revival (Literature) I. Title.
PN3435.B78 2005
809'.9164—dc22
2004003969

Original Printing 2005

Last figure below indicates year of this printing:
14   13   12   11   10   09   08   07   06   05

To my family, near and far.

CONTENTS

PREFACE

Horace counsels cellaring one's writings for nine years. Portions of this book have more than doubled the Horatian term. While the delay is not intrinsically either good or bad, it does yield a different kind of book from one written at fever pitch. My initial notion was that Kant and the gothic together discovered a new dimension of human consciousness. Internal differentiation and chance encounter have both played their part in ramifying a text that now feels to me something between an organism and a construction. Consequently, this preface will offer both a genetic and a structural overview of the book to follow.

Early on in that long period, I began a chapter about *The Castle of Otranto* for my book *Preromanticism*. That book concerns milestones of literary composition from the 1740s through Wordsworth. Walpole's little novel was surely a milestone, among the most eccentric of its era's many oddities. Reading for form, I was struck by its early and extensive use of indirect discourse. I tried pairing Walpole's unprecedented, and seemingly unremarked, focus on his characters' thoughts with the great philosophical exploration of consciousness in the work of Immanuel Kant. Those two bachelors seem an odd couple. Yet they weren't so far apart in age (Kant was seven years younger) or in literary predilections (Kant's taste ran to Pope and the

German Thomson imitators), and it was suggestive that Kant's own most eccentric work, "Dreams of a Ghost-Seer," followed *Otranto* by not much over a year, and that (as K. K. Mehrotra showed long ago) *Otranto* peaked in popularity as a psychological novel in the 1780s, the decade of Kant's Critiques. The Critiques both construct and keep at bay an imagined, "transcendental" realm that haunts the borders of our experience. As I say in my introductory fantasia (Chapter 2 below, which weaves together motifs from later in the book), it doesn't seem a great leap from the transcendental to the supernatural, let alone from the noumenal to the numinous. With these initial ideas, the planned *Otranto* chapter had already grown too large to be included in *Preromanticism* and became instead the germ of *The Gothic Text*.

Projecting Walpole into the philosophical future proved to be a double endeavor: I had to bring Kant to the gothic and the gothic to Kant. This meant reading around the edges of Kant's texts, looking for keys to a chamber he wanted to keep locked. That in turn led to actual research, as I explored the image and reception of Kant in the psychology of his day. It turned out that he looked to his medical contemporaries and followers much the way he looked to me but has never looked to philosophers, as a bold yet guarded explorer of the unknown. Meanwhile, the conjuncture of Walpole and Kant, if it had any utility, would shed light on the rendition of consciousness in the gothic novels of the romantic period. To see why Walpole mattered to this history, and why Kant matters to Walpole, it was necessary to consider structures of thought and consciousness in the main line of gothic fiction. What Walpole began found its meaning in the uses to which later writers put it.

The phenomenon of *The Castle of Otranto* still remained puzzling. To be sure, Kant, too, kept his genius bottled up until late in life, but eventually it poured out. Walpole, as an artist, neither prepared for nor continued his great success. His one-time literary achievement is typically accounted a stroke of luck, and not very good luck at that. Yet it must surely have arisen from something. I have always believed that to understand a work of art, one must be able to see it at work, layering its moments of innovation on top of familiar strat-

egies. But where is one to look for the roots of a wayward, even va-
grant creation?

Walpole's inspiration turned out to lie right on the surface. Seeking secrets, historians of literature have found mysteries. There were
no novels like *Otranto*. But Walpole's interests, plain as day, lay in the
theater. His novel is built on a dramatic plan, and its closest models
—numerous models—come from the early-eighteenth-century playhouse. The works are no longer well known, but (unlike the works of
Kant's commentators) they are mostly not hard to locate, and they
illuminate the subbasement of romantic conceptions of the ego. By
carefully sifting what emerges in his book, we can cast new light on
Walpole's accomplishment, and through him on the meaning of the
gothic novel and on the romantic achievement all the way to Freud (a
link well made by David Morris in "Gothic Sublimity").

Nearly two decades ago, though still not even half done, my study
of Kant and the gothic novel had already grown too big for its prero-
mantic breeches. In the meantime, critical books on the gothic novel
have flooded in. They examine gender and politics, domesticity and
tyranny, reception and influences (from science in particular). All are
studies of encounter. They read the gothic novels in the light of the society of their day, hence not as daydreamy recreations to immerse oneself in privately, nor as serious inquiries into and models of the mind.
Understandably, the critics seize upon highlights and harvest much
insight thereby. Yet the better, and better known, romantic gothic
novels are not thrillers; one slogs to the occasional fireworks through
marshlands of descriptive or even analytical prose. Reading the novels
slowly, I became increasingly absorbed by the murky expanses where
the characters wait for the other shoe to fall. They seem to me far
more speculative constructs than appears from most of the writing
about them (with the notable exception of some of the post-Freudian,
deconstructive studies of particular novels or themes). All readings
are partial; I found myself more partial to the words actually filling
the pages than to the incidents that only intermittently spark them or
to the fantasies buried beneath.

Having examined the sources of the gothic in this book's first part
(the second written) and, in Parts II and III, its philosophical reso-

nances, I turn in the fourth part to the gothic novels as writings. In these chapters I try to take seriously the artistry of Ann Radcliffe and of Mary Shelley. I consider how gothic style produces its effects in the work of Radcliffe, as the writer who forged the manner out of Walpole's base metal, and then I examine how *Frankenstein*, the most tightly wound of the gothic novels, is composed. In 1800, as now, there were many bad ghost stories, often silly in the *Northanger Abbey* vein rather than scary, contrived rather than haunting. Having considered what kind of meditation the best gothic novels practice, in these chapters I examine what distinguishes a gothic novel from a mere supernatural diversion. Since a craft cannot be divorced from its materials and its purposes, these chapters continue my book's consideration of gothic meanings, insofar as they arise from technique rather than imagination.

Finally, if the gothic advanced from its forebears, and if its meaning emerges from an intentional structure, it also has a momentum beyond itself. One heir to the romantic gothic is of course the Victorian sensation novel, followed by the Edwardian supernatural romance. But by exploring the hidden reaches of consciousness, the gothic promotes understanding and not just a more exciting mystification. At the end of this book, therefore—following up some suggestions in the introduction—I turn to Goethe's *Faust*, a play that ought to have been gothic but isn't, in order to ask where the gothic leaves off, and where it leaves us in doing so.

The Gothic Text, then, while it contains the study of Kant and the gothic novel that I once envisioned, goes far beyond it. What unifies the book is my desire to take the gothic enterprise literally. As I say again at the beginning of the *Frankenstein* chapter (Chapter 15), my concern is not what transcendental fictions show us about daily or historical existence but what they show us about the transcendental dimensions of experience. Style and form, origin and ideas come together in an identity that has been misrecognized because it wears its depths on its sleeve. I have come to feel these works deserve and repay close attention. To highlight that conviction, I have abandoned my numerous working titles for the simpler and franker one that now appears on the cover.

Since even the best gothic novels are formulaic, I discuss in depth only a limited number here. But many others that I mention merely in passing could have been studied. (Some other examples, briefly treated, can be found in my essay "Philosophy and the Gothic.") In my experience of reading and teaching, the scrutiny of mind and consciousness really does pervade the genre; consequently, the kinds of analysis I offer can easily be extended to numerous works of the period, with ever varying but not dramatically different results.

Although my focus here is restricted to a relatively few works, I have made a point of including fiction from France, Germany, and Russia in the mix. My original goal in *The Gothic Text* was to illuminate connections between English novels and German philosophy and psychology—a project that naturally becomes more palatable if Continental novels are kept in view. Among them are marvelous works that it is a shame to overlook. But beyond tactical utility for the argument and subjective judgments of quality, it is useful simply to recognize the breadth of the romantic gothic endeavor. The gothic novel was the one truly international literary mode remaining as Europe entered its great era of nationalism. As I stress in "Three Theses on Gothic Fiction" (Chapter 1), the gothic was a Western cultural universal in the romantic period, and that fact in itself licenses a reading of gothic fiction in terms of abstractions rather than particular situations.

Each chapter or section strikes a different balance among my several interests: literary history, history of ideas, form, style, and ideology. I hope that readers will welcome the variety of approaches. At the same time, I hope that the overarching thrust of the book will be clear. To that end, I complement the account I have given of the growth of my manuscript with a conspectus of the argument.

Initially a diversion for the culture in which it took shape, the gothic novel over the course of several decades became an enterprise. Writing a new novel always meant exploiting the genre by means of its formulas; in the important cases it meant exploring the genre as well. In the fantasy worlds of the gothic, remote from ordinary experience, material existence plays a secondary role. Gothic characters rarely eat or work; the economic circumstances in Godwin's *St Leon* and the dinner scene in Balzac's *The Wild Ass's Skin* are, in generic terms, transitory contaminations. From the start in Walpole, consequently, the gothic found the essence of humanity in the mind. Perception and imagination are the focal issues. How that came to pass, as an almost casual result of Walpole's self-enclosed dilettantism, is the subject of my analysis of his novel.

The contents and operations of the mind are, however, hardly at issue yet in Walpole. Subsequent novelists explore them in diverse ways. While most critics of the gothic novel have highlighted social, political, and sexual themes reflected in the novels, in fact few gothic novelists were serious thinkers, and those who were wrote their finest novels early in their careers. Consequently, my readings approach the gothic preoccupation with the mental on a general level, transcending specificities of situation and historical location. As their chaotic events unfold, the novels return insistently to problems of orientation in time and place, to coherence of experience in a world of magic or mystery, to participation in a community under the threat of isolation—in short, to the various continuities of meaning that stabilize a world at risk. I analyze what the novels imagine and represent in the terms of a different though contemporaneous discourse, originating in or deriving from the writings of Kant. German romantic writers on the medical and psychological sciences of mind construct an understanding of the problems of consciousness readily applicable to the situations of gothic fiction, and indeed directly adopted by some Continental novelists. In a series of readings beginning with novels explicitly in the orbit of German speculative thought, I survey representative forms of the gothic exploration of experience, differing in their manifestations and emphases while uniting in their fundamental impulse.

Originally my aim was to establish the pertinence of philosophical analysis and to characterize the formal or constructive drive within the gothic enterprise. But form, while significant, is never self-sufficient. If a structure is created, a meaning comes to inhabit it. As I demonstrate within the survey of psychology in the wake of Kant, once a transcendental domain is imagined, and no matter how empty and negative its conception initially is, an impulse begins to give it a local habitation and a name. The chapters on *The Italian* and *Frankenstein* resume issues of sensibility that emerge throughout the earlier chapters—the frivolous play of gothicism, the self-absorption, the child's perspective—and show how these became significant concerns of value, not just of form and motif. In Radcliffe automatic writing—formula and cliché—gathers psychic energy as it becomes a motivating shell. In my reading (as in that of many of her contemporaries), Radcliffe's popular landscape descriptions trump her crude narration. Background becomes foreground so as to sketch out a transformed picture of psychic mechanisms of self-projection and defense. As a plot-writer, she has always seemed at best typical of a group, and as a crafter of sentences perhaps even less than that. She achieved her singular reputation, I claim, by putting the formal structures of gothic style in the service of a strikingly new set of personality mechanisms, not fully theorized before Freud. For her part, Shelley, a well-connected and brainy writer, has won ample praise, but typically it situates her in proximity to intellectual currents of her day. I see her instead as having intuited with peculiar insight how the childishness of the gothic impels a view of childhood that seems (at least so far as scholarship on the history of childhood goes) unique in its time. And even more emphatically than *The Italian*, *Frankenstein* finds the terms for a final understanding—at least with regard to this topic—in the work of Freud. These authors are of their time in their choice of literary modes, but strikingly new in the ways they develop them.

My epilogue, finally, echoes many previous epilogues to the gothic in suggesting how the gothic feeds into broader, more public, and more experiential concerns. That nineteenth-century realism draws on the gothic will not be news. But it is not normally recognized that the greatest literary work of modern times actualizes the insights of the gothic. As a sequel to my study of the thrust of the gothic form, the discussion of *Faust* (in which my wife has joined me) may suggest additional dimensions of gothic realism. Gothic novels were not just escapist; they led their readers to a new anthropology. It would take a different book to chart the channels of the abundant delta created by the gothic stream; but our study of *Faust* should at least indicate the direction of flow.

Two topics remain to be discussed. The first is convergence. What does it mean to claim that gothic novels—British gothic novels above all—and German philosophy illuminate one another? How can categories and analyses from one domain legitimately be introduced into an alien domain? Some readers of my work have been concerned about the disparity of the materials with which it operates. Surely one response lies in simple pragmatism: if the examination is clear, the source of its terms should not matter. Certainly a critic willing to "apply" a modern theorist to old works should be untroubled if another critic's theorist happens to come from the writers' contemporaries. Nor is my contextualizing inherently freer than that of many historical critics nowadays. Do we know how many conduct books Jane Austen or Emily Brontë read? How much economic theory Fielding perused? How many colonial reports Pope digested? Some certainly, in each case, but it is impractical and implausible to limit contextual studies to documented authorial sources. Surely it is hard to imagine Kant reading many gothic novels, but then it remains uncertain even how much of Hume he may have read, and he certainly was informed about the mystic Swedenborg and regularly corresponded with some of the figures whose responses to him I discuss. And it is hard to imagine that Kant and many of his younger contemporaries had *not* read Schiller's *Ghost-Seer*. British novelists probably had no direct knowledge of Kant but were in varying degrees aware of empiricist and idealist currents in medical literature and undoubtedly aware of devotional tracts like Zimmermann's *Solitude*, which I cite in connection with Ann Radcliffe. However indirect its sources, a well-established image of Kant was reflected, for instance, in an oft-cited passage in Thomas Love Peacock's *Nightmare Abbey* describing the Coleridge figure, named Flosky:

> He lived in the midst of that visionary world in which nothing is but what is not. He dreamed with his eyes open, and saw ghosts dancing round him at noontide. He had been in his youth an enthusiast for liberty, and had hailed the dawn of the French Revolution as the promise of a day that was to banish war and slavery, and every form of vice and misery, from the face of the earth. . . . He plunged into the central opacity of

Kantian metaphysics, and lay *perdu* several years in transcendental darkness, till the common daylight of common-sense became intolerable to his eyes.   (Peacock, *"Headlong Hall" and "Nightmare Abbey,"* 144–45)

Terms like "cause," "time," and "sleep" are in everyday usage and ubiquitous in the novels I discuss, and it seems to me beyond question that they could have been used consistently and purposefully and that it is legitimate to compare and contrast them with their equivalents in Kant.

So far, so good. But my claim that the gothic and Kant converge goes beyond comparison and contrast. In the later romantics it is doc-umentable that Hoffmann and Balzac, along with Poe and others whom I don't discuss in this book, drew explicitly and in some detail on high or middling philosophical tracts. And my study of the Kant-ian milieu stands or falls on explicit documentation of gothic tenden-cies in his texts and their immediate reception. That section, whether surprising or not, whether correct or not, operates as pure intellectual history. There remains, then, chiefly the contention that Radcliffe, Shelley, Maturin, and their ilk could be regarded as thinkers, albeit in an imaginative vein, who might even have contributed significantly to major currents of ideas in their period. Isn't it irresponsible to name them in the same breath with Kant? Doesn't doing so illicitly exalt them and impertinently debase him, denaturing both? To those ques-tions I answer, simply, no. A level playing field belongs here, as it does in the many other kinds of contextual study that have currency today. Philosophers do imagine; novelists do think; and even if European culture was less international around 1800 than it had been earlier, it retained more than enough lines of communication for us to re-gard the diverse literary and philosophical explorations of mind as a shared enterprise. The writers in question did not all agree, of course, but they did share common questions for debate and inquiry even across the English Channel, at least within the decades-long time frame encompassed by this book.

The second and more problematic aspect of the book is my refusal to confine the significance of authors to their own time. Since even be-fore *Preromanticism*, I have spoken out in favor of teleological understandings. It seems wrong to me to limit the meaning of either Kant or Radcliffe to the thoughts they knew how to express compactly or the accomplishments they felt settled in. A work of consequence is measured by its consequentiality: its innovations with respect to predecessors and its entailments upon successors. The imagination is always looking ahead, trying to make a mark on posterity. Recent rehabilitations and recoveries of women writers of the past acknowledge teleology implicitly and sometimes explicitly: we see the writers as mattering to our understanding of their time in the light of their importance to us. We read them because their present speaks to its future, which is our present—and it does so, in some cases, across a gulf of long-standing neglect or ignorance. At least in some of its varieties, the reader-response mode of reading likewise recognized the orientation of writing toward the future, though it was limited by restrictive canons of evidence. Even a contemporary resonance is a teleology, as one really ought not to need to say. But the larger consequences emerge more gradually and reverberate further in time.

But if my advocacy of teleology is really nothing more than a commitment to enduring freshness, it has been misunderstood as slighting the accomplishments of great writers and thinkers. Did they not have value in themselves, beyond or in advance of what future readers made of them? Did they know less well what they said and meant than the often lesser folk of later times? Did they not grow out of and address themselves more consciously and visibly to their predecessors than to the unknown races of later years? The last question has been put directly to *Preromanticism* by David Fairer, in a splendid essay on Wordsworth and the school of Warton. The accomplishment of "Tintern Abbey," he argues, is to sum up the intuitions, insights, and even phrasings of the many poets in whom Wordsworth was immersed. Poetry absorbs and consolidates and thereby creates an imaginary community, on the model of an imaginary nation. Fairer's recovery of this context for Wordsworth is precious. Yet I do not find Wordsworth strongest and most distinctive when he is writing as a member of a group. The Wordsworth who echoes others is not the poet whose lines Coleridge would have recognized running wild in the desert. Even when he echoes himself, Wordsworth is not his true—that is, his most original—self. As I noted in *Preromanticism*, Wordsworth absorbs a line of "Tintern Abbey," "Once again I hear these waters rolling with a soft inland murmur," into a line of *The Excursion*, "Feebly it tinkled with an earthy sound." No one, I dare to assert, would prefer the later, retrospective version.

The confusion lies in equating value with accomplishment. I claim that the significance of an imaginative creation lies always ahead of it, not in some intrinsic perfection. While I might hesitate with Milton, or Dante, or Goethe (though Goethe withheld the bulk of *Faust* to be read and appreciated after his death), I would not hesitate with most of the writers in *Preromanticism*—Goldsmith, Sheridan, Sterne, and the others—to assert that their writings meant more than they realized. They certainly meant more than their contemporary Samuel Johnson was ever willing to concede. *Preromanticism* culminates, however, not in high romanticism but in an unknown late sonnet by Wordsworth. Much as I love "Mark the Concent'red Hazels," not even I would prefer it to *any* of the earlier texts my book studies. This really is a sonnet that looks backward; it consolidates earlier accomplishments and helps us to recognize and integrate them. In that sense, the one sonnet is the goal of preromanticism, or at least of *Preromanticism*. Value, however, lies in works that have not yet reached their goal but instead have opened new paths, saying what has never been said before, imagining what could not yet be formulated. Not even Kant was altogether satisfied with his formulations; he rewrote major portions of the *Critique of Pure Reason*, and perhaps no subsequent reader has found that book perfect. Its significance lies in what it enabled its future readers to see, in what arguments it provoked, and—if I may believe my own upcoming arguments—in what dreams it stimulated. A teleology is not a putdown; to say that later writings unveil new insights and values within a text is not to denigrate it. Indeed, it is inherent in my notion of teleology that it is not statically telic. Seeking distances, a teleology does not come to rest but instead finds in any goal we posit for it only a temporary respite.

In that spirit, I have found myself turning in this book repeatedly to Freud's texts as resting places for romantic values. Freud's immersion in romantic fiction is well known, and I imagine that some readers may find him less out of place than Kant in a study of gothic novels. But Kant, whom I have studied (though not, certainly, as a professional philosopher), is generative in this book, while Freud, whom I have merely and rather casually read, is more nearly a figure of convenience. So was it with "Mark the Concent'red Hazels," and so it is with teleological goals. The last thing a teleological reading envisions is a single point-goal.

Teleology means looking forward, not stopping. The resting places of my books are way stations of futurity, not—I cannot repeat too often—final repositories of value, let alone definitive truth. So long as a work's value endures, it will continue to find new receptors, new goals. Teleology does not singularize and reduce; it pluralizes and opens. And that, to return to the questions evoked in the previous paragraphs, is because the values of the imagination outsoar and outlast the powers of definition. Comprehending the indefinite is the challenge of literary criticism.

Portions of this book have appeared in print. The introductory chapter appeared in approximately the same form in Italian under the title "Kant e i demoni della notte," trans. Daniela Carpi, *Studi di estetica* 12 (1984): 155–65. The paragraph about Tieck's *William Lovell* is drawn from a review essay, "Gothic Readers versus Gothic Writers," *Eighteenth-Century Studies* 35 (2002): 615–22. Much of the documentation of Kant's reputation was published as "Kant and the Doctors," *Bucknell Review* 39 (1996): 151–69. Pieces of an essay in which I first tried out my approach, "A Philosophical View of the Gothic Novel," *Studies in Romanticism* 26 (1987): 275–301, reappear in this preface, in the discussion of the *Critique of Pure Reason*, and as part of the reading of *Melmoth the Wanderer*. (I have not, however, reused the very preliminary reading of *Frankenstein* at the center of that essay.) Excerpts from my chapter on Radcliffe's clichés appeared in Italian as "I paesaggi di Ann Radcliffe: In difesa del cliché," *Parametro*, no. 245 (May/June 2003): 60–61. "*Frankenstein*: A Child's Tale" was published in *Novel* 36 (2003): 145–75; Nancy Armstrong's editorial intervention pointed it in the right direction. The chapter on *Faust* that concludes this book originated as "*Faust* and the Gothic Novel," written together with my wife, Jane (hence the first-person plural pronouns, retained in this book), and appeared in *Interpreting Goethe's "Faust" Today*, ed. Jane K. Brown et al. (Columbia, S.C.: Camden House, 1994), 68–80. The quotation from Herder's letters about Kant's onanism also appears in *Preromanticism* and is the hinge between the two books.

How does one give adequate thanks for an intermittent, decades-long project? *The Castle of Otranto* was the topic of one of my first conference papers, which I presented at an MLA conference in a session chaired by Ed Block; in another guise, also in the early 1980s, that paper led to my acquaintance with Mona Modiano and thus eventually to my current position. Subsequently I had many opportunities to try out most segments of this book at conferences and lectures, most importantly a week-long series of talks at the University of Bologna, hosted by a great gothicist, Giovanna Franci. A faculty fellowship from the University of Colorado enabled me to draft much of what has become the center of this book, and a small grant from the same institution sent me off to the National Library of Medicine. More recently, fellowships from the National Endowment for the Humanities, the Woodrow Wilson International Center for Scholars, the Deutsche Forschungsgemeinschaft (under the generous sponsorship of Prof. Herbert Grabes), and the Walter Chapin Simpson Center for the Humanities at the University of Washington freed more time for this project and others. I am also indebted to libraries in the U.S., starting with the wonderful Hoose Library of philosophy at the University of Southern California, and to collections in Münster, Munich, and Tübingen, where I pursued my passion for post-Kantian arcana, and to my home libraries, especially at the University of Colorado and the University of Washington, for much generous assistance. Even more than to institutions and collections, I am indebted to many undergraduate and graduate students, in Colorado, Washington, and Tübingen, with whom I could not only pursue but also share my passions. And then, too, as always, how many friends and casual acquaintances have discussed things gothic, answered questions, read drafts? I no longer know, though I can never forget that anything philosophically acceptable I may chance to have said about Kant derives from some relentless critiques by Marjorie Grene, and some needed encouragement from Berel Lang. For this book, Jane doesn't get the usual sort of heartfelt thanks for stimulation and love because she didn't just back it up; she actually wrote part of it. I no longer know which pages of the *Faust* chapter are hers and which are mine: it is a product "of neither, and of both at once."

Nancy Atkinson Young copyedited this book, as she did my previous one. She rubs tirelessly with both sandpaper and a soft cloth; her ministrations could turn wormwood into mahogany. Ivan Kidoguchi shared proofreading woes; Caitlin Rippey actually volunteered to prepare the index.

My dedication is a singular plural. Disproving gothic example and Tolstoyan precept, I am blessed with a family that finds many and idiosyncratic ways to happiness. My family is domestic, filial, fraternal, lateral, transverse. It is enriched by hilarity, warmth, companionship, and brilliances I can only envy, not emulate. And, even after their death, it is held together by parents whose light shone into their late eighties equally on their professional associates, their many devoted friends, and their relatives. Everyone should be so fortunate in their ghosts.

A NOTE ON SOURCES

While I have tried to acknowledge the work of the now many other scholars working on the gothic novel, at the request of my wonderful editor Helen Tartar, whose departure from Stanford University Press I regret as much as do countless others, I have also generally limited citations, especially of articles, to the most pertinent or most valuable ones. The version of the *Frankenstein* chapter published in *Novel* shows what a more fully documented investigation might look like. In the quotations, all translations not otherwise cited are my own, while all italics not specifically exempted represent emphasis in the original texts. In many cases I cite passages by standard divisions (e.g., book and chapter numbers), followed by a semicolon and page numbers. For a few key works, page references are given for both original-language editions and English translations; except for *La Princesse de Clèves*, the quotations come from the translations, modified only where it seemed essential. Kant's works are cited in the conventional system, by page numbers in the first (A) or second (B) edition of each work. *Faust* is cited by line number. Full information on sources cited parenthetically in the text is provided in the bibliography.

The Gothic Text

Three Theses on Gothic Fiction

URING THE ROMANTIC DECADES, gothic fiction flourished not only in Great Britain and the United States but throughout much of Europe. Works such as Honoré de Balzac's *Wild Ass's Skin*, E. T. A. Hoffmann's *Devil's Elixirs*, and numerous tales by Tieck, Kleist, Nodier, Pushkin, and Poe, for example, are exemplars as fine as any written in Britain. Given the international compass on the romantic gothic, it is perhaps surprising that scholarship of the genre has been largely parochial, confining itself to the literature written within specific national or linguistic borders. Certainly exceptions exist, most notably Mario Praz's classic study of the heritage of Marquis de Sade, *The Romantic Agony* (first published in Italian as *La Morte, la carne e la diavola* [Death, Flesh, and the Devil]), which examines works produced throughout the major literatures of Europe. But for the most part, books on the gothic, especially those by Anglo-American scholars, remain sturdily monoglot in their choice of subject texts.[1] At best, English-speaking critics may nod toward German influence, idealist philosophy, or the French Revolution. But one looks long and hard for scholarly recognition of the romantic gothic as a common enterprise developed by an international community of writers.

To some extent this scholarly reticence about the romantic gothic

is understandable. The romantic period was an age of growing nationalism, which bred an attendant sense of cultural separation. We
take it for granted that Enlightenment artists of lasting importance
were known across Europe: Mme de La Fayette, Daniel Defoe, Samuel Richardson, Henry Fielding, Jean-Jacques Rousseau, Laurence
Sterne, Johann Wolfgang Goethe, and many others were European
novelists, not just national ones; Nicholas-Despréaux Boileau, Alexander Pope, Matthew Prior, James Thomson, Edward Young, Thomas
Gray, Voltaire, and many others (though not yet Dryden) were European poets; Handel was trilingual and tricultural, and Haydn and
Mozart garnered commissions and celebrity both at home and
abroad. But after the revolutions, things changed. William Wordsworth and Jane Austen are pretty exclusively national treasures; likewise Friedrich Hölderlin, Jean Paul (J. P. F. Richter), Heinrich von
Kleist, Novalis (Friedrich von Hardenberg), and Joseph von Eichendorff. Many great writers of the romantic era remain mostly untrans-
lated to this day. Immanuel Kant and G. W. F. Hegel swept intellectual
Germany off its feet with astonishing rapidity; they were much slower
to penetrate abroad than had been their predecessors John Locke, David Hume, and the philosophes. Romantic paintings rarely crossed
the Channel or the Rhine. For Beethoven, triumph meant Austria; for
Rossini, Italy and, fitfully, France. Of course there were others of the
romantic era—Goethe (in some of his works), Sir Walter Scott, eventually Edgar Allan Poe—who became international darlings, but they
appear to have been exceptions and no longer represented the norm or
the goal of artists, generally speaking.

Yet the gothic (together with its dramatic counterpart, the melo-
drama) remains the one form of literary endeavor that was not then
and should not now be divided into national schools. Gothic fiction
began unequivocally in England, with Horace Walpole's *The Castle
of Otranto*, but it is a work that bears its internationalism in its title
and in its original preface. (Imagine Austen setting a novel abroad,
even fancifully. Consider what happened to Scott's work when he
did.) William Beckford, Ann Radcliffe, and Monk (Matthew G.)
Lewis were European or even global in their settings, as in their repu-

tations (and, in the men's case, in their formation as well). Scott's folk magicians find their original inspirations in German ballads; Wordsworth blames the depraved taste for sensationalism on German writers; Mary Shelley was inspired to write *Frankenstein* after reading German ghost stories in French translation; Charles Robert Maturin's devil ranges the world; Charlotte Brontë's madwoman came from across the seas; Hoffmann and Eichendorff at times transported their wonders to a fantastic Italy or (in Eichendorff's case) to mysterious oceans. Even Balzac travels abroad for some of his gothic realms—setting *Seraphita* in Norway, "Jesus Christ in Flanders" in the Low Countries, "Massimilla Doni" and the inserted tale in "Sarrasine" in Italy; and drawing upon a seething Italy for the background of "Sarrasine" and an inscrutable Irish provenance for "Melmoth Reconciled"—because the gothic would dwindle into normality in the French bureaucracy. In an uncharacteristically uneven recent essay, Terry Castle has claimed, "To affirm, with Addison, that there is something distinctively 'British' about the Gothic mode is undoubtedly true," but to my mind her claim is undoubtedly false.[2]

In this book I have sought to respect the international character of the mode, using examples from several non-English-speaking nations in addition to those from Great Britain and the U.S. Romantic fiction from the Continent does substantially alter the balance of what one sees in the gothic. It is from the experience of reading romantic-era gothic fiction in its broad extent that I propose the three theses that follow.

1. *Romantic gothic fiction is not exciting.* Authors of the romantic period were quite capable of crafting page-turners and cliff-hangers. Sophia Lee's *The Recess* abounds with amazing turns and gripping plot lines; like virtually all writing in the period it does have gothic elements, but taking it as a gothic paradigm distorts its accomplishment as a historical novel and sheds little light on the accepted classics.[3] Elizabeth Inchbald, for once breaking free of her depressingly conformist drama, constructed a plot of ever-growing intensity and excitement for her masterpiece, *A Simple Story*; here, too, a powerful

psychological study of temptation and persecution would be flattened by being measured against Ann Radcliffe, and vice versa. Fascination rather than excitement is the hypnotic core of the great gothic novels. Radcliffe was known as much for her landscapes as for her ghosts, which hardly even tried to avoid the charge of hokeyness, and it was acknowledged in her own day that "her best style is essentially pictorial; and a slow development of events was, therefore, necessary to her success."[4] The big-boned novels of Lewis and Maturin have vast empty regions; both authors also wrote more concentrated fiction and drama, which was very popular in their day but has been little read or performed since. The violence in *Frankenstein* looms but then takes place offstage; vast tracts of scenery make large pauses in the action; months elapse in waiting that tries to forget the lurking dangers. Especially if you come to these novels from the even slower-moving long fiction of the Germans, the protracted vacancies in the action, lyrical interludes, and romance motifs seem integral to the genre, not irritants along the way. Gothic novels are to be savored and even reflected upon; their psychosexual fantasies are more like those of Richardson than like those of the grotesquely overheated Sade.

Ghost stories can be exciting, of course. Some of the tales that Shelley and her companions read in Geneva are. They are quick and shallowly sensational. Some novels squarely in the gothic camp are sensational as well. Charlotte Dacre's *Zofloya* is more compact than its model, Lewis's *The Monk*, with much shorter chapters and many more climaxes; Radcliffe's *Sicilian Romance*, similarly, is shorter and more adventure-filled than her better novels. William Godwin's *Caleb Williams* eventually builds up a pretty head of steam; still, it earns a place in this book by virtue of its reflective dimension, which is much more in evidence than in Godwin's more plot-filled later novels, such as the overtly supernatural *St Leon* or the historical romance *Fleetwood*. Eventually, madness and cruelty grew together with a swift pace in novels like *Wuthering Heights*, and supernatural fiction blended with adventure plotting in *Dracula* and Rider Haggard's novels. But if there is a comprehensible reason why Poe dismissed long fiction as an impossibility, it is perhaps because the novels in his gothic mode do in fact constitutively lack the excitement that he sought. The failure of his apparently incomplete novel, *The Narrative of A. Gordon Pym*, shows how difficult it could be to imagine gothic fiction as a world of frenzy. Consequently, I arrive at a second thesis.

2. *Gothic novels are not ghost stories.* In her 1831 introduction to *Frankenstein*, Shelley speaks of "my ghost story—my tiresome unlucky ghost story." It isn't clear whether she is speaking of the nightmare that begot the novel, of the kernel episode in the book, or, retrospectively, of the entire book. What is clear is that the ghost story, if there is one, is the book's jumping-off point, not its essence. If, indeed, there is a ghost story, for it is palpable that there are no actual ghosts in the book. One may well conclude from Shelley's self-disparagement that she regarded science fiction as one way of rejecting supernatural sensationalism, or of transmuting it into richer metal. Similar tendencies are pervasive in the romantic decades. One of the signature novels of the 1790s, Ludwig Tieck's *William Lovell* (English in title, setting, and inspiration), contains an episode of posthumous manifestations, doppelgängers, and a mysterious portrait that comes to life (bk. 3, letter 11). The episode reads as a throwback, not of serious consequence in the plot, and it is eventually "explained" in the novel's concluding wrap-up. At the same time, it points toward the novel's central problem of the borders between error and madness, *Irrtum* and *Irrsinn*. The novel's dark protagonist is led astray not by this early supernatural silliness but by a sadistic manipulator masking himself in the pretense of visionary illumination. Serious psychological probing replaces juvenile dalliance. About Tieck's novel Friedrich Schlegel had this to say in *Athenaeum Fragments*: "The whole book is a contest of prose and poetry. . . . The absolute fantasy in this novel may be misunderstood even by devotees of poetry and scorned as merely sentimental, while its sentimentality by no means appeals to the rational reader who, in exchange for his money, demands to be touched and who finds it very wild [*furios*]" (frag. 418). A contest of values occurs in serious novels such as *William Lovell*, *Frankenstein*, and Radcliffe's *Mysteries of Udolpho* or *The Italian*. It is not supernatural elements but rather displacements and renegotiations like Tieck's and Shelley's that are fundamental to

the "romanticism" of the gothic. Of course, the transformations of expectation take widely varying forms, and (even in the early Tieck) they operate on political, social, and philosophical planes as well as on the psychological. All the better gothic writing has a method in its madness, an intent replacing the empty theatrics of popular supernatural fiction. For surely, even as they sought the approbation of readers and reviewers to dignify their enterprise, writers also had to endow their works with a content and a purpose. Of my three theses, this one is the true foundation of this book.

3. My third thesis is perhaps the most controversial at present. It is also the least integral to my argument. It justifies omissions rather than explaining what is included here. It is this: *Gothic novels are not women's writing.* In England, to be sure, women are prominent among the leading exponents of gothic fiction. "It is an odd fact," a usually meticulous scholar has written, that gothic novels, with their powerful sexuality, "were, for the most part, written by women and gay men" (Perry, "Incest," 269). But odd facts with sample sizes under a dozen are merely odd. Ruth Perry here leaves out of account Charles Brockden Brown, William Godwin, James Hogg, Edgar Allan Poe, Friedrich Schiller, Ludwig Tieck, E. T. A. Hoffmann, Honoré de Balzac, Charles Nodier, and Aleksandr Pushkin, among others. (She does specify her terrain as "English," which might refer to the country rather than the language despite some historical material from the U.S., and she later accommodates Godwin, and could have accommodated Brown, under the ad hoc rubric "feminist men," 270.) Even in England, much of the finest fiction by women is not best regarded as gothic, though it was of course in touch with gothic impulses, as essentially all literary writing in the period was. The leading women writers in French, Mme de Staël and, later, George Sand, were not gothic novelists, nor were most of the more prominent women writers in German. It unduly limits our sense of women's literary accomplishments to single out a popularizing mode like the gothic as their particular terrain, and an exclusive focus on feminist issues (or, in a related tendency, on "feminization" and hence on gayness) limits our sense of gothic novels.[5] This is in no sense to contest the impor-

tant presence of feminist and other gender concerns in gothic novels. The sexes, the genders, bodies, and social roles are inescapable in almost all novels, and certainly in most gothic fiction. Other critics, including some of the most powerful and most influential on my own approach, have examined gender issues in detail. I have chosen, rather, to explore avenues that have remained outside the scope of the proliferating writing on gothic fiction. I have no polemical intention in adding a new perspective to the many already in circulation. But it remains important to point out that I am not betraying some imagined essence of the gothic by turning the focus away from sexuality. There is more than one way to skin the black cat of the gothic novel.

2

Fantasia
Kant and the Demons of the Night

I

LISTEN, for a moment, to the demons of the night. Their accents have become worn with time and familiarity; let them recover the sharp freshness of the dawning of dream and madness.

> Night envelops the earth. . . . The noise of the wind crying or whistling through the ill-jointed planks of the casement is all that remains of the ordinary impressions of your senses, and at the end of some instants, you imagine that this murmur itself exists within you. It becomes a voice of your soul, the echo of an undefinable but fixed idea that blends with the first perceptions of sleep. You begin this nocturnal life that takes place (O wonder!) in worlds ever new, among creatures whose form the great Spirit has conceived without deigning to complete it, content to sow them, flighty and mysterious phantoms, in the limitless universe of dreams. . . . For a long while you see the transparent and motley dust escaping like a little luminous cloud in the middle of an extinct sky. . . . The imagination of a man asleep, in the power of his independent, solitary soul, participates to some degree in the perfection of spirits. It springs up with them, and, miraculously carried into the midst of the aerial chorus of dreams, it flies from surprise to surprise until the instant when the song of morning alerts its adventuresome escort to the return of light. Frightened by the premonitory cry, . . . they fall, rebound, reascend, cross like atoms driven by contrary powers, and disappear in disorder in a ray of sun.   (Nodier, "Smarra," in *Contes*, 84–85)

At the end, the gothic dies into life—either the living death when ghoulish terror triumphs or the even more terrifying sunlight that reveals the demons to have dwelt with us in our daytime world all along. But until the end, the gothic exists in the state of suspense—of questioning and questing—that we have come to call the fantastic. What kind of crucible is the gothic, this dust storm of the mind? What does it say, this murmuring sublanguage, the brooding of the great Spirit, the perfect but undefinable idea? What are these dream pictures, whose transcendental aesthetic converts a pulsing time without direction into a space without dimension? "They are not enemy demons," the spokesman says before the nightmare begins in earnest. "They dance, they rejoice, they have the abandon and the outbursts of madness" (*Contes*, 99). But then they prove to portend a harvest of death. "'Arise,' they said to me laughing insolently, and they shattered my oppressed bosom by striking it with a straw bent off into the shape of a flail, which they had snatched from the hand of a gleaner" (118–19). What hold do the demons have on us? What riveting truths are forged within their cauldron? Here is a modern philosopher's meditation on a gothic painting:

> Always the object, always matter. . . . The material cloud with its aleatory edges becomes a squall, and the water in the tank, driving rain. For a moment the engine dissolves into the world that resembles it: it passes like a scourge of time. Man has constructed a thing-nature. The painter makes one see the entrails of this thing: stochastic bundles, dualism of sources, winking fires, its material entrails, which are the very womb of the world, sun, rain, ice, clouds, and showers. Heaven, sea, earth, and thunder are the interior of a boiler which bakes the material of the world. At random. . . . The other, the same . . . the love-making of fire and water.   (Serres, "Turner," 60–62)

What, Michel Serres particularly impels one to ask, comes out of the gothic engine? What does it fashion, produce, engender?

We are inclined to take the artificial hallucinations of the gothic too superficially. Too readily ensnared by shimmering, slender-threaded thrills, we neglect its representations of the dark powers at play in the womb of the world—the inside of things, and not the material universe as we know it. I would like to reverse the priorities of our gothic criticism, treating, for instance, Frankenstein's monster as a thought, not a thing. Paul Sherwin has written of the monster "not only as a signifier in search of its proper signification but as a literal being that means only itself" and as "apparently the thing itself" ("*Frankenstein*," 891, 886). But the thing itself, *das Ding an sich*, is precisely an eternal signified that is never a signifier; it is not an object of real experience, but a mysterious hypothesis of our reason, the conjectural substratum perpetually hinted at by the world we know. What kind of stone, after all, is free, a *Frankenstein*? The gothic substance is a thing whose materiality has been sublimated into a freedom from all conditioning factors, making it at once madness, dream, and play. "Critics have called the story unclear," writes Nodier; "they say that the end leaves only a vague and nearly inextricable idea; that the narrator's spirit, continually distracted by the most fleeting details, gets lost on any pretext in digressions without object; that the transitions of the tale . . . seem abandoned to the whim of language like a stake in a game of dice. . . . This is the praise I would have desired. These characteristics are precisely those of a dream" ("Smarra," Préface nouvelle, 79).

The hauntings and torments of the gothic make man a plaything of higher powers. But behind their sadism lies a reduction of the physical. The body is kneaded until it is desiccated and inert, and at that point a mysterious residual freedom of the spirit arises from the petrified corpse. "True happiness lies in being a stone—Nobody can complain of me—all day long I do nothing—am a stone."[1] This gothic condition has nothing to do with the world of ordinary experience; its "stony Dread" (Blake, "Earth's Answer") lies beyond any recognizable pity and fear. Yet even when sensation and sentiment are annihilated, the gothic relieves us of the utter featurelessness attributed by Immanuel Kant to the thing in itself. For, indeed, the gothic lavishes its most colorful eloquence precisely on the limits of experience, where the in-itself resides:

> I had no thought, no feeling—none—
> Among the stones I stood a stone,
> And was, scarce conscious what I wist,
> As shrubless crags within the mist;

writes Lord Byron ("Prisoner of Chillon," sec. 9), and so on for a dozen more lines that utter the unutterable, describe the indescribable, feel the impalpable. The churning entropy seems like a denial of everything, yet from it emerges an impassioned speaker and a voluble poem.

In the gothic, physical destruction and mental resistance are mutual and inseparable: the reduction to stony essence reveals to the eye of the understanding precisely the impalpable energy within the crucible of nature, or what Hegel, in the *Science of Logic*, artfully calls the "unknown *thingness-in-itself behind* knowledge" (*Schriften*, 6: 500). Precisely at midnight, in Nodier's "Inés de las Sierras," the ghostly heroine appears, and her soulless madness a-stonishes the travelers: "We must have resembled those petrified figures of Oriental tales whom death has gripped in the midst of life" (*Contes*, 469–70). Yet gothic petrifaction comes accompanied by exaltation: "The two essences of my being separated distinctly in my thought: the one, inert and clumsy, that was held fast by its material weight on one of Ghismondo's chairs; the other, already transmuted, mounting to the sky with the words of Inés, and receiving, at their will, all the impressions of a new life, inexhaustible in delights" (472). The mysterious performer known as la Pedrina (the little stone) then begins to dance, and her leaps reveal the freedom ordinarily locked up within the stony materials of the world:

> She came back, she turned about herself, like a flower that the wind has plucked from its branch; she leaped from the earth as if it lay in her power to leave it forever; she descended as if it lay in her power not to touch it; she did not jump upon the soil; you would have thought that she did but spring up from it, and that a mysterious decree of her destiny forbade her from touching it other than to flee. (474)

Persecuted by malicious relatives and deprived of her patrimony, Inés, la Pedrina, finds her freedom as a dancing stone.

I would agree, then, with Francis Hart's contention that "the demonic is no myth, no superstition, but a reality," but not that it is "a reality in human character or relationship" ("Experience," 99). Instead, the gothic confronts us with a transcendent reality, the reality of the thing in itself, of the stone in its freedom from empirical conditioning. The gothic is perhaps the most sublime of all our literary modes, transcending the merely human sublime of the psyche. The psychology of nineteenth-century novelists often exploits a practical sublime, but in the gothic of the romantic period we find a pure metaphysical sublime, epistemological or even ontological rather than merely psychological. The terrors of gothic demons are great, but greater yet is the power of human invention that imagined them; the gothic novelists open to view real powers that lie beyond experience.

II

Suppose, then, that we consider gothic novels as thought experiments that test the limits not just of human endurance but more specifically of human reason.[2] Typically, after all, the early gothic novels devote far more space to the thoughts and feelings of the victim and sometimes also to those of the persecuting demon than to the mechanisms of punishment and torment. What would be left of a person, these novels ask, if all human society were stripped away, all customary perception, all the expected regularity of cause and effect? They ask, in other words, what are people in themselves, when deprived of all the external supports that condition ordinary experience? What resources, if any, does the mind retain in isolation? What is the nature of pure consciousness? If we pose the gothic question in this fashion, we might begin to glimpse how the greatest of the gothic novelists is none other than Kant. It may seem surprising, even alarming, to suggest a link between the meticulous German professor and the wild imaginings of novelists in England and France, even if Michel Foucault has done so long since.[3] But after all, the distance from the transcendental of the philosopher to the supernatural of the novelists is not necessarily so great, perhaps no more than the distance from a noumenal object to a numinous one.

Indeed, all throughout Kant's major writings are scattered temptations toward transcendental speculation. To be sure, Kant warns repeatedly against the lure of personifying the transcendental ideals—God, freedom, and immortality. It is a "paralogism," a "subreption of hypostatized consciousness" (*Critique of Pure Reason* A 402), to imagine supernatural beings who actually incarnate the ideals. But clearly, the very act of denial acknowledges the impulse. Kant's imagination is haunted at its edges by a mysterious world beyond the limitations of reason. This world is inhabited, for instance, by that shadowy "something = X" repeatedly invoked by the *Critique of Pure Reason*; this ghost of Kant's system is a presence somewhere in the mind, yet not within the bounds of experience. Kant's last influential essay, "On Eternal Peace," to take another example, is devoted to "dream[ing] that sweet dream" in which this world beyond reason becomes habitable, where the "mad freedom" of savages proves to be rational after all, where "even a race of devils . . . must bring about the condition of peace in which all laws have force" (A3, 31, 60–61). Such language shows how closely the transcendental imagination can approximate a gothic vision.

"Did the Sage of Königsberg Have No Dreams?" asks one of our leading Kant scholars, Lewis White Beck, in a thorough essay that endeavors to keep within the limits of Kant's text. His answer is in effect: No, Kant never slept; he only suffered from periods of deficient wakefulness. Yet one of the effects of Kant's writing was unquestionably to stimulate imaginative speculation. Here is how Kant looked in his own day, to a philosophical psychologist writing in 1788: "I thought of Kant's 'Dreams of a Ghost-Seer' in relation to his present writings. Kant now realizes his fantasies and dreams through serious, cold philosophy; which is all the more comprehensible since it was a philosopher who fantasized in that book and philosophers are said frequently to reason better in dreams than awake."[4] Kant's thought of the limits is a dream of pure reason, yet also a dream beyond the bounds of ordinary rationality, a realm of spirit inhabited by spirits, a world where mad savages and devils live at eternal peace.

Every step of Kant's itinerary represents or is represented by the gothic vision. Incarcerated in darkness and cut off from concrete experiences, gothic victims regenerate from within their own space and time, Kant's pure forms of sensible intuition. Pursued by doppelgängers and haunted by demons, they test the categories of quantity and quality. Confronted by supernatural powers, they experience the birth of causality. Cut off from their roots, they remain categorically linked to the universe by the transcendental power of what Kant calls community. And above all, the gothic world remains inexplicable, as does Kant's world, because it is pervaded by contradiction. Fate and chance, limitlessness and confinement, the persistence of unreal essences and the annihilation of real ones—the gothic is preeminently the world of the antinomy. All these strands link Kant with the gothic in an epistemological sublime.

The antinomies are the copestone of Kant's architectonic, even occurring at the physical center of the *Critique of Pure Reason*. I would like to suggest that the essence, the true sublimity, of the gothic too lies in its play with unreconciled antinomies.[5] It is not the final triumph of good or evil, explanation or irrationality, free will or fate that makes a gothic atmosphere, but the lingering uncertainties along the way. To be sure, terror is a characteristic component of the gothic, but it is far more the terror of suspense—of some mystery held in reserve—than the full power of terror in action.[6] The gothic does not break butterflies upon a wheel but dangles them on a string, toys with them, plays at the exercise of power. The range of play in the gothic is great, extending from the self-deprecating prefaces of Walpole or Mary Shelley—"Swift as light and as cheering was the idea that broke in upon me," she writes, recollecting her moment of inspiration—to the gothic spawn of Tantalus and Job, butts of the most cosmic of jokes. From the gambling that launches Radcliffe's *Romance of the Forest*, Schiller's *Ghost-Seer*, and Balzac's *Wild Ass's Skin* to the tennis match in James Hogg's *Private Memoirs and Confessions of a Justified Sinner* and Rip van Winkle's ninepins, motifs of gaming pervade both the centers and the odd corners of gothic fictions. The greatness of the gothic—inseparable from the seeming frivolity of all its greatest exemplars—is not that it plays with *terror* and the limits of reason, but rather, precisely, that it *plays* with these things, that is, that it *imagines* them.[7]

At the end of its game the gothic dies into life. Among the writers who dealt the deathblow to the romantic gothic is Pushkin, in his tale "The Queen of Spades." This story pushes the antinomial speculation of the gothic to its limit. The victim here, who is not only of German descent but actually named Germann (Herman in English), is a figure of the gothic itself, "a truly novelistic figure, with the profile of Napoleon and the soul of Mephistopheles" (*Sochineniya*, 3: 409). When he is driven insane at the end, the whole story loses its bearings. A conclusion in the present tense contaminates the distancing or framing effects that are intrinsic to the gothic and destroys the speculative purity of the genre. What is concluded in this conclusion? (The Russian word that Pushkin uses for "conclusion" also means "imprisonment"; it is as if the final opening of the mode to present-day reality was also its final confinement to the dungeon of literary history.) The mad symmetries of the story never end: Herman, incarcerated in a specific room of a real hospital, wildly mutters the order of the fateful cards, while Lizaveta Ivanovna "somewhere" marries a husband with an "orderly livelihood." The patterning extends to the syntactic and phonetic levels: Elizabeth's fate, "Lizaveta Ivanovna výshla zámush" (a simplified phonetic transliteration, meaning "Lizaveta Ivanovna has married," literally, "has gone after a husband"), reshuffles the sounds of his fate, "Germann sashól s'umá" ("Herman has gone out of his mind," 417). The antinomies here, as throughout the story, however, are above all tonal. It is as if Pushkin had set out to demonstrate the ultimate generic antinomy, whose thesis is that everything is at stake in the gothic and whose antithesis is that the gothic is a never-never land of pure fantasy. It is all a game, but what kind of game? "'It was all a joke,' she said at last. 'I swear to you! It was a joke!'"[8]

"'There's no joking about it,' answered Herman angrily. 'Remember Chaplitsky, whom you helped to win the game'" (*Sochineniya*, 3: 406; the scene is prefaced by Herman's turning to stone, "on okamenel"). And the play of the cards, silly or superficial as it seems, correlates well with the play of deep feelings. "The whole time he joked about her passion for officers of the Engineers, . . . and several of his jokes were so successfully aimed that sometimes Lizaveta Ivanovna thought her secret was known to him" (408). It was the secret life of consciousness that Kant set out to uncover and display in the frenetically orderly structure of the three Critiques. Half a century afterward, the avaricious Herman could well be seen as the last and most enigmatic in the line of speculators born of German idealism. Old scores are settled; the demonic books are balanced (as they are in Balzac's "Melmoth reconciled," a delightful tale of the devil's failure with an accountant); the "sweet dream of reason" has dreamed itself out. "Tomsky [has been] promoted to captain and [is to] marry Princess Pauline" (*Sochineniya*, 3: 417; no finite verbs appear in Pushkin's terse Russian). Short and sweet. It is the end of the story. The gothic has awakened at last into the fairy tale of eternal peace we otherwise know as the mad savagery of bourgeois society.[9]

NOTE ADDED IN PROOF. I regret having overlooked Liliane Weissberg's *Geistersprache* until too late. The first half of her book supplements and enriches many aspects of my discussion of Kant. In particular, I had profited long ago from reading a version of her second chapter without remembering to acknowledge it.

PART I

Origins
Walpole

3

The Birth of *The Castle of Otranto*

ALL SERIOUS STUDENTS of the gothic talk about Horace Walpole's *Castle of Otranto*, yet hardly anyone has a good word to say about it. When so poor a book spawns so long a line of fascinating, if slightly naughty, successors, distinctive questions arise about literary origins and creativity. Novels, it need hardly be said, are made, not born. Especially the crudely contrived works in the tradition begun by *The Castle of Otranto*. Especially *The Castle of Otranto* itself. If that piece of clanky machinery was born, then surely nature has lost her touch. What kind of birth might such a book or such a genre have— what kind of gestation, what kind of genesis?

Walpole originally published *The Castle of Otranto* anonymously, in 1764, with a brief preface claiming it to be a translation from an Italian manuscript. When the novel succeeded, Walpole republished it under his own name, with a second preface justifying its form, notably its mixture of the comic and the serious. He now claimed to have "created a new species of romance" (*Castle*, Penguin ed., 48) through his "attempt to blend the two kinds of romance, the ancient and the modern" (43). Now, "blend" is not the sexiest word in the English language, though it does occur at perhaps the sexiest moment in all of English literature, in Keats's *Eve of St. Agnes*, when Porphyro approaches Madeline as the rose blendeth its odour with the violet.

Blending kinds is what horticulturists or animal breeders often do to improve their stock: in controlled conditions, existing kinds are blended to give birth to new kinds. Birth through scientific selection is, indeed, a recurrent fancy of breeders of gothic tales: Mary Shelley appeals to such a fancy in the prefaces to *Frankenstein*, Edgar Allan Poe in "The Anatomy of Composition," Henry James in his account of "The Turn of the Screw." You risk your reputation when you write a gothic novel, and you need to convince yourself and your public that your monstrous brainchild is a viable, well-behaved creature after all.

Students of the gothic tend to focus on themes rather than forms: on political tyranny and oppression, on sexual deviation and violence, on psychological abnormality and revelation. These more seductive issues are all very well when you find them, and the books and articles that focus on them can be very compelling. Often, indeed, they are more compelling than the novels. To unprepared readers, Ann Radcliffe's novels may seem long and crawling, and even Walpole's short novel tedious. The back cover of the Collier-Macmillan paperback of *The Castle of Otranto* proclaims in red, "A Bleeding Statue, A Praying Skeleton, A Castle of *Horror*!" But most of the horrors appear only briefly, as glimpsed by comically foolish servants; and the bloody sculpture has only a mild nosebleed—"three drops of blood fell from the nose of Alfonso's statue" (Penguin ed., 130). As the second preface declares, Walpole conceived the supernatural as a foil for the ordinary: "he wished," as he says, to make "the mortal agents in his drama . . . think, speak and act, as it might be supposed mere men and women would do in extraordinary positions" (43–44). If you want sadomasochism, you are much better off with *Dracula* or with your corner newsstand. My purpose here is to attend to Walpole's expressed concerns with form and to the actual conduct of his book and thereby to show how the form is the essential ground of Walpole's imagination. The form is, so to speak, the matrix of his intermittent horrors—their context, and the mother that gives them birth. Finally, I will argue, the blending of kinds is the most powerful agent in the novel.

In his *Essay on the Origins of Human Knowledge*, Etienne Bonnot de Condillac presents an account of creation more elaborately considered than Walpole's. It summarizes some of the commonplaces that Walpole's preface would later evoke:

> Invention consists of knowing how to make new combinations: there are two kinds of it; talent, and genius.
>
> Talent combines the ideas of an art, or of a science in such a manner as is proper to producing those effects, which should naturally be expected from it. . . . Genius adds to talent the idea in some sense of a creative mind. . . . It examines things in a point of view peculiar to itself; it gives birth to a new science; or, in those already cultivated it carves out a road to truths, which it never expected to reach.[1]

Talent, in other words, produces offspring that resemble their parents by natural consequence. The fruit of genius, by contrast, seems unnatural: it is the unforeseen, the mutation, the bastard that manages to legitimate itself as truth. An adequate theory of creation along such lines will never be entirely comfortable, since it needs to satisfy two contradictory demands. The work of genius is bound to be at least slightly awkward; it does not fit into known and predictable categories; it can't have too reassuring an outcome. Here is what Walpole says about the new road to the new birth:

> As the public have applauded the attempt, the author must not say he was entirely unequal to the task he had undertaken: yet if the new route he has struck out shall have paved a road for men of brighter talents, he shall own with pleasure and modesty, that he was sensible the plan was capable of receiving greater embellishments than his imagination or conduct of the passions could bestow on it.   (*Castle*, Penguin ed., 44)

Yet the diffidence is balanced by moments in Walpole's correspondence where he describes the book as the product of an unrepeatable moment of vision. Consistently inconsistent, he calls it both a realistic portrait of medieval manners and "a world that bears no resemblance to the world of affairs" (*Corr.*, 5: 398). The insecurity of Walpole's gothic—the feebleness of its inventions, of its passions, and of its characters—guarantees the authenticity of its author's invention.

Walpole's language of kinds can be just as suspect and just as provocative as the metaphor of birth in my title. Books have grown frail, Walpole tells us in his preface, and they need to be reinvigorated. In his words, "the great resources of fancy have been dammed up," and

"Nature has cramped imagination" (*Castle*, Penguin ed., 43). Potency is at issue, and not only at the level of form. For *The Castle of Otranto* deals with a feeble race, exhausted by conflict and oppression. Walpole's characters, like his book, begin cramped and squeezed. To regenerate the form is to regenerate the race and the state. The "new species of romance" is simultaneously a new kind of book and a new kind of emotion. Walpole doesn't explore forms on the surface and then, separately, the interesting things beneath; rather, he explores the interesting things by exploring forms.

Fielding's *Tom Jones*, which was published some fifteen years earlier, serves as a model for *The Castle of Otranto*, with respect both to the blending of forms and to the issues of paternity. Walpole expressed hostility toward Fielding's novel, and as a writer he may be considered a kind of "natural son"—that is, an illegitimate child—of Fielding's. The resemblance and the difference begin with the claims the authors make. In advertising his "new species of romance," Walpole alludes to Fielding's well-known claim to have discovered a "new province of writing" (*Tom Jones* 2.1; p. 41). The difference between these phrases measures the distance between Fielding, a noted justice of the peace and keeper of public order, and Walpole, the dilettante son of one of England's greatest and most corrupt prime ministers. With a verve that seems to belie any anxiety of creation, Fielding relates the story of an illegitimate son who proves worthy after all. *Tom Jones* is an anti-gothic romance: in the midst of the Man of the Hill episode, a moral fable of corruption and repentance at the center of the novel, Fielding has his superstitious barber Partridge mangle an appallingly bad tale of an executed murderer who returns from the dead to thrash his accuser (*Tom Jones* 8.11). For Fielding, a well-told story can dispense with terror.

Tom Jones combines the kind of extravagant adventure found in picaresque novels with the kind of unified plot characteristic of (or at least attributed to) ancient epic. Subsequent generations have canonized Fielding's newly delineated province of writing with the name "novel," but Fielding's title calls his book a "history," and his prefatory chapters offer only awkwardly amalgamated names like "prosaicomi-epic writing" (5.1; p. 159) for his bastard form. Since ancient times the epic had focused on a whole society. Fielding's combination takes the picaresque hero, who was traditionally pitted against his society, and projects him as the unified focus of a unified world. In this fashion, the new combination displaces the center of value from the surrounding, outer world to the world of the individual. The offspring of two flamboyantly externalizing literary forms, *Tom Jones* traces a new course by moving inward. Hence in Fielding's book the literature of action gradually yet unexpectedly yields to the literature of character.

This is, to be sure, not the most usual view of *Tom Jones*, for only toward the end of the novel does the character virtue of a good heart triumph over the action virtue of prudence. Critics often downplay this development; Ian Watt devotes pages of *The Rise of the Novel* to Fielding's "avoidance of the subjective dimension" (273), and Robert Alter writes, "The refusal to render inner states is a conscious decision on Fielding's part" (*Fielding*, 63). Yet in fact the narrative is structured precisely to create the novel possibility of rendering inner states. *Tom Jones* features a series of monologues by its hero; most of them are uttered aloud, but they point directly toward a silent monologue at the pivotal moment of the plot when Arabella Hunt unexpectedly proposes marriage. For the first time, Tom's feelings of responsibility toward Sophia outweigh worldly temptations as he inwardly debates and finally rejects the proposal. "But to abandon Sophia, and marry another, that was impossible; he could not think of it upon any account. Yet why should he not, since it was plain she could not be his?" (15.11; p. 733). And we continue in this vein to overhear his inmost thoughts until the answer is reached. The character knows his world through knowing himself, reversing the ancient pattern of the epic. Here at last the bastard has grown up, and Fielding's new species has found its new voice, which Fielding pointedly calls "the voice of nature, which cried in his heart" (ibid.). Through its formal experimentation, *Tom Jones* searches for the inner self, for the nature and the voice that conventions of writing have cramped and dammed up.

The Castle of Otranto furthers and radicalizes Fielding's endeavor. What Fielding develops very gradually, with patience and tact, Wal-

pole thrusts into the forefront of his tempestuous short novel. Both
books, for instance, concern the discovery of true parentage; both
pivot on suggestions of incest; in both, the denouement consists of a
succession of narratives by various characters, each revealing a portion of the hero's history. And Manfred's castle could almost be one of
Fielding's inns: both are meeting places for wanderers and sites of battles between brave civilians and cowardly soldiers; in both, identities
are mistaken or concealed and people stumble into the wrong bed-
room or escape out a back exit. Madness and accusations of madness
lurk all about the fringes of *Tom Jones*. But whereas in *Tom Jones*
only Partridge is fool enough to believe in ghosts, in *The Castle of
Otranto* everyone does. While Fielding's allegorical Allworthy and his
representative Tom Jones are men seen as Man, the ideal universal,
Walpole's tyrant Manfred is man freed from all civilized bounds, and
his hero Theo-dore is an unexpected gift from God. From Walpole's
perspective, the trouble with *Tom Jones* is that it naturalizes the illegitimate son, reabsorbs him into the tradition, and thus robs him of
his originality. The true genius refuses the compromises that are fundamental to Fielding's endeavor.[2]

Like most gothic novels, *The Castle of Otranto* is an intricate and
confusing narrative. Surprising revelations are more the aim than orderly development. The facts emerge piecemeal and are hard to remember even shortly after a fresh reading. Retelling the plots will further my exposition, but to make sense of the scrambled events of the
narrative I must reverse Walpole's order of presentation by tracing the
history from its inception.

The book tells the story of three families. The first is that of Alfonso the Good, the former ruler of Otranto, whose statue stands in
the chapel of St. Nicholas. Under way to the Crusades, Alfonso was
stranded by foul weather in Sicily, where he fell in love with the virtuous Victoria and secretly married her. Alfonso then died in Palestine.
We never learn the name of his unacknowledged daughter, who eventually married the Count of Falconara. They had a son named Theodore, who is the rightful heir to Otranto. But when Theodore was five,
he and his mother were captured by pirates. The Count, Theodore's
father, moved to Otranto and entered the church under the name of

Father Jerome. Years later Theodore is freed from slavery and wanders about Italy in search of his father. As the novel opens, he has just arrived in Otranto, in shepherd's attire.

The second family is that of the reigning usurper, Manfred. Manfred's grandfather Ricardo was chamberlain to Alfonso the Good. He poisoned Alfonso and forged a will bequeathing the principality to himself. Following a storm-tossed voyage, St. Nicholas appeared to him in a vision and granted his family the rule of Otranto, as the prophecy has it, "until the rightful owner should be grown too large to inhabit the castle, and as long as issue-male from Ricardo's loins should remain to enjoy it" (Penguin ed., 146). Manfred, the eventual successor, is now married to his cousin Hippolita. He has two children, a daughter named Matilda and a feeble son, Conrad, who is betrothed to a woman named Isabella.

Isabella, Conrad's fiancée, belongs to the third family. Her father is Frederic, Alfonso's closest known surviving relative and thus a claimant to the throne of Otranto. He, too, was taken prisoner in Palestine and was believed dead. In an attempt to secure the succession, Manfred has bribed Isabella's guardians to engage her to the unlovable Conrad. Meanwhile, Frederic was ransomed in Palestine. Guided by a dream, he discovered a giant buried sword inscribed with an injunction to rescue his daughter Isabella.

We have, then, three families—one that has perpetrated treachery, two that are the victims of war and spoliation. And two storms, two dream visions, two lost fathers in disguise, two weak and tyrannical overlords. Two generations after the treachery in Otranto, peace has not yet come to Europe, to the principality, or to the three families.

These are, to be sure, only the background stories that emerge piecemeal in the course of the novel. Gradually each of the men—Theodore, Frederic, Jerome (who is really the Count of Falconara), and finally Manfred—is brought to tell his part of the whole, which we must patch together from the odd bits of narration. As with other tales of oedipal curses, the novel looks backward to set a disordered past to rights.

The narration opens on the day before the planned marriage of Conrad and Isabella. The absurd events of the foreground action begin when Conrad is crushed to death in the palace courtyard by a giant helmet like that on the statue of Alfonso. Theodore, as yet unknown but resembling the statue in appearance, is accused by Manfred of mischief and is imprisoned under the helmet. The helmet, however, has broken the pavement, and Theodore is able to escape into the palace cellar. There he encounters Isabella; she is fleeing from Manfred, who has had the idea of divorcing Hippolita and marrying Isabella himself. Theodore helps Isabella escape into a secret passage to the church, but he is trapped behind, caught by Manfred, and condemned to death. Jerome comes to confess Theodore, recognizes him as his son, and bargains for his life. Suddenly, Frederic arrives in disguise, accompanied by an enormous procession carrying the enormous, unearthed sword. Taking advantage of all the confusion, Isabella, afraid of being handed over to Manfred, escapes to a cave. All three fathers leave in pursuit. Abandoned by his guards, Theodore wanders free, meets Manfred's daughter Matilda, and falls instantly in love. She dresses him in Manfred's armor; he goes to defend Isabella, and mistakenly wounds the disguised Frederic, who panics and confesses his identity. While Frederic is recovering, Manfred persuades him to make an exchange: each father will marry the daughter of the other, Manfred Isabella, and Frederic the irresistible Matilda. During all these confusions, portents of doom keep intruding: the feathers on the giant helmet wave wildly; mysterious voices sigh; huge body parts are glimpsed wandering about the castle; and Alfonso's statue suffers its nosebleed. It would all be very funny if the stiff and awkward prose did not effectively stifle the tumultuous bustle of the action.

The novel ends with an earthquake.[3] More portents finally dissuade Frederic from connivance with Manfred. Manfred comes upon Theodore in the church with a female figure. Manfred jealously suspects that Theodore loves Isabella, and he stabs the girl, only to discover that it is his own daughter. As the unfortunate Matilda lies dying, the statue of Alfonso swells to enormous size, the castle walls collapse, and the final parts of the background story are told as the prophecy is fulfilled. Manfred and Hippolita take holy vows, while Theodore, deprived of his true love, makes do with Isabella, "with whom," the novel concludes, "he could for ever indulge the melancholy that had taken possession of his soul" (Penguin ed., 148). Having opened with the great uproar over Conrad's death and continued with various public displays and pursuits, the novel concludes with these dreary solitudes. We are left to wonder who will take care of the poor inhabitants of Otranto.[4]

This bare account of the book's plot hardly conveys what it is like. When slogging through the crowded incidents, one wonders how such an insane mishmash could have gained popular success. Much is totally unprepared, and nothing is adequately motivated; there is little consistency in the types of incidents, and the focus of interest shifts radically from moment to moment. Far from a coherent undertaking, the novel is best seen as an attempt to comprehend within a tiny compass as great a variety as possible.[5] To this extent Walpole's aim of blending ancient and modern romance means conceiving a book that summarizes all previous kinds of narrative.

Walpole does, to be sure, attempt to master the book's profusion. For blending also means combining disorder with order. While one side of the equation is the turbulence of the new romance, the other side is classic symmetry. Both of Walpole's prefaces harp on dramatic models, and the work they introduce marries the inclusiveness of prose with orderly Aristotelian form. The five chapters, all of equal length, are the five acts of a drama conveyed more through dialogue than through narrative report; terror and pity are the avowed goals; the three Aristotelian unities of time, place, and plot are carefully observed. As the preface to the anonymous publication says, the author's "talents . . . were evidently proper for, the theatre" (Penguin ed., 41). In this combination of picaresque sweep with classic focus, Walpole is again following Fielding's example. Fielding, however, took his Aristotle lightly. Walpole outdoes him in modeling his unity so strictly on the canons of the drama. If his content is too wild, his form is too mannered. Summarizing the novel's plot highlights a crucial fact on which the book is predicated: just as the gothic world is set in the shadowy past, so the gothic elements of Walpole's plot represent the novel's past, as long dead battles resurface and are refought. Repetitions deny or threaten advance, and the goal of the narrative is to quell them. In this novel, the battle against the past succeeds only at the cost of utter exhaustion. Still, what has been repressed does not threaten to return. Disenchanted it may be, but the world has at least emerged from enchantment.

Blending might be supposed to be a merely additive and value-neutral process. Features of the novel are combined with features of the drama; a drama is narrated and a narrative dramatized, and the result is a product that has some of each. If that were all that *The Castle of Otranto* amounted to, then we could not speak of a birth or of a new species of writing. *The Castle of Otranto* would be neither the natural nor the unnatural son of *Tom Jones*—and I am proposing that it is both natural and unnatural at once—but just a feeble copycat. However, in Walpole's hands the generic hybrid is not a balanced compromise. Quite the contrary, it achieves a genuine transformation, in which two potentially opposed developments merge through mutual reinforcement into a single development. The result is a displacement, specifically a displacement inward that radicalizes the carefully emerging inwardness of the parent novel, *Tom Jones*. Attention to the flamboyant—but silly—externals of the gothic novels has blinded critics to their distinctive achievement: the preservation and reaffirmation of the human inside of things, or, as Walpole's preface phrases it, the preservation of the "human character" even amid the "dispensation of miracles" and "the most stupendous phenomena" (Penguin ed., 44).

The novel, as Walpole inherited it, traditionally took place outside, on the open road. Novelist, hero, and reader became fellow travelers on the path toward virtue. Fielding defines the focus as "a certain relative quality which is always busying itself without-doors" (*Tom Jones* 15.1; p. 690). In prose narratives as diverse as Alain-René Lesage's *Gil Blas*, Samuel Richardson's *Clarissa*, and Fielding's *Tom Jones*, interiors function primarily as places of confinement and moral darkness. In neoclassical drama, on the other hand, the enclosed space of the theater and of the stage seems to encourage a contrasting distribution of values. Interior scenes are the norm, and exterior scenes tend toward violation and violence. It is when George Lillo's *London Merchant* moves out of doors, for instance, that the unfortunate Barnwell is murdered. And Walpole's own frenzied play, *The Mysterious Mother*, is set entirely outdoors. When Walpole took a novel and cast it into dramatic form, therefore, one effect was to displace narrative onto internal spaces. His book is renowned for its subterranean passages, but it is arbitrary to single these out. More characteristic of the whole book is that the exteriors are places of danger—the courtyard where Conrad is killed and Theodore is imprisoned, and the forest through which Isabella is pursued—while crypt, cave, and chapel are all sought as places of refuge. Virtue is covered, as when Theodore is imprisoned under the helmet; the truth is buried, as was the giant sword; identity is veiled in obscurity, as is Matilda when Manfred mistakenly stabs her, or as is Theodore, who, despite his resemblance to his grandfather Alfonso, is not recognized until a birthmark hidden under his clothing is exposed. As it moves inside, the illuminated world of the novel is dimmed.[6]

The half-light of the theater has a magic aura; when you step into the playhouse, you enter a world of wonders. But in the novel the glamour is lost, and we are left with the prevailing moonlight that generates melancholy throughout the book. It subdues the drama by eliminating the immediacy of dramatic spectacle. Plays parade action and articulate emotion; narratives describe action and analyze emotion. To be sure, as I have said (and as Walpole's first preface observes), many parts of the novel preserve the animated dialogue of the drama. But these are primarily the comic scenes with the servants. In many other parts, action seems to pause, while we wait anxiously for another ax to fall or another statue to clank. Narrating the drama thus reinforces the consequences of dramatizing a narrative; both techniques displace the focus inward.

In Walpole's generic hybrid everything that was healthy in either the novel or the drama becomes furtive. Characters deriving from the picaresque, for instance, become dramatically ennobled yet do not acquire dignity. The current ruling family is really a race of wily servants who have triumphed over their master, while the true heir not only is reduced to the guise of a clever peasant with a quick tongue but inherits the throne only through a secret and obviously inferior maternal lineage. "*Hereditary* and *bad* are almost synonymous," Walpole had once opined, after all (*Corr.*, 15: 51), and "Anybody with two or three hundred years of pedigree, may find themselves descended from whom they please" (9: 69). Theodore's nobility of character is real, but it is all inward, and has nothing to do with his upbringing as a slave. ("In the present refined or depraved state of human nature, most people endeavour to conceal their real character, not to display it," 16: 256). The sexuality in the novel, too, takes on an unexpectedly furtive quality. Incest had appeared as a tragic danger—and sometimes even as a comic foible—not just in *Tom Jones* but in numerous Elizabethan and eighteenth-century plays and novels. In the displaced world of Walpole's novel, incest becomes an unspeakable horror. Manfred's first-cousin marriage would be unproblematic in England —in 1769 Walpole termed the scruples of Horace Mann's nephew about marrying his illegitimate first cousin "ridiculous" (*Corr.*, 23: 100)—but displaced to Catholic Italy the union's status as incestuous becomes the pretext for his divorce petition.[7] And his proposed marriage to Isabella, his son's betrothed, calls down anathemas from the priestly Jerome. Through so many channels, the hybrid form comes to feel inbred and almost automatically foments the book's atmosphere of secretiveness and of political and sexual repression.

At the end of the novel, to be sure, the marriage of kinds is consummated in a tidy conclusion. Hidden matter is brought to light as all the secret histories are narrated; the supernatural is brought on stage when the statue bleeds and the murdered Alfonso speaks in the presence of numerous witnesses. And the displaced ruler is restored to the throne, in a sentimentalized transposition of the thematics of works like Shakespeare's *Macbeth* and Racine's *Andromaque*. Yet Theodore's beloved Matilda has been murdered; he is forced to make do with the less attractive and more childish Isabella (her name coyly calls her "equally beautiful," but Theodore seems not to believe it); and no renovation of the public world is in sight. What has happened to render the contamination of types irreversible?

So as to stage my own surprise, I have left the novel's principal mood-creating agent for last. For as I see it, Walpole's greatest originality lies in the parts of his book to which the least attention has been paid, and in which the least appears to happen. *Hamlet*, the Shakespearian drama to which much of Walpole's preface is devoted, is distinguished, among other things, by the dramatic monologues in which characters' thoughts and motivations are brought into the open. These monologues, too, are reflected in the novel. But they are silenced as they are converted back into narrative. I described earlier how inward thoughts become the focus for one moment at the pivot of *Tom Jones*. That device, which has been called psycho-narration— the direct transposition into third-person narrative of the immediate thought processes of the characters—becomes all-pervasive in *The Castle of Otranto*.[8] All the featured personages take their turn thinking. Most often the diction generalizes a bit, giving a delicate sense of a narrator bridging the path to the interior. I excerpt the earliest example out of a great many: "Yet her own situation could not help finding its place in her thoughts. She felt no concern for the death of young Conrad, except commiseration" (Penguin ed., 53–54). And so it goes, as the narrator transmits the inward reactions to us. But at least once, early in the novel, as if to set the stakes, Walpole gives us thoughts with all the abruptness of an immediate transcript, syntactically even more extreme than the questioning thoughts of *Tom Jones* at Fielding's climax: "Yet where conceal herself! How avoid the pursuit he would infallibly make throughout the castle!" (61). The continuation, "As these thoughts passed rapidly through her mind," rather self-consciously insists on the effect of immediacy Walpole is striving for. A character like this—and all Walpole's characters approach this frequently—is pursued by her own internal desires and fears more than by any external monsters and demons. Walpole's supernatural is as juvenile and silly as is the pretense in his first introduction of giving a faithful report of a foreign country in a time gone by. That is the mode of the epic, a form for which Walpole professed scorn: "Epic poetry is the art of being as long as possible in telling an uninteresting story: and an epic poem is a mixture of history without truth and of romance without imagination."[9] The externals don't matter, except as a provocation. What matters in his novel is what his second and more honest preface says matters, namely the genuinely human way in which his characters react to even the most inhuman of events. What really haunts them is what drives them from inside. Naturally, almost mechanically, yet to astonishing effect, Walpole has displaced the center of human concern from behavior and action to the private resources of the mind and the emotions. The histories of literature that attend to such things tell us that Jane Austen's novels and, simultaneously, Goethe's *Elective Affinities* were the great discoverers of the narrative of consciousness. But in truth, they were only its naturalizers. Though Terry Castle has brilliantly traced the narrative discovery of consciousness back to Radcliffe, no reader seems hitherto to have recognized what I take to be its true source, in Walpole's slender and seemingly harmlessly sensational novel.[10] What we have here is a new conception of character, not yet mature enough to make an effect or to belong by rights to the family of literature. The bleeding statue and the giant form of Alfonso are not the true innovations of Walpole, nor is the gothic novel in general best understood as supernatural fiction. Indeed, "Ghosts in the Flesh" (Chapter 5 below) will discuss the roots of such plots outside of narrative fiction altogether. Rather, the supernatural serves as pretext for the focus on the thoughts and feelings of isolated individuals; that is the true genius of Walpole's invention.

The formalism of *The Castle of Otranto*, however, is the matrix, not itself the product; the mold, not the fully baked cake. The juvenile silliness of Walpole's book is essential to its character. This natural son is a conception that has not yet grown up. Resentment against parents pervades the narrative (as, indeed, anxiety about his father permeates the correspondence). Time and again the imagery suggests the confinement of the budding vigor of youth by the repressive machinations of the older generation. The gigantic statue gives us the infant's perspective on adult sexuality, as Theodore must learn to wear the giant helmet and to wield the giant sword.[11] Walpole's supernatural is full not so much of ghostly bodies as of body parts—an arm here, a leg there, a nose elsewhere. Even the castle acquires something of the aspect of a body without organs, waiting to be animated by its rightful master: Walpole's preface reminds us that corridors have hands and staircases, feet. You have to learn how to inhabit your buildings and your inheritance, as you have to learn how to inhabit your body. Falling and rising movements alike evoke the mysteries of physical process. It's not just exterior happenstance, then, that links this family curse and regressive narration to the psychic structure of the Oedipus myth. Nor is the displacement inward in the novel merely a discovery of the primacy of thoughts and feelings in general. Rather, it will turn out, particular structures of a sort ultimately analyzed only by Freud and his successors are in question—structures of thought and feeling, of consciousness as mastery, and of the rebelliousness of maturation.[12]

In evoking the patterns that coalesce out of the seemingly random impulses of form, of plot, and of imagery in *The Castle of Otranto*, I have been constructing the novel as a signifying machine, or a discourse network. A writer without any obvious attainments begets a book whose buried subject is the constitution of an identity that must be presupposed by the sort of accomplishment to which, for a millennium, the name of masterpiece has been awarded.

> To master the painful event, someone may say—but who masters, where is the master here, to be mastered? Why speak so hastily when we do not know precisely where to situate the agency that would undertake this operation of mastery?. . . . On the contrary, we see here a point that the subject can approach only by dividing himself into a certain number of agencies. One might say what is said of the divided kingdom, that any conception of the unity of the psyche, of the supposed totalizing, synthesizing psyche, ascending towards consciousness, perishes there.
>
> (Lacan, *Four Fundamental Concepts*, 51)

That inchoate *there*, I suggest, is the thrashing, stabbing, disordered narration of the gothic novel, intuited here by an author who himself never entirely grew up, who never mastered or understood the monster he was creating, and who could not have created it if he had understood it, because it is in the nature of genius to invent what has not yet been found.

4

Excursus
Notes on the History of Psycho-Narration

THE ROMANTIC GOTHIC NOVEL is a theater of mind. None-theless, Dorrit Cohn's *Transparent Minds* opens with the claim that the "avoidance of psycho-narration . . . dominates the third-person novel well into the nineteenth century" (22). While her exam-ple of avoidance is explicit—"How Miss Sharp lay awake, thinking, will he come or not to-morrow, need not be told here"—her claim is clearly mistaken. I have illustrated Walpole's exploration of psycho-narration, the technique that his novel shapes for purposes explored by subsequent writers of gothic fiction. Still, it would be inaccurate to claim that Walpole invented psycho-narration. As John Bender and Nicholas Paige reminded me in conversation, related techniques were widespread in earlier French fiction and were certainly familiar in En-gland as well, through many early examples in addition to the defin-ing moment in *Tom Jones*. I do think, however, that Walpole's narra-tion is distinctive, particularly with respect to the most important forebear, Mme de La Fayette, and it is worth taking the space to show how. (I consider only passages describing momentary reflections, not those that summarize thoughts over a period of time.)

Narration of consciousness pervades Mme de La Fayette's *Prin-cesse de Clèves* (1678). In some respects it appears more complex than Walpole's narration, in other respects less. The incomplete infinitives of passion that I cited from Walpole ("Yet where conceal herself! How

34

avoid the pursuit he would infallibly make throughout the castle!") are very likely a gallicism: because the French infinite lacks a marker comparable to the English "to," a bare infinitive is more normal in French, but consequently belongs to a more settled kind of reflection, punctuated (in the following passage) by a question mark rather than Walpole's exclamation point: "Elle ne pouvait douter qu'il n'eût conté cette aventure au vidame de Chartres. . . . Comment excuser une si grande imprudence . . . ? [She could not doubt that he would have told this adventure to the Vidame of Chartres. . . . How to excuse so great an imprudence . . . ?]."[1] This passage issues in an articulation of thoughts, moving away from psycho-narration toward the more self-conscious device of monologue: "Il a été discret, disait-elle [He was discreet, she said]" (351; 116). Quotation marks were not yet in use, so nothing graphically signals the boundary separating psycho-narration from monologue, and the whole passage consequently gives the effect of a series of explicit reflections. Here Mme de La Fayette's report of consciousness is less emotive than is characteristic of Walpole.

As a first generalization, subject to subsequent qualification, it can be said that consciousness for Mme de La Fayette consists of thoughts, whereas for Walpole it is a distinctive mixture of thoughts and feelings. Thus, one passage in her novel proceeds with the following markers: "il résolut [he resolved]"; "disait-il [he said]"; a bare infinitive: "Pourquoi me réduire à la voir . . . ? [Why confine myself to seeing her . . . ?]"; a clearly thoughtful continuation: "J'ai dû respecter la douleur de Mme de Clèves; mais . . . [I ought to respect Mme de Clèves's grief, but . . .]"; and a concluding summary pointing to the thoughtful nature of the passage: "Après ces réflexions [After these reflections]" (381; 146–47). Thought can be extensive; one passage beginning "Quand elle pensait . . . [When she thought . . .]" continues for more than a page, moving temporarily to narrative summary of the heroine's thoughts ("Elle avait ignoré . . . [She had not known . . .]"), marking as monologue the return to her perspective ("disait-elle [she said]"), and characterizing the upshot as a decision, "cette résolution [this resolve]" (329–31; 93–95).

Such reports of thought are possible only with a degree of self-possession that is denied Walpole's agitated characters. Perhaps the longest episode of thought in the *Princesse de Clèves* follows a moment of agitation too great to be penetrated. The episode begins, "On ne peut exprimer ce que sentit M. de Nemours dans ce moment [It is impossible to express what M. de Nemours felt at that moment]." In the next paragraph the narrator insists, "Ce prince était aussi tellement hors de lui-même [This prince, too, was so greatly beside himself]." But then the fit subsides and the thinking begins: "Quand il fut un peu remis, il pensa . . . [When he was somewhat calmer, he thought . . .]." M. de Nemours is tempted to run away; as the narrator says, "il fut prêt plusieurs fois à prendre la résolution de s'en retourner sans se faire voir [Several times he was ready to make a resolution to return without showing himself]." But, as the narrator continues (analyzing feelings rather than narrating them as Walpole does), "Poussé néanmoins par le désir de lui parler, et rassuré par les espérances que lui donnait tout ce qu'il avait vu . . . [Urged nonetheless by the desire to speak with her, and reassured by the hopes given him by all that he had seen . . .]." Since the atmosphere remains sufficiently peaceful, thought can continue, though the focus passes to Mme de Clèves. She passes through a state of agitation but speaks aloud (though she is not quoted) to calm the situation enough that thought can resume: "Quand elle eut fait quelque réflexion, elle pensa . . . [When she had reflected for a while, she thought . . .]." A moment of excitement disrupts both thought and psycho-narration, but within the same sentence it is conquered enough for thought to continue: "Peut-être souhaitait-elle, autant qu'elle le craignait, d'y trouver M. de Nemours; mais enfin la raison et la prudence l'emportèrent sur tous ses autres sentiments, et elle trouva . . . [Perhaps she wished, as much as she feared, to find M. de Nemours, but finally reason and prudence won out over all other feelings, and she found . . .]" (367–68; 133–35). Mme de La Fayette presents a clear hierarchy here: "sentiments" fall beyond the reach of articulation, whereas thought and reason remain articulate and reportable.

Indeed, thought is not just reportable but readable. There are moments when not just the narrator but also characters can see what is going on within the mind of another. The most notable is this: "Mme de Clèves . . . crut voir dans ce moment ce qui lui passait dans l'esprit [Mme de Clèves . . . believed she could see at this moment what was

passing in his mind]." And lest we put too much weight on the qualification "she believed she could see," confirmation of the thought is
forthcoming: "Les questions que fit ce prince le confirmèrent encore
dans cette pensée [This prince's questions confirmed her further in
this thought]" (365; 132). Feelings as such, by contrast, lie out of ken,
not just of the characters but occasionally even of the narrator.[2] Feeling is then characterized as inexpressible, inconceivable: "L'on ne
peut exprimer la douleur qu'elle sentit . . . [The grief which she felt
can not be expressed]" (275; 36). The richest resource of Mme de La
Fayette's narrator as a reporter of states of mind lies in this sensitivity
to the mysteries of personality. The heart has its reasons that reason
cannot know. The characters tremble on the verge of abysses of emotion. "Elle ne pouvait s'empêcher d'être troublée de sa vue, et d'avoir
pourtant du plaisir à le voir; mais . . . il s'en fallait peu qu'elle ne crût
le haïr par la douleur que lui donnait cette pensée [She could not keep
herself from being distressed at the sight of him, and yet from taking
pleasure in seeing him; but . . . she was little short of thinking that she
hated him from the grief this thought gave her]" (277; 38). As hard as
the characters struggle to retain their reason, it is always threatened
by powers they cannot control. Mme de La Fayette's characters exist
to the extent that they think, and their feelings remain cordoned off in
a world beyond experience.[3]

First-person presentation (narrative or epistolary) was probably
the dominant mode in European fiction of this period—it was certainly far more prevalent than in the nineteenth century—and of
course lacks the third-person narrator's capacity for omniscience. But
the third-person narratives I have inspected from the first half of the
eighteenth century leave no doubt that psycho-narration was much in
use. Thus, for instance, in Claude Crébillon's early story "Tanzaï et
Néadarné" (1734) it is possible to find scattered reports of thought.
The following is typical, and it is worth noting that the verb *crain-
dre*, which might have an emotive cast, here remains a modality of
judgment:

> Au milieu de tant de joie, des réflexions tristes sur les menaces de Barba-
> cela se firent sentir à Tanzaï; il considéra que sans la consulter, il avait
> non seulement choisi, mais même annoncé son mariage à tout le monde,

avant que de lui en faire part. Il craignit qu'elle ne le punît, en cessant de le protéger, du peu d'égards qu'il avait eu pour elle. Il était occupé de ces idées, lorsqu'on vint.

[Amid such joy, sad reflections on Barbacela's threats made themselves felt; Tanzaï reflected that without consulting her he had not merely thought, but even announced his marriage to everyone before telling her. He feared she might punish him by ceasing to protect him on account of his lack of consideration for her. He was occupied with these ideas when a messenger arrived.]   (Crébillon, "Tanzaï et Néadarné," 287)

A longer episode of reflection begins as a report of conscious feelings, such as I have not found in Mme de La Fayette: "Elle sentait avec douleur qu'elle ne le haïssait pas, et le craignait d'autant plus qu'elle écartait l'idée de Tanzaï quand elle se présentait avec trop d'avantage. . . . Quelquefois, elle pensait . . . [She felt with grief that she did not hate him, and she feared it so much the more that she dismissed the idea of Tanzaï when it offered itself to her too advantageously. . . . Sometimes, she thought . . .]." The passage then continues with a long paragraph of interior monologue, introduced with "se disait-elle [she said to herself]" and punctuated, in the middle, with the self-listening gesture "Mais que dis-je? [But what am I saying?]." The episode concludes, however, with a distancing gesture that limits the immediacy of the narrator's access: "Pendant que Néadarné faisait ces réflexions, ou d'autres semblables . . . [While Néadarné made these reflections, or other similar ones . . .]" (410–12).

English examples that I have noted are similar. They move closer to emotions at the cost of Mme de La Fayette's powerful sense of repressed turmoil, and remain occasional rather than systematic. Here is one example, from Delarivier Manley's *New Atalantis* (1709). It begins with Madam de St. Amant's feelings, though a long temporal perspective leaves the boundary between narration and more distanced explanation fluid at the start:

Berintha had named to her that terrible disease, which she had so long felt, and yet could give no name to. Jealousy had discovered it to be love, because he never appears in a place where love is not, because in a moment [here is the slip into more obvious immediacy] she passed to an aversion for her cousin, who before had been very well in her kindness.

What should she do? . . . She saw she was in a moment going to lose that long-valued reputation. . . . But what most amazed her was . . . She hoped . . . [Her husband] had ever been so extreme respectful that she had reason to think him ignorant.   (67–68)

From here the narrative proceeds briefly to Berintha's thoughts (followed by her exit, singing and laughing though not quoted) and then to the seducer, Baron de Mezeray, with a substantial paragraph that mingles reported (but not quoted) conversation between Madam de St. Amant and the Baron with actions and mental impressions. The piquancy lies in the casualness of the passage among feelings, words, and deeds. Everything has an emotional and risqué coloration, and nothing goes too deep. The frivolity is equally evident in a longer, potentially more intimate paragraph of amorous feelings (33), where an unnamed Duke suffers the "hostile fires" of love and spends a sleepless night fretting. The expressions are passionate, but (like everything else in this salacious, libertine novel) not serious; time passes swiftly, and an epidemic of exclamation points adds a satiric coloring to his thoughts and the subsequent emotions of the seduced damsel: "the nimble beatings of his heart, apparently seen and felt through his open breast! the glowings! the tremblings of his limbs! the glorious sparkles from his guilty eyes! his shortness of breath and eminent disorder—were things all new to her. . . . Nor had she leisure to examine his disorders, possessed by greater of her own!" (36). Manley moralizes the Duke's lust with several italicized sentences at the end of his paragraph, but the conduct of her narration purposefully turns the narrative resources of Mme de La Fayette against any earnest moral, social, or political scrutiny.

The hectic pace is characteristic of the amorous fiction of the period. Eliza Haywood's *Love in Excess* provides a last example:

She had not 'till now, had a moments time for reflection. . . . She was ready to die with shame, when she considered . . . [She considers for one quick sentence ending this paragraph, followed by further reflections, as follows:] But these thoughts soon gave way to another, equally as shocking . . . [A paragraph of complicated, quick thinking ensues, leading Melliora to a device to plug the lock against her would-be seducer. And the pace keeps up:] Melliora thought she had done a very heroick action,

> and sat her self down on the bed-side in a pleased contemplation of the
> conquest, she believed her virtue had gained over her passion. But alas!
> How little did she know the true state of her own heart? She no sooner
> heard a little noise . . . , but she thought . . .   (129–30)

Feelings run rampant, but again without any stability and consequently without any psychological intensity.

Walpole is no stranger to frenzy, to be sure. Emotions burst out. Indeed, nosebleeds such as that suffered by the statue were a conventional sign of feeling: "The Duchess's . . . resentment burst out into
a bleeding at her nose" (Manley, *New Atalantis*, 25). And Walpole's
passions lack the complexity found beneath the surface of Mme de La
Fayette's characters; inexpressibility formulas occur several times, but
only for evident "astonishment," "horror," and the "passions" ensuing on the revelation that Jerome is Theodore's father (*Otranto*, 58,
62, 91). On the other hand, thought occupies a proportionately larger
space in *The Castle of Otranto* than it does even in *La Princesse de
Clèves*, especially if Walpole's comic servants are discounted. All the
serious characters have thoughts or feelings reported, via one technique or another and at lesser or (mostly) greater length: Frederic, Jerome, Hippolita, Isabella, Matilda, Manfred, and of course the hero,
Theodore. Even if the reflections are not profound, these characters
dwell in them in a way I have found to exist previously only in Mme
de La Fayette. And Walpole no longer recognizes her separation of
thought from feeling. Emotions are continually in motion, agitating
and destabilizing personalities. The last paragraph of the first chapter
of *The Castle of Otranto* merits quoting at length to illustrate the
sense for the uncertainty of personality and the fluid boundary between conscious and subconscious moments, aware and repressed responses, deliberation and feeling:

> Manfred, though persuaded, like his wife, that the vision had been no
> work of fancy, recovered a little from the tempest of mind into which so
> many strange events had thrown him. Ashamed too of his inhuman
> treatment of a princess, who returned every injury with new marks of
> tenderness and duty; he felt returning love forcing itself into his eyes—
> but not less ashamed of feeling remorse towards one, against whom
> he was inwardly meditating a yet more bitter outrage, he curbed the

yearnings of this heart, and did not dare to lean even towards pity. The next transition of his soul was to exquisite villainy. Presuming on the unshaken submission of Hippolita, he flattered himself that she would not only acquiesce with patience to a divorce, but would obey, if it was his pleasure, in endeavouring to persuade Isabella to give him her hand— But, ere he could indulge this horrid hope, he reflected that Isabella was not to be found. (71–72)

The episode ends with a purported return of self-possession: "Coming to himself, he gave orders . . . " But once the action has been launched, it is evident that neither Manfred nor anyone else is ever really himself. Walpole did not invent the technique of psychonarration, but I continue to believe that *The Castle of Otranto* dwells in it with an extraordinary extensiveness and fluidity of movement (supported by the long arch of many of Walpole's sentences). He makes identity at once deeply problematic, embedded in the surge of time, and coextensive with mental processes, known and unknown. That, I think, is the true originality of his novel.

But the matter is ripe for further investigation.

NOTE ADDED IN PROOF. In *Lyric Generations* (155–58), Gabrielle Starr discusses the rendition of consciousness in early fiction, giving a wonderful example from Frances Brooke's novel *The Excursion* (1773). She alleges earlier instances in John Bunyan and in Richardson but provides no evidentiary material, and the earlier studies she cites were unavailable to me. On quick inspection, I see reports of judgments in Bunyan—"he thought . . . " or "they thought . . . "—and reported speech in Richardson, but not reports of thought processes and inward feelings.

5

Ghosts in the Flesh

Looking up, I view'd
A vast, gigantic spectre striding on
Thro' murmuring thunders and a waste of clouds,
With dreadful action.
   —Mark Akenside, *The Pleasures of Imagination*
                                    (1744), 2.506–9

EVERYONE MORE OR LESS AGREES that the gothic novel begins with *The Castle of Otranto* and likewise that *The Castle of Otranto* is a pretty poor book. The traditional view is that in writing a supernatural fiction Walpole did something very new, even if he didn't do it very well. Eventually, after a couple of decades, his innovation caught on, and other people started writing supernatural fiction and rapidly got much better at it. Walpole's unremarkable novel turned into a remarkable forerunner that gave birth to offspring far superior to itself. The logic of such accounts mostly remains unarticulated, probably because there isn't much logic to articulate. The picture is further clouded by the fact that virtually nothing in Walpole's "rather frothy little romance" (MacAndrew, *Gothic Tradition*, 9) forecasts what contemporaries and posterity would find admirable in Radcliffe, Lewis, or Shelley—not their slow crescendo of tension, their intricately motivated plotting, their richly meditative landscapes, nor their nuanced sociology. The incoherence of conventional literary histories led me to suspect that Walpole's actual accomplishment is something other than the supernaturalism with which his name is almost always linked.

The preceding chapters discussed some crucial elements of Walpole's innovations in relation to earlier fiction. Earlier fiction, however, does not offer ghost stories that much resemble Walpole's. But the Aristotelian theorizing in his prefaces, the unified, five-part structure of the plot, and the Shakespeare echoes all make it clear that his models are really to be sought in the playhouse. An avid watcher and reader of plays, Walpole wrote in a letter of 1775, "I am Methusalem in my memory of the stage" (*Corr.*, 32: 233). While the scholarship includes many routine acknowledgments of the novel's theatricality, I think only Giovanna Franci has given the dramatic aspect of *The Castle of Otranto* the attention it deserves (*Messa in scena*, 29–64). But not even she has related the novel to the playhouse. Yet in looking at Walpole's theatricality, we should not hesitate to look to the theater for models. Gary Kelly has pointed the way, in a book on the romantic novel that is at once thorough and original. Kelly calls attention to dramatic sources, specifically the Restoration heroic dramas and she-tragedies by Nicholas Rowe that were revived in the later eighteenth century. Along with prose romances, he says, these "influenced the grand air and somewhat operatic dialogues, the complex intrigues, exotic and 'historical' settings, and basic character repertory of Gothic novels, as well as conflicts of domestic and public loyalties and duties, conflict of the generations, and the theme of romantic love as a personal absolute running against social and political institutions and motives" (*English Fiction*, 50). Kelly's list of gothic motifs is admirable; nevertheless, in the desire to avoid cliché he leaves out what is surely the single defining attribute of gothic fiction—its ghosts and other supernatural mechanisms. And so, I suggest a second caution: in looking for backgrounds to the gothic, we should not hesitate to look for gothic backgrounds.

Therefore I propose examining supernatural devices in Restoration and eighteenth-century tragedy. Elizabeth MacAndrew continues her disparagement by noting, "*The Castle of Otranto* has several immediate antecedents—works that show an early use of historical setting, a ghost here and there," and so on. "These and other predecessors," she continues, "have, of course, been traced" (*Gothic Tradition*, 9). Beware "of course." An outstanding general survey first published in 1915, which discusses all the tragedies I managed to find on my own except for the two closest to Walpole, and an essay of 1937 do not, between them, say everything.[1] There is still work to be done.

Certainly, tragic theater in Greece, Rome, and England (as well as in Spain and Germany) frequently employed ghosts and other supernatural devices. However, Walpole's assorted body parts and gigantic manifestations do not seem all that close to Seneca's premonitory phantoms or Shakespeare's brooding specters and witches.[2] The gothic novel has not been persuasively linked with the earlier supernatural stage effects because in fact its emphases are different. The earlier ghosts trouble the state, typically at the outset of their tragedies; Walpole's Alfonso rises at the end of the novel in order—after the mode of heroic tragedy—to set things to right. The gulf that appears to divide Walpole from Shakespeare shows up in one eighteenth-century favorite, Nicholas Rowe's *Fair Penitent*. Act 5 of Rowe's play opens in an Ophelian vein: the "disordered" Calista contemplates Lothario's corpse with all the trimmings: she sings a song summoning "midnight phantoms, . . . pale and wan," then has a long solitary "meditation" evoking "frenzy," "madness," "ghosts, fantastic forms of night," and "dreadful shapes." Such kindred specters that reflect a character's mood are distinctly Shakespearian and little resemble Walpole's pompously sententious Alfonso. The act closes, however, with a different, much more Walpolean pose in Calista's pious self-accusation and tearful reconciliation with her father. Here the play suddenly seems to enter the new century as "epidemic madness" (as one character calls it at 5.240) indulges in sentimental rhetoric altogether different from the previous Elizabethan supernaturalism. This is the new emotional and rhetorical air that Alfonso also breathes. On the other hand, in one crucial respect Alfonso still resembles his dramatic predecessors and differs from his narrative imitators: whereas subsequent gothic demons and villains are typically evil, furtive, and deceptive, Walpole's Alfonso follows the earlier convention: he knows and tells the truth in order to exact a justified retribution. Devices and values both count, and Walpole's half-religious sublime is clearly in transition between an old rhetoric and a new psychology.[3]

With these observations in mind, I started looking for predecessors that are closer in spirit to Walpole than is *Hamlet*, even if they are less familiar. The ensuing examples suggest a set of conclusions that I will now state as theses, in advance of the evidence. The supernatural elements in *The Castle of Otranto* belong to its most traditional layer, not its innovation. What Walpole undertakes with the supernatural in his novel is not invention but borrowing. Consequently, as Kelly rightly intuited and as I argued in "The Birth of *The Castle of Otranto*" (Chapter 3 above), his genuine innovation was not in the supernatural but in the response to it. Inevitably, ghosts on the page are less immediate than ghosts in the flesh, if any exist; old dramatic plots provoke a changed reaction when given a narrative presentation. In relation to the plays I am about to discuss, *The Castle of Otranto* appears more nearly a pensive transmutation than a smashing innovation. *The Castle of Otranto* succeeds primarily by imbuing fiction with an aura, not by cranking up the mechanism.

The Castle of Otranto turns out to belong to a group of works employing what I shall call the prodigal-infant plot. A valiant youth, torn from his parents in infancy, wanders into a state suffering from misrule and beset by strife and evil omens. The youth falls magically in love with the princess or (in other versions of the story) with the widowed queen. After the usurping ruler or a surrogate attacks him as an enemy of the state, tokens, divine portents, or actual manifestation of a supernatural spirit reveal the hidden truth of his parentage— he is the rightful ruler, long concealed by the forces of evil—and the usurper is overthrown. Three outcomes are possible. If the usurper was an outsider such as an ambitious general, leaving the princess's own heritage untainted, then prince valiant may get his girl and live happily ever after. If the beloved princess comes from the usurping stock, then the prince may lose her and be forced to live unhappily ever after, as happens to Walpole's Theodore. Finally, if the prince has been so unfortunate as to marry the queen, he may find himself at once hero and victim, for if he is the true prince and she is the true queen, then she is his mother. That is notably the situation of *Oedipus*, the most compact and hence the most knotty of all these plots, as well as their earliest model.

Three comments are in order on this group of plots. First, the unsullied youths of sentimental versions are necessarily younger than King Oedipus. Their offstage exile has typically been uneventful, and their triumph comes quickly. The ruler, on the other hand, is older, and the time he has spent on the throne alienates him from his inborn character. Justice rolls the clock back; its task is to abolish the past, not to prepare the future. The virtuous youth belongs to space and action and therein appears pitted against an older generation that is subject to corruption, time, and suffering. Second, the love plot is an emotional necessity, not a logical one; it is conceptually independent of the political plot, and generally dramaturgically independent as well. A wronged and rightful ruler really doesn't *have* to fall in love with *anybody* in order to be dramatically returned to the throne. The youth was beset by a mysterious male persecution and lost his identity; he is rewarded by an equally mysterious female bonding. In these plots love is not a natural growth that counters unnatural persecution but rather an opposing enchantment, instant and inexplicable. Like time, affection is unexplained and denaturing—positively or negatively charged electricity. Third and finally, as the *Oedipus* plot shows, no simplification is possible. With more figures and less time the oppositions are externalized; in *Oedipus* the figures merge, leaving fewer plots and counterplots, but the affections only grow murkier and the characters more self-divided. One explanation for the besetting darkness of *Oedipus* is that outer threats have fallen away and inner threats cannot be seen, or can be seen only with the eyes of the mind, in a blinding revelation. There is no way to unravel the knots. Generically, nature lies outside these plots; it lurks on the periphery as a pure, savage exteriority outside experience, outside the family, outside the social community. Nature has no natural place on the neoclassical stage.

One predecessor play has been previously cited. In a 1947 study entitled *Gothic Drama from Walpole to Shelley*, Bertrand Evans mentions John Home's 1756 tragedy *Douglas* as a forerunner to Walpole. Home's durably popular work was much admired by Walpole. It concerns the noble Matilda, who, years before the action of the play, had secretly married her hereditary enemy Douglas. Douglas was immediately slain in battle, and his posthumous child was lost with the nurse bearing him to safety. At the start of the play the now grown son arrives and rescues Matilda's second husband, Randolph. Though unrecognized, the hero makes an instant impact on Matilda, who says that "a spark from fancy . . . kindle[s] up a fondness" for him in her (2.169–70). While Randolph is more virtuous than most such improper rulers, he is burdened with a vicious heir, Glenarvon, who foments jealousies. Glenarvon stabs young Douglas from behind; Douglas kills him; and Matilda jumps off a cliff, leaving the despondent Randolph to depart for a doomed battle against the English. The play features gloomy outdoor settings—"The court of a castle surrounded with woods" in acts 1–4, "The Wood" at midnight in act 5— and a pervasive sense of time that is both static and compressed: feelings long bottled up blaze out of control, and too much happens too suddenly for ready comprehension or emotional development. In a world beset by enemies domestic, internal, and foreign—respectively, Glenarvon, the Douglas clan, and the English—none of the hostilities has a rational origin or explanation. Yet despite much wild talk, including several references to ghosts and supernatural visitations, no specters actually tread the stage. For in *Douglas* the gothic is under way toward a later dispensation—an atmosphere of irrationality and a delusion of power. Similar rhetoric becomes the staple of some of the most intensely psychological creations of the German romantics, including many of Heinrich von Kleist's stories and plays and Friedrich Schiller's *Maid of Orleans*, a play set in the distant past and climaxed by an actual stage ghost. Evans is right to invoke *Douglas*, for Home lies further along the trajectory that Walpole also pursues.

In introducing *Douglas*, the editors, Dougald MacMillan and Howard Mumford Jones, mention Aaron Hill's 1749 *Merope* as a predecessor to Home. Hill was an important literary figure in his day, a friend of both Pope and Richardson, and one of Handel's librettists. Though not so popular as *Douglas*, *Merope* held the stage throughout the 1750s and was published in several editions. In plot it is even closer than *Douglas* to *The Castle of Otranto*—so close, indeed, as to seem a direct precursor. Hill's source is Voltaire's *Mérope*; Walpole regretted missing a performance on account of gout in 1765 but finally managed to see it staged in 1769 (*Corr.*, 35: 122; 31: 60), and he discusses Voltaire's extensive prefatory epistle to *Mérope* in the preface to the second edition of *The Castle of Otranto*. Yet despite the striking anticipations of *The Castle of Otranto* in Hill's *Merope*, and despite the hint in the Jones-MacMillan anthology, the play has gone unnoticed by literary historians. Hill, a wretchedly overheated writer, merits only a few dismissive comments in Walpole's correspondence, but *Merope* stands somewhat apart from Hill's other works and deserves, if not better, at least different strictures.[4]

Again the plot concerns the secret identity of a noble youth. Eumenes, the long-lost prince brought up as a shepherd, returns to Mycene. He fights off attackers at the border, but since he wields the dead king's sword, he is himself arrested on suspicion of murder. Though he reminds Queen Merope of the king, she is about to execute him when his foster sister reveals his identity. The villain in all this is the general Poliphontes, who had killed the king and has long sought to marry the queen. With the people on his side, Poliphontes tells Merope that if she marries him, he will acknowledge Eumenes, but if she refuses, he will execute Eumenes. Eumenes chooses death, but his foster sister, looking out at the temple courtyard, sees a deus ex machina: thunder and darkness terrify the crowd, the roof shakes and "seem[s] to *bow*" (Hill, *Dramatic Works*, 2: 255; 5: 4). Poliphontes is overthrown and killed, and Eumenes' divine ancestry is recognized. This divine intervention closely resembles the opening of *The Castle of Otranto*, where an offstage courtyard manifestation punishes a tainted bridegroom to the amazement of a crowd. But then Hill's scene changes to the temple itself, in a scenic effect both spectacular and disturbing, and amid a hubbub of voices and trumpets, "A loud clap of thunder"—forecasting the thunderclap that brings down the Castle of Otranto—confirms the verdict of the gods.

Hill's Poliphontes is an overweening rationalist who has been willing to calculate opportunity and to wait decades for the moment to force marriage on Merope. Her own advisor, Euricles, likewise rationalizes, recommending that she placate the usurper for the sake of future peace. By contrast, Eumenes says, "my fix'd hate was *instinct*" (*Dramatic Works*, 2: 235; 3.3). Along with his foster father, Eumenes speaks the language of passion, fury, and madness; long before he learns his true identity, he is irresistibly drawn to his fate, his honor, and the idea of royal legitimacy. Thus, throughout the play comprehensible evil confronts mysterious, angelic virtue. A seemingly supernatural steadfastness of resolve, arriving from outside the city, triumphs over base manipulation; it is then confirmed by the concluding manifestations of the heavens. The deus ex machina merely corroborates what the omniscient audience has long known. In this play supernatural forces do not overturn the human determinations of the protagonist as they commonly do in classical and Elizabethan tragedies. Rather, in Eumenes, the descendant of gods, human persistence overcomes the natural surge of feelings.

The staginess of Hill's deus ex machina is essential to the play's message. None of the thematic and theatrical elements I have been describing is taken from Voltaire's *Mérope* (1743); in particular, Hill's rapid, precisely rendered description of the first (offstage) deus ex machina replaces a long, typically French *tirade* that narrates an irresolute scene of utter confusion. Voltaire does have Hill's second deus ex machina, the thunderclap, but without the change of scene, so that it relieves confusion instead of adding to it. Hence Mérope calls the thunderclap the voice of heaven, whereas Hill's Eumenes says that it "make[s] voice needless" (*Dramatic Works*, 2: 255; 5.5). Hill suspends reason, as his incessant, prosy ranting yields to unexpected, transcendently manifested powers of the heart, instinct, and morality, exceeding anything that can be formulated in words. Poliphontes, who knows how to manipulate courtiers, women, and crowds, is wise in the ways of the world, but the *coup de théâtre* installs a more commanding truth. As in Home's *Douglas*, but with a more Walpolean flamboyance, we catch sight of a realm beyond experience. The past is restored to the present, the low to the heights, and errant virtue to the city. Yet the play is not a celebration of human accomplishment. Eumenes exercises his valor offstage, before the action begins; onstage his triumph is linked to a readiness to endure martyrdom. In the more naturalistic *Douglas* the hero is capable of resolute action, but he and his society suffer the consequences. Hill's conclusion turns the clock back to enforce an ancient order threatened by the otherwise ceaseless flux of time. The supernatural finds its place in a temple; it is architectural and stabilizing. So was the sanitized, mother-son bond that Voltaire had already preferred to risky exogamy and polluted incest alike. But the clarity of speech in Voltaire allows his play to end with a consoling restoration, whereas the deafening spectacle leaves Hill's *Merope* to sink into Walpolean melancholy.

It has become common in recent decades to think of the gothic as a revolutionary mode. Whether the verdict is radical (as in Godwin and Shelley) or reactionary (as in Burke and Maturin), the supernatural becomes the language of a destructive uprising. Thus David Punter, for instance, says that in Walpole "the supernatural itself becomes a symbol of our past rising against us" (*Literature of Terror*, 53). It's true that Manfred's past rises against him, but it is *our* past rising against *us* only to the extent that we identify with Manfred. Punter takes off from verse antecedents where such a personal focus makes sense. But on the neoclassical stage the embodied supernatural is inescapable, hence never what Tzvetan Todorov calls fantastic, and it invests the theatrical order with an absolute authority. Consequently, in the vein preceding and including Walpole, the supernatural is not the historical past in opposition but the timeless past rising up to rescue us. By the solidity or dramatic immediacy of its stage representation, it interrupts not regular process but rather dramatic conflict and confusion. It is a suspension of the disorder of nature and of human corruption.

Actual ghosts grow scarcer after the Restoration because they might upset the applecart. Alfonso's dilation is great to read about, but in performance Hill's thunderclap is impressive enough. Anything further risks falling into farce, as do the five ghosts of John Gay's 1715 parody, *The What D'Ye Call It*. After all, unlike Fielding's Partridge, many in the enlightened public did not really believe in ghosts; they were always a figure for something. And yet, there were ghosts on the neoclassical stage. To be sure, most of them were the ghosts in Elizabethan or classical revivals that form part of Walpole's context without being in his mode. But despite the pressures for verisimilitude, there are neoclassical ghosts as well. And they do confirm that the gothic begins neither as a revolutionary anti-society nor as an irrational anti-nature, but rather as the provocation to exploring a deeper, more complex humanity.

The great arbiter of neoclassicism was Voltaire. In the same year that Hill's *Merope* appeared (1749), Voltaire returned to the prodigal-infant plot in *Sémiramis*. (*Sémiramis* itself was translated into English in 1776, in a fairly skillful version by George Ayscough, later Lord Littleton; the Lewis-Walpole Library contains an unmarked and unbound copy.) Though not intended for music, *Sémiramis* is more operatic than dramatic: Voltaire's prefatory essay begins by praising Metastasio's librettos for their powerful naturalism (not the quality posterity associates with them), and the supernatural devices must be seen in this context. *Sémiramis* is a long and ranting text, at its worst in the flaming apothegms supposed to epitomize human understanding and at its relative best in the confused emotions and pacing of act 4. Language claims a delusory absolutism; thus, as Sémiramis is about to select a consort, she conceives of her word as the world, with the hollow social symbolism of a stage court: "When I have said the word, the earth will lie at his feet. . . . I wed him, and give him the world in dower. Finally my glory is pure, and I can savor it."[5] The absolutist's pure fiat compels the past to oblivion. Indeed, on the theory that to forget is to forgive (the hero's utterance, "I wish to ignore everything," "Je veux tout ignorer," at the end of act 4, unconsciously puns on the Latin verb for forgiving, *ignosco*), the characters share an interest in abolishing knowledge—the culprits' knowledge that they had poisoned the father; the heroine's knowledge of her status, which stands in the way of marrying the déclassé hero; and the hero's knowledge of his entanglement in political and family intrigue. Along with these creating and uncreating fiats come illusions of regularity and continuity, to the degree that even a rare mid-act scene change (in act 3) from private cabinet to crowded reception hall falls in the middle of a couplet whose rhyme serves to bridge the interruption. But spectacle proves more decisive than the incessant flow of speech: a dark tomb, a bloody sword, and a triumphantly punctuating thunderbolt finally quash the tyrannical exertions, and suddenly, in thunder, the ghost of the murdered father, Ninus (not listed among the dramatis personae), stops the show. Ninus doesn't talk much: his two speeches of cryptically ambivalent exhortation to the hero and warning to the guilty widow total 6 lines in all. His crucial line, "Remember thy father," "Souviens-toi de ton père" (3.320) is a *Hamlet* echo that cannot be missed, since Voltaire's preface discusses Shakespeare's play, praising its ghost while blaming the rest. But Ninus does not proclaim the reinstatement of patriarchal reason here. For whereas Hamlet recognizes his father and knows what he is talking about, Voltaire's hero knows only his foster father and therefore misunderstands the message. Hence, even though the plot would seem to point toward a restoration of order, Voltaire's preface declares the essence of the supernatural to lie in its disruptiveness. "I should wish above all that the intervention of these supernatural beings not appear absolutely necessary. Let me explain myself: if the knot of a tragic poem is so tangled that the author can only escape from his difficulties with the aid of a wonder, the spectator feels his embarrassment, and the lameness of the expedient" (*Théâtre*, 464). Voltaire describes his artifice in formal terms. A ghost demanded by the logic of the plot is not what the author wants.

Where form goes, ideology cannot be far behind. A motivated deus ex machina would be a dependent god, not a truly independent divinity. Voltaire's dead father proclaims his law with peremptory artifice that suspends the corrupt course of reason. Such a ghost does not participate in plotted action as Elizabethan and romantic ghosts do; his form of justice is not continuous with human experience. The shock of a play like this thus strikes at the foundations of empiricism. It is a challenge the eighteenth century did not often make and perhaps did not know how to make very well, but it is real and was felt at the time to be theatrically effective. The ghost comes from a world that we would now designate as not just morally transcendent but epistemologically transcendental—a world in which sound abolishes sense. An irresistible yet inscrutable truth like this is a sublime tinged with religious feeling but unsupported by institutions, doctrine, or orthodoxy. I think it is best categorized in terms of recent psychoanalytic theory. Of course, Voltaire did not anticipate Freudianism in any formal or articulate way; nevertheless, his crude theatrical device makes the kind of impression that post-Freudian, specifically Lacanian, theory has set out to analyze. The ghost of Ninus is a figure of what Jacques Lacan calls the Real, the primal world unprocessed by any of our psychic rationalisms. In the terms of one of Lacan's best explicators, Slavoj Žižek, the ghost is the sublime object of ideology, or it is one of those traumatic symptoms that we love to hate, rising as Other to check illusions.

Enlightened specters don't fit the usual conceptions of their intellectual world. In the face of such operatic effects, one scholar, Charles Whitmore, gives up the ghost. "The supernatural in the Restoration period," he says, "is a meaningless survival from a better time, with no real relation to the new age" (*Supernatural*, 298). Looking for meaning, he finds only vacancy, artifice devoid of ideology. That suspension of reason is, however, just the point proclaimed by Voltaire's praise of the unnecessary ghost. With that in mind, I turn next to the example that Whitmore, in the same passage, dismisses as inarticulate: "Non-speaking ghosts, it may be noted, also occur at the end of Otway's *Venice Preserved* (1682)."

Venice Preserved; or, A Plot Discovered, by Thomas Otway, concerns an impoverished commoner named Jaffeir, who had earlier rescued Senator Priuli's daughter Belvidera from a shipwreck. They married and had a son, without recognition from Priuli, who is now trying to confiscate Jaffeir's remaining possessions. The frustrated Jaffeir is drawn into a conspiracy by his friend Pierre, but turns coat upon discovering that the conspirators are as corrupt and violent as the senators. The friends escape through a suicide pact, and in the famous conclusion, their ghosts, accompanied by "soft music," silently confront first Belvidera and then her father. She collapses and dies; he repents his paternal cruelty.

There is much additional byplay, but nothing that really integrates the two plots. Indeed, a prologue Dryden wrote for a performance of the play articulates the separation: "A Tyrant's Pow'r in rigour is exprest: / The Father yearns in the true Prince's Breast" ("Prologue to His Royal Highness," ll. 8–29). On the one side lies the conspiracy that preexists the stage action; it is apparently doomed even without Jaffeir's treachery, since conspirators are already being apprehended offstage while he is revealing it onstage to the senators (act 4, scene 2), and its consequences are unreported (hence the title words "preserved" and "discovered" rather than "restored" or "punished"). (*The Fair Penitent* involves a similar disjunction: offstage crowds imply a political dimension that is never actuated.) On the other side are the silent ghosts, who are too firmly attached to the sentimental domestic conclusion to function as Elizabethan fate figures. Rather, in their refusal to speak even when addressed, they refute any pretensions to rational and knowable truths. In addition there is a comic sideshow that underscores the separation of plots and the lack of rational order. It concerns Pierre's beloved Aquilina, who has been betraying him for a wealthy, pathetically foolish, and grotesquely sadomasochistic senator. While Aquilina's infidelity drove Pierre into the conspiracy, the potential conflict of politics and love, high and low, remains as indecisive in Pierre's case as in Jaffeir's. What matters—and what remains onstage at the end—is the purity of their sentiments in a world that has no place for purity. A void commands experience, physically represented by the bloody, silent ghosts. When they sink out of sight, they draw Belvidera after them into the unconscious depths—"They've hold on me, and drag me to the bottom," she says as she dies (5.2; p. 304), as if undoing all events since being saved from drowning. Her father concludes by invoking the darkness. "Uncanny" is not the right term for the powerfully stabilizing effect, but no discursive decoding is possible for figures that have no meaning and do not organize a plot.

The ghosts in Otway's *Venice Preserved* fulfill Voltaire's demands better than the one in his own *Sémiramis*. Voltaire claims that ghosts are most effective as supernumeraries, and he contrives to make the ghost seem arbitrary: testamentary evidence shows up independently after the ghost's exhortation, and the ghost's manipulations remain persistently associated with confusion and darkness. (As he is being led offstage to his punishment, the villain stages the final coup by revealing Sémiramis as the unintended—though also justly punished—victim. Ayscough's English version lets the hero defeat the villain onstage to the accompaniment of thunder and lightning—a more conventionally moralized, less abrupt and arbitrary ending.) Yet the dead Ninus still appears to pull all the strings, both in the deceptive call for the hero to remember his father and in various manifestations that lure the doomed Sémiramis into the sacred precincts where he will mistakenly kill her. By contrast, Otway's Belvidera is already dying and her father already apparently repentant by the time the dead heroes' ghosts put in their brief appearance. The ghosts really aren't needed; their bodily presence projects the permanence of the inexplicable passions governing human destinies and infecting the audience from the stage, as the final couplet says: "Sparing no tears when you this tale relate, / But bid all cruel fathers dread my fate" (304).

I do not think the eighteenth century had an adequate vocabulary for describing the effect aroused by ghosts such as these. "Ruling passion" was its nearest term, but a ruling passion remains both personal and nameable, unlike the fatal but scarcely moral energies of silent or laconic ghosts. Possibly, indeed, the eighteenth century brooded so much about ruling passions precisely because the concept remained inadequate to the intuition it was trying to characterize. The ghosts I have been describing—central yet inexplicable, the meaningless ground of meaningful order—seem to me better understood in terms that chronology makes us perhaps too reluctant to apply to incoherencies three centuries old. A famous passage in Freud's *Interpretation of Dreams* sounds remarkably like what Voltaire struggled to express, and the anachronism will be less troubling if we concede that Freud had developed a logic, a locale, and a method for analyzing what the Enlightenment barely found a primitive means to suggest in representation. The passage I mean is the one describing the "navel" of dreams, that point where the irrational persistently gives notice of itself. What is important is that the irrational is always there, that it cannot be rationalized or interpreted, that it nevertheless resides beneath our daily actions and is the source of their primary impulses, as an arbitrary point of stabilization.

> In the most successfully interpreted dreams a passage must often be left in the dark because we note in the interpretation that a knot of dream thoughts starts there which does not permit unravelling, yet also makes no further contributions to the dream content. This is then the navel of the dream, the place where it sits atop the unknown. The dream thoughts that we come upon through interpretation must very generally remain without conclusion. . . . Like a mushroom out of its mycelium, then, the dream wish arises at a place where the weave is quite close.

Here Freud cautiously says this uninterpretable knot occurs only "often," but elsewhere he insists on its universality: "There is at least one spot in every dream at which it is unplumbable—a navel, as it were, that is its point of contact with the unknown."[6] It is tempting to regard the navel of the dream as a point of failure, where nothing more can be known. But Freud is explicit that the point where dream contents stop making sense is the point where the enabling wish is rooted. That is why Lacan, describing this point as a node of stability, coined the phrase "quilting point" (*point de capiton*) to name it. The node, as Lacan stresses, is "mythical" (*Speech*, 274), yet it is, as Žižek observes, entrusted with the "interpellation of individuals . . . into subjects" (*Sublime Object*, 101). It "is not a point of supreme density of Meaning . . . : its role is purely structural, its nature is purely performative. . . . The element which . . . is experienced as a kind of transcendent Guarantee, . . . which is in its bodily presence nothing but an embodiment of a certain lack, is perceived as a point of supreme plenitude" (*Sublime Object*, 99). Clearly, eighteenth-century ghosts do not fully work out this psychomythology, but they explore primitive, undeveloped versions of it.

Perhaps the most remarkable supernaturalized neoclassical reworking of the prodigal-infant story is the 1678 version of *Oedipus* by John Dryden (who is presumed to have written the scenario) and Nathaniel Lee. In this turbulent play Dryden adds to the spare Sophoclean and Senecan plots a second incestuous liaison: Creon pursues Jocasta's daughter (and his own niece) Eurydice, to whom he was betrothed in her infancy. She, however, loves Adrastus, an enemy prisoner from Argos with whom Oedipus is bound in friendship. Fickle crowds, scheming nobles, hypocritical allies, and an abundance of partial and deceptive revelations create one of the most sullen versions of the political instability Dryden so often evoked in his satires and of the skeptical rationalism leading toward *Religio Laici* (1682). Unlike the doctrinal poem to come, the play lets fate prevail over faith and darkness preempt vision, as happens early in act 5. Here Haemon, captain of the guard, reports watching through a chink as Oedipus tears out his eyes. "When Haemon weeps," as Creon says, "without the help of ghosts / I may foretel there is a fatal cause" (*Oedipus*, 207).

Ghosts, however, abound, and the question to be asked is what purpose they serve in a world so full of fatal causes. The play presents a whole gamut of such causes, from irrational passions, omens, prophecies, haunted sleepwalkings, nightmares, prodigies of nature, and conjurings, to Laius's ghost in four incarnations: as an offstage voice challenging Oedipus and Jocasta, as a private onstage voice accusing Oedipus, as a confessional speaker unwillingly summoned by Tiresias and his daughter Manto, and finally as a thundering celestial vision denouncing the incestuous couple in the last act. The last manifestation closely resembles Alfonso's more public assumption into the thundering heavens in *The Castle of Otranto*, and, curiously, Dryden gives Oedipus's rustic stepmother the name Merope, evoking the other prodigal-infant myth later dramatized by Voltaire and Hill. But the psychology of *Oedipus*, at least in Dryden's portion of the text, is far subtler than that of any of these later works, and the political and sexual dynamic would have sufficed to drive the tragedy without any supernatural infusion. To be sure, Lee had recently used ghosts to some effect in *The Rival Queens* (1677)—a Banquo-like stage walker in act 1 and an accusing chorus of spirits opening act 5. But these seem almost disjunct from the action: Lee's King Philip does not appear in the cast of characters, and the spirits warble death in anapests. And in any case, the ghosts in *Oedipus* appear in both authors' portions and form an integral part of the atmosphere despite seeming superfluous to the action.

That disjunction of atmosphere and action, surely, is just the point. In the subsidiary plots of politics and love, with their animated crowd scenes and intense confrontations, the protagonists (Creon, Euridice, Adrastus) jockey to seize emotional and tactical advantages. Their struggles to hasten or delay catastrophe culminate in the middle of the final act with a series of sudden moves: all three are stabbed on stage in quick succession, with Euridice and Adrastus prating of love and pleasure and Creon continuing to adjure "the dictates of my daring mind" and "the god, ambition." But all of this action in time is mere foreground. Divine fury manifest in the ghosts repeals mere human desire. The parting curtains reveal Jocasta and her children, already multiply stabbed, with the "groping ghost" Oedipus standing above, then plunging amid thunder, "Swift as a falling meteor, . . . downwards to the darker sky." The epilogue is wryly clear-sighted about the displacement of the one kind of spectacle by the other, whose "treat is what your palates relish most, / Charm! song! and show! a murder and a ghost!" (*Oedipus*, 222). The back stage and the

upper stage become worlds out of nature. The play opens with the ee-
rie terror of the plague, but by the end even that miasma is virtually
forgotten in the "horror / And pity" (220) aroused by the inflexible
destiny of the cursed individuals. Charm, song, and ghost return the
stage to a primitive physicality before which those left on stage can utter only meaningless pieties. Oedipus dies asking the gods to admire
him, to "Shout and applaud me with a clap of thunder," which they
do. Nothing here is plausibly motivated, and Haemon's ensuing reaction, "O cursed effect of the most deep despair," remains so woefully
inept, even for Lee's slender abilities, that the contrast must be intentional. Oedipus's death, in this play, is not the result of any definable
cause. Rather it is a manifestation of the kind of ineluctable force that
Percy Shelley was later to call both "the one Spirit's plastic stress"
(*Adonais*, l. 381) and then, with his own tragic irony, "The Triumph
of Life."

By quoting Shelley I do not mean to make a romantic of Dryden.
Juxtaposing the two authors should, in fact, evince exactly the reverse: what is most striking is the failure of neoclassical ghosts to
inspire any articulately transcendental thoughts. The theatrical aim
of manifesting or embodying a force subverts the emotional aim of
imagining it. Unlike the spare Elizabethan theater stage, the spectacular visual and aural effects of the neoclassical stage (and their predecessor in the masque) offer little leeway for empathic speculation. It's
hard to imagine suspending disbelief, willingly or unwillingly, while
the thunder is roaring at Oedipus's behest.[7] Rather, the spectacular
machinery compels visceral admiration. Indeed, to understand the
erstwhile success of these plays we must attribute to their audience a
kind of attention we can no longer muster. The spectators cannot
have sunk into the atmosphere like the deluded Partridge, but can
have enjoyed the displays only by retaining distance. The primary impact is material: the actor's body and vocal declamation, the spectacular scenic tableau, the noise. If these things are to claim any deeper
impact, it is essential to disbelieve the first impressions of the senses.
We find it puzzling why Johnson's and Coleridge's arguments for literary empathy were not always self-evident, and perhaps yet more
mysterious that Dryden's criticism could sometimes articulate similar
sentiments without their taking root. But in fact romantic absorption

presupposes particular forms of staging and spectatordom and displaces other forms. Hence it is not altogether foolish to describe neoclassical stage ghosts as the romantic imaginary caught in a straitjacket of enlightened representation. They are the continent that would later be rediscovered as the unconscious; their romantic successors are the hallucinatory visions climaxing Goethe's *Egmont* (with the hero "wrapped in pleasing madness") and Kleist's *Prince Friedrich of Homburg*. But in their own day the ghosts remained outside rather than buried within the mental universe. To the extent that we see the neoclassical ghost plays as unsuccessfully self-divided, we would have to say that the ghosts are released into their destined nature when they escape their bodily fetters.

But such a romantic perspective on neoclassical ghosts fails to explain their durability on the eighteenth-century stage. Understanding them on their own terms requires respecting rather than criticizing their internal divisions. Emotion versus passion, natural sentiment versus supernatural body, character versus fatality, temporal development versus spatial immediacy—in all these dualisms, neoclassical ghosts make the second element the one that counts and that masters the first. In its unaccountability, the second or ghostly element could be mistaken for the romantic unconscious. But the unconscious is an irrational force with an etiology rooted in the contingencies of infantile experience. The eighteenth century, by contrast, uniformly regarded consciousness as the contingent, associative, and irrational side of experience, underlain by a rationality to which it had only imperfect access. Dryden's Tiresias expresses the polarity in a speech that foreshadowed Pope's *Essay on Man* and that Dryden later revised into a famous set-piece in *Religio Laici*:

> The gods are just;
> But how can finite measure infinite?
> Reason! alas, it does not know itself. . . .
> Whatever is, is in its causes just;
> Since all things are by fate. But purblind man
> Sees but a part o'the chain.
>
> (*Oedipus* 3.1; p. 174)

Walter Scott's introduction to his edition of Dryden's *Oedipus* singles out this speech for admiration, presumably responding more to the intuitive mystery of reason than to its secret solidity. What the neoclassical refutation of experience performs is something quite different from the miraculous illumination of dark mysteries to which much romantic gothic (including the gothic element in Scott) tends. In their full-bodied obstinacy, neoclassical stage ghosts trumpet a doctrine of order imposed from beyond awareness. The senses do not give sense; rather, an arbitrary and inescapable lineage determines the limits within which meaningful action becomes possible. Romantic meaning emerges from the twilight and imperfect knowledge generated by uncertain human endeavor; it remains as a future horizon constantly being approached as it ever recedes. (The philosophical expressions of romantic futurity include Kant's regulative ideals, Fichte's asymptotes, and Hegel's dialectical equating of being with beginning; its poetic expressions include the themes of awakening in Goethe and Keats and the morning suns of Wordsworth and Thoreau.) Conversely, the limits of Enlightenment reason are a constraint from the past, or from a timeless realm experienced as past—whether Leibniz's watchmaker-God at one end of the period or Burke's custom at the other. Meaning is granted by arbitrary separations that must be honored without recuperation. Incest (or confusion of identity) is the first danger; Jocasta's crucial achievement and provocation of the evil Creon in Dryden's play—until her delusion is tragically revealed—is having apparently married a "stranger" (1.1; p. 134). For the romantic there is no other or outside world without a self: time and again, loss of identity becomes equated with solipsism or loss of the outside world. Conversely, in the Enlightenment there is no self without an other to give boundary and shape to identity.

Classical and Elizabethan ghosts are as prone to be political (*Macbeth*) as familial (*Hamlet*). Romantic ghosts and their avatars ("The Turn of the Screw," *The Sound and the Fury, Beloved*) externalize the drives buried within the region of the psyche that Freud was to call the id. In the later nineteenth century these ghosts often blend with or get replaced by mythic powers like Guy de Maupassant's Horla, Bram Stoker's Dracula, or Rider Haggard's She. In contrast to all these, the concentration of neoclassical ghosts in the prodigal-infant plot—as in the familial, antipolitical dimension of *Venice Preserved*—indicates their distinctive function. Representing established origins, they quell the turmoil or chaos toward which human interactions inherently slide (and reach at the end of Pope's *Dunciad*, as the ghosts of human endeavor dissolve into meaningless farce); thus, they do not so much deny as declare and direct. The prodigal infant has grown up as a tabula rasa; hence his curious combination of purity and aimlessness (this is also the nature of Otway's Jaffeir). The inscription that should have established his identity internally must instead now come from strange signs—tokens to be deciphered and words uttered in thunder. Opposing the natural causal order of experience, fatality appears in a supernatural guise. The deus ex machina stands in as the institutor of meaning in a world violently cut adrift.

Dryden, Lee, Otway, and others included additional supernatural figures in plays (and operas as well)—ghosts of the dead, divinities, spirit choruses.[8] My discussion has concerned the plays that remained most popular in the eighteenth century or that share the plot structure of *The Castle of Otranto*. Such retrospect highlights a hardly surprising shift in attitude. Coming late in the game, Home's *Douglas* preserves the spirit of this myth even while anthropologizing it. Arbitrary and confusing tribal and national enmities overlay the deprivation of familial identity. The catastrophe dispenses with a supernatural revelation; its open-air setting preserves only the aura of spirituality; as the hero says in the opening monologue of act 5:

> In such a place as this, at such an hour,
> If ancestry [ancient lore] can be in aught believed,
> Descending spirits have conversed with man,
> And told the secrets of the world unknown.
> (*Douglas* 5.9–12)

Thus it indicates a desire to arrive at organic founding gestures and a natural understanding of the institution of identity.

In relation to this line of forebears, *The Castle of Otranto* looks like a throwback, not an innovation. With predominantly indoor settings, an artificially stagy deus ex machina (whether or not directly borrowed from Hill), and an ascension resembling that in the Dryden-Lee *Oedipus*, the plot outline of Walpole's novel offers little that was unfamiliar. Its original reception as a historical fiction seems, in retrospect, like readerly wish-fulfillment, as does Scott's praise of it for its realistic portrait of manners. On the contrary, in comparison with works of the romantic generation, it appears strikingly littered with residual features that block fulfillment of naturalistic yearnings like Home's. And even its supernatural side offers novelty only in the incidental devices of terror. As hoary as the prodigal-infant plot are the accusing voices and the commanding ghost; even the vaunted underground passages have analogues in Sémiramis's (offstage) crypt and, more directly, in the burial-room setting in act 5 of Rowe's *Fair Penitent*. To these Walpole adds merely fragmentary foretastes that can't be shown onstage—loose body parts and a walking picture. These were novelties, perhaps, but in terms of literary history they evoke Gilbert and Sullivan's *Ruddigore* rather than anything more earnest; no one claims that Walpole's fame rests on the attack by a giant helmet or the bloated pageant of Frederic's arrival with hundreds of men carrying a giant sword.

We are left, then, with a simple but surprisingly overlooked observation. In his novel, Walpole took a variant of the long-familiar Oedipus story and changed it chiefly by presenting it in narrative rather than dramatic form. In Chapter 3 I considered Walpole's innovation as inward displacement, but it can now be understood also as a silencing. Adapting the novel for the stage was easily accomplished but doomed to failure. Elevated diction diversified with comic patter, long formal declamations, and intense monologues occupy the bulk of the novel's text, to a degree incompatible with live performance. As in *Douglas*, events in *The Castle of Otranto* arrive with the preternatural rapidity prompted by the required unity of time, and the prospect to the future in the brief last paragraph is even emptier than most theatrical epilogues of the period. Worst of all is the narrative voice itself, which compensates for the lack of acting with cumbersome analyses of the feelings that would be displayed in an actor's face and body. A giant ghost can hardly be a subtle demon; the repetitiousness and stiffness of Walpole's supernatural are marks of ghosts that don't work as they ought. Narration does not create the supernatural as it was known to Walpole but undermines it.

Walpole's ghost has size and scope in abundance. What it most strikingly lacks is a body. The servants report seeing limbs; more directly narrated manifestations are only attributes, a walking portrait, and the final dilating "form of Alfonso" (145). (By contrast, Frankenstein's monster, while similar to the Walpolean specter in being large and originally molded from body parts, appears as an integral, tangible bulk. Still, he cannot be looked at with impunity.) To be sure, Alfonso's sway is secure; it would be wrong to deny to Walpole's supernatural the absoluteness of earlier ghosts. But the locus of the absolute has changed. In narrative, fate takes precedence over form. Identity is innate rather than inscribed; hence Theodore's origin is established not by preserved and rediscovered documents and tokens but by an accidentally revealed birthmark. Neoclassical tragedies achieve their finest effects in turbulent stage confusion—the plague scene opening *Oedipus*, the jockeying of the conspirators in *Venice Preserved*, Isménie's broken narrative of the first climax in Voltaire's *Mérope*. Not until the middle of the nineteenth century would narratives like *War and Peace* and *Mme Bovary* attempt to recapture in prose the confused simultaneity of disparate actions and responses routinely achieved by neoclassical stage crowds. Altogether different is Walpole's precise, analytical rendition of climactic events that would necessarily be impenetrable on stage. Though Manfred's thoughts are "distracted" and his speech momentarily characterized by "wild confusion," we know exactly what is on his mind; the ensuing long-winded speeches are necessary to explain not him but the vanishing ghost. Scenic stability is denied as the house is torn asunder, and the supernatural becomes a dynamic whirlwind rather than a binding presence.

Walpole's accomplishment in *The Castle of Otranto* was the creation of a mood, not a mechanism. Narrative dissolves bodies and silences spectacle. Its analytic sequentiality compromises the hustle of the stage even though Walpole maintains dramatic unity of time and the accompanying rapidity of action. The play drawn from the novel, Robert Jephson's *Count of Narbonne*, is torn between atmosphere and corporeal sensation; it mostly opts for atmosphere, but no satisfactory compromise was achievable on stage, and indeed the playwright quarreled with Walpole about how to manage the final *coup de théâtre*. As a suppressed prologue to *The Count of Narbonne* acknowledges, "The pond'rous statue, if beheld too near, / Would but a huge, misshapen mass appear."[9] In the novel, Walpole found the way to convert majesty into mystery.

Indeed, one of the difficulties for us in experiencing the classical Oedipus plays, let alone their neoclassical avatars, lies in the foregrounded immediacy that the drama brings to them. "Oedipus" is our name for both a tragedy and a complex, yet these are separated by the difference between dramatic encounter and the timelessness of the unconscious, between an individual curse and a universal destiny. Perhaps the ritualized performance conditions of Greek tragedy bridged the allegorical gap, but that is harder to do on modern stages. Walpole's novel achieves its peculiar kind of success by means of a remoteness exceeding anything in his dramatic models. The historical and geographical distance of his Otranto are surface reflections of the novel's abstraction from empirical experience, and the primitive beliefs and emotions of the servants likewise gesticulate beyond the graspable. Even more, the narrator's awkwardness reflects embarrassment at a trauma that cannot be remedied and a sin that will not speak its name. Hence formulas like "words cannot paint" (58, 62, 91, always beginning a paragraph) are anything but trivial. Indeed, the novel lies not just beyond dramatic representation but even beyond narrative designation. It is not quite a satire or a joke, but it is some kind of uneasy folly that undermines rational cognition of its objects. The prodigal-infant plays enact Burkean sublimities—vast, crowded, sudden, dark, loud. Walpole's sublimity is different; it expresses the unanchored affect of "thoughts crowded on [a] distracted mind" (62), awash in seas of speculation. The dramatic *coup de théâtre* illuminates the truth "in a blaze of glory" (145), yet in the novel something goes awry. Light conceals as much as it reveals: the figures are "soon wrapt from mortal eyes," and in being so they are darkened; as the text says with remarkable precision, the heavenly "form of St. Nicholas . . . receiv[es] Alfonso's shade" (145). By the end all are infected with the melancholy spreading initially from Manfred's children.[10]

Judgment and punishment are no longer moral and personal or familial, but psychological and generic.

Dramatic spectacle is like the "clap of thunder" that breaks off the first interview between Theodore and Matilda, at the exact center of the narrative (107). But the moonlit world of the novel is dark and empty at its core. The "deep and hollow groan" of the tower (107), the "hollow and rustling sound" of the waving plumes (59), and the "hollow voice" of the skeleton with its "fleshless jaws and empty sockets" (139) are the novelist's answer to the theater's garrulous display. The characters are most eloquent when they sigh (and most foolish when they converse): "I cannot speak," cries Frederic when the skeleton warns him *off* marriage—"Oh! Matilda!" (140). In counterpoint to the dramatic settings of courtyard and portal, the vast spaces of castle, crypt, cavern, and church project an enveloping maternal world of identities lost. In this reverberant world, guilt is tellingly distanced from present consciousness. For while the comic Frederic is a father, the two greater stories concern grandfathers and grandsons;[11] Manfred's intermediate lineage is unmentioned (nor is Frederic's relation ship to Alfonso clarified), and Theodore is connected via a tenuous maternal line. This is no longer a tale of paternal injunctions, arbitrary order, castration, and language. Its plague neither fulfills a prophecy nor is assuaged by answering a riddle. Rather, this wordy yet short book moves toward an unvoicing, after which its author, for all his voluminous correspondence, hardly ever again addressed the public with a literary expression.

PART II

Kant and the Gothic

6

At the Limits of Kantian Philosophy

I TURN NOW to the convergence of a certain strand of Kantian philosophy with the aims of the gothic novel. As marginal as the gothic may sometimes appear to be, it nevertheless originated as an exploration of recesses hidden at the very center of human experience. It probes the nature of man in isolation, the uttermost resources of individuals deprived of the society of their fellows. The gothic, in other words, strips away collectivities in order to make the individual into a representative of the species. The results of what may be called gothic anthropology vary, of course, with time; early romantic exemplars tend toward an idealizing, Rousseauist view of human nature, while later gothic victims appear more obviously in conflict with themselves and complicit with their fate. But the aim of studying the mind of man—the mind in general and not the mind of a particular individual in a real, carefully delimited setting—remains a constant.

The convergence of the gothic with philosophy occurs within the sphere denoted by the Kantian phrase *das allgemeine Bewußtsein*, consciousness in general. General consciousness is a transcendental or limit concept. Though all experience is filtered through consciousness, consciousness itself can be experienced only as it is conditioned by particular perceptions and never in a pure state. For this reason, Kant never reflects directly on the nature of the pure, or transcendental, human personality. Even his *Anthropology* concerns itself with how man behaves in society rather than with what man is in himself, for instance with egotism as a way of acting rather than as a way of thinking, or with what dreams and dreamers do rather than with what feelings dreams engender. Kant repeatedly dismisses pure forms of self-involvement as pathological—the lectures on pedagogy go so far as to indulge in a telltale diatribe against masturbation (*Über pädagogik* A140–42)—and he categorically excludes them from his ken: "To investigate what *sleep*, what *dream*, what *somnambulism* . . . is in its natural constitution lies outside the scope of a *pragmatic* anthropology" (*Anthropology* A104).[1]

Yet one tenet of Kant's philosophy is that human understanding is impelled toward its limits. We inevitably imagine those transcendental entities that haunt the margins of experience. We do so via a "transcendental illusion"—a phrase that has the positive as well as the negative connotations of "illusion" (*Schein*). Only with great vigilance can we refrain from the "subreption" (illegitimate substitution) of attributing empirical reality to the transcendental domain. The essence of Kant's dialectic and the dynamic aspect of his psychology lies in the interplay among experience, necessary illusion, and delusive subreption. In the act of demarcating the confines of the understanding, Kant is drawn to the very concept of pure consciousness that he means to exclude from philosophical investigation.

The literary investigation of pure consciousness found in the gothic novel complements the philosophical investigation of consciousness found in the rational discourse of philosophy. To be sure, in at least one moment of vindictiveness, reviewing *Ideen zur Philosophie der Geschichte der Menschheit* by his apostate student and former friend Johann Gottfried Herder, Kant appears to warn against any contamination of philosophy by the literary imagination:

> We will not investigate here whether the poetical spirit that animates the expression has not also at times penetrated into the author's philosophy; whether here and there synonyms do not pass for explanations and allegories for truths; whether instead of natural transitions from the realm of the philosophical into the district of poetical language at times the boundaries and possessions of both have not been totally deranged [*verrückt*]; and whether in many spots the fabric of bold metaphors, poetic

images, mythological allusions does not serve rather to conceal the body of thought under a *farthingale* than to let it pleasingly gleam forth as if from under a transparent garment.   (A154)

This passage seems categorically to forbid any such reading of Kant as I propose: poetic language promulgates spurious virtues (virtue in masquerade is surely the etymological pun lurking in the *Vertügade* or *farthingale*) that trivialize philosophy, corrupt it, and ultimately drive it mad. But Kant's diatribe against poetic metaphor, which continues for two pages of the modern edition, is itself clearly an irrational outburst, full of the metaphoric rhetoric that it denounces, an outburst of the philosopher gone mad and not a rational demarcation of the true boundaries of philosophy. Only at the end does Kant salvage the rationality of his discourse by coyly withdrawing from defining the limits he has appeared to insist on: "all this we must here, mindful of the limits that are placed on us, leave untouched" (ibid.).

In sober truth, the limits of philosophical discourse are narrower than the limits of thought. Kant leaves us free, after all, to speculate about what happens at the margins of his philosophy. Literature, as Kant writes at a more relaxed moment, supplements philosophy by pushing at the limits of experience and daring to dream what philosophy has never known: "for even though [plays and novels] are not actually founded on experience and truth, but rather only poetic invention, and it is permitted here to set up exaggeration of the characters and the situations in which men are put, just as in a dream image, and those thus seem not to teach anything for the knowledge of man," still, despite all these objections, Kant says that writers like Molière and Richardson base their poetic imaginings on experience and thus may promote and facilitate a philosophical anthropology (preface to *Anthropology*, A xi–xii). And not just poets. Kant knew that Descartes's philosophy originated in a dream, as Plato's culminated in ecstatic myth. In this and succeeding chapters I propose to exaggerate the character and situation of Kantian philosophy so as to reconstitute the dream vision of the human condition that lies at its root.[2]

In fact, Kant's writings do occasionally push toward the margins of his thought and hint at the poetic vision that is chastely excluded from his rational discourse, perhaps even from his conscious thought.

The hints, naturally, are found largely in the prefaces, essays, and lectures that surround the main edifice of the three Critiques. And beyond Kant's own words there is also the evidence of Kant's early readers. The writings of commentators, disciples, admirers, and followers reveal what Kant's texts implied but left unsaid. I will draw on writings of numerous types, but above all on extensions of Kant's thought into one field that he left untouched, namely psychology. For I want to reconstruct here what would have been Kant's doctrine of the soul. The writings in question leave much to be desired as philosophical exegesis, and consequently they have been little utilized by modern exegetes. But they are invaluable as indicators of the direction of Kantian thought. For Kant's work functioned historically not as a summation and resting place but rather as an enabling act that unlocked the doors of speculation. Here, as in my study of preromanticism, I wish to keep in view the movements of mind and imagination. Therefore the true subject is the Kantian style rather than the substance of Kant's doctrines—Kantianism, not Kant. Echoing the art historian Heinrich Wölfflin's famous call for an "art history without names," I am tempted to call it an "intellectual history without intellects."

Caught in a web of fate, gothic heroes (or victims) can do nothing to improve their lot. Their passive condition condemns them to a life of observation. The generic topos sounds like this: "When enabled at length to attend to the information which my senses afforded, I was conscious, for a time, of nothing but existence. It was unaccompanied with lassitude or pain, but I felt disinclined to stretch my limbs, or raise my eye-lids. My thoughts were wildering and mazy, and though consciousness were present, it was disconnected with the loco-motive or voluntary power."[3] Such characters observe themselves with an introspective obsessiveness whose lineage can be traced back to Samuel Richardson; and when they can, they also observe the world around them. But in typical gothic novels—in contrast to Richardson's and still, to some extent, Walpole's—what the typical gothic hero observes is static. The outside world is reduced to a series of unchanging, discrete pictures; a natural landscape, often seen framed by a window, and often even the social world that is so frequently represented by portraits of ancestors and miniatures of long-lost lovers. As for self-observation, gothic heroes play a waiting game. Their greatest accomplishment is simply to survive, physically and morally. Or if they are corrupt, Byronic villains, then their self-observation leads to a recognition of what they have always been. In either case, the true action lies not in deeds but merely in continuing to exist, and the end of action is the protagonist's knowledge of his or her moral being.

The counteraction that provokes heroic resistance consists of villainy or satanic violence. Stasis clashes with frenzy. Like stasis, frenzy is divided into an inner and an outer aspect; it comprises both the anxiety of imminent persecution and the turmoil of battle, hallucination, and murder. Natural time does not exist in the gothic except in the form of a simple illusion; all true experiences in the novels are filtered through the grid of four types of unnatural time: inner and outer stasis, inner and outer frenzy. As I discuss later in connection with *Frankenstein*, continuity is a problem for the gothic, which knows only repetition and disruption. In the end the discontinuities of gothic tear the hero in two, or at least threaten to do so, and eventuate in torment (*Zerrissenheit*), despair (*Verzweiflung*), and ultimately madness.

The exclusion of authentic selfhood from nature, the association of self-knowledge with passivity and mere continuity of existence, with a temporal experience compounded of stasis and frenzy, and ultimately with madness—this is the complex of characteristics that typify the gothic personality and that will also be found in Kantian philosophy. To set off the distinctiveness of this complex, here is a montage of associationist (or sensationalist) tenets of pre-Kantian or non-Kantian psychologists.

1. In what appears to be the first work written specifically on insanity, *Treatise on Madness* (1758), William Battie carefully distinguishes madness from stupor and anxiety.[4] Madness is a cognitive disorder, false perception or disordered sensation. It may have either external or internal causes—Battie calls the two types consequential and original madness—but both types of causes are physical and thus would count for a Kantian as external; a typical cause of original madness is continued muscular constriction. And the cures that Battie recommends are likewise all physical and physiological: the aim is the

restoration of the proper nerve tone. Thus for Battie, and for associationists generally, madness is a way of behaving, not a way of feeling,
and hence unrelated to reverie; it is an intellectual, not an emotional
or moral disorder; it pertains to individuals as they relate to the world
and not to individuals in isolation from the world. It is a disease of the
body or of the brain, not of the mind. "No one is born mad," as one
nosology puts it, and "rarely does the primary cause of madness appear to reside in the brain"; it appears rather in other organs.[5] Even
late in the century, an authoritative treatise could still conclude:
"Madness consists in faulty judgments and conclusions, which have
their basis in an idiopathic injury to the general sensorium" (Chiarugi, *Wahnsinn*, 1: 34). And, later yet, "The soul cannot fall sick, any
more than it can die" (Spurzheim, *Observations*, 101).

2. For Kantians the most direct access to the mind in its pure state
lies in reverie and in dreams, when we are unaffected by the external
world. If associationists discuss reverie and dreams at all, they do so
only to deny them any primary status. Thus for Erasmus Darwin day-
dreaming is an active state of the soul:

> It appears that these concatenations of ideas and muscular motions,
> which form the trains of reverie, are composed both of voluntary and
> sensitive associations of them; and that these ideas differ from those of
> delirium or of sleep, as they are kept consistent by the power of volition;
> and they differ also from the trains of ideas belonging to insanity as they
> are as frequently excited by sensation as by volition. (*Zoonomia*, 1: 170)[6]

Insanity is volitional. Reverie is volitional. But it turns out that
dreams are likewise volitional. Or at least, most dreams are, insofar as
they have anything to do with our identity. To be sure, "in our complete dreams we neither measure time, are surprised at the sudden
changes of place, nor attend to our own existence, or identity; because
our power of volition is suspended" (*Zoonomia*, 1: 160). But normally when we dream we remain active and therefore retain elements
of self-consciousness; these are what Darwin calls incomplete dreams.
"For then we attend a little to the lapse of time, and the changes of
place, and to our own existence; and even to our identity of person;
for a lady seldom dreams, that she is a soldier; nor a man, that he is
brought to bed" (1: 160). The sensationalist views the imagination as

an intentional, worldly faculty, "the brain of man enriched with ideas, signs, and pictures of things," in explicit contrast to the later view that denies any intentionality or sign character to the contents of imaginative reverie: "With open eyes, or somewhat closed senses, we sometimes give ourselves over . . . to the aimless representations of our aroused fancy. I by no means mean here the . . . disposition of the soul in which we build so-called castles in the air. Rather a condition of even less spontaneity, even more passive, in which we accede to all represented ideas, observe all with similar indifference."[7]

3. For Kantians the passive, unthinking mind is the seat and focus of life. Kant calls its activity spontaneous: it appears to be inert (as in Hume's famous portrait of the mind watching the spectacle of the world passing by) but works in secret. No such conception existed previously. Instead the emphasis was on the separate activities of the mind; the mind in itself was at best an occult quality, unknowable if it existed at all.

> As it is certain that an extent cannot measure itself; that light never lights itself: it is equally certain that the soul cannot know itself; but it knows its capacity by the reflection it makes on its Operations, like an eye which, unable to see itself unaided, sees itself reflected by a mirror. Thus *we shall not endeavor to know the nature of soul, nor what is its constitutive or internal essence*, since no possible means exist by which we could arrive at this knowledge.[8]

Against the background of such late empiricist doctrines it becomes evident that Kant's novelty as a philosopher of mind lay in the assertions of transcendental productivity, whereas his drawing of limits to investigations was more traditional. The text of the *Critique of Pure Reason*, in particular, displays a reluctant fascination with this "third thing," which Kant did not know how to define, but which shows clear affinities with the "life force" of subsequent writers. "A third thing [*ein Drittes*] is necessary," writes Kant, "in which alone the synthesis of two concepts [and hence any real experience] is possible. But what now is this third thing but the medium of all synthetic judgments? It is only an essence [*Inbegriff*] in which all our representations are included, namely the inner sense, and the form of the same, a priori, time."[9] The telltale "only" is Kant's signature word, barring further progress. Yet from here it is only a step to identifying life and time—not, of course, time as change, but the pure form of temporality, distinct from any form of action—with self-consciousness and soul. For the Kantian, following where the master feared to tread, "life is *internal* [*ein Inneres*]" (Reil, "Begriff der Medicin," 229), and this means that it is neither physiological nor supernatural, neither empirical nor irretrievably transcendental. While it is no discovery to point out that the romantics envisioned selfhood vitalistically, I should like to quote one relatively unfamiliar passage, from Robert Browning's first poem, as a measure of the distance that had been traversed since the time of Jean-François Dufour and other sensationalists:

> I strip my mind bare, whose first elements
> I shall unveil—not as they struggled forth
> In infancy, nor as they now exist,
> When I am grown above them and can rule—
> But in that middle stage when they were full
> Yet ere I had disposed them to my will . . .
> I am made up of an intensest life,
> Of a most clear idea of consciousness
> Of self, distinct from all its qualities,
> From all affections, passions, feelings, powers;
> And thus far it exists, if tracked, in all.
> (*Pauline*, 1833, ll. 260–65, 268–72)

4. Since sensationalists have no distinct, unified conception of mind, they also have no distinct, unified conception of mental illness. Madness as such does not exist, but only different madnesses, whether these are classified by symptoms (dementia, melancholia, mania, and hypochondria in Dufour), by the locus of derangement (diseases of the imagination, of genius, of volition, and of the passions in Alexander Crichton), or by some combination of the two. The latter approach is taken by the inimitable Benjamin Rush, who discusses hypochondria, mania, and dementia side by side with derangements in the will, in the "Principle of Faith, or the Believing Faculty," and in memory, and with other derangements that are designated as fatuity, "Dreaming, Incubus, or Night mare, and Somnambulism," "Illu-

sions" (i.e., supernatural voices), "Reverie, or Absence of Mind," derangement of the passions, the sexual appetite, and finally the moral faculties.[10] As one can read explicitly in William Cullen, such rationalist accounts of madness have no place for demonic possession.[11]

While Kant himself did not write on psychology, his concept of consciousness in general turned his followers toward the development of a science of mind in general. Indeed, the effects of this trend are noticeable even where psychiatric practice remained strictly empirical and unsystematic. Even Rush, when writing about a noted German figure, the pietist Johann Caspar Lavater, is capable of evoking the pure, empty sensations of dementia: "The mind in this disease may be considered as floating in a balloon, and at the mercy of every object and thought that acts upon it" (*Medical Inquiries*, 260). In the 1790s works like William Falconer's *Dissertation on the Influence of the Passions upon Disorders of the Body* began superimposing an idealist conception of the centrality of mental life on an old-fashioned empiricist or even atomistic nosology, capable of discussing, in this sequence, epilepsy, cramp, hiccup, hysteria, melancholia, mania, scurvy, jaundice, and the Swiss national ailment, nostalgia. John Haslam's *Observations on Madness and Melancholy* illustrates further effects of the new way of thinking. A practitioner who stresses that the physician's role is to make decisions about confinement, not to theorize, Haslam nevertheless incorporates a definition of madness into his treatise. And in his definition he explicitly turns away from a recognizably cognitive theory of madness as deluded imagination and substitutes a unified, "metaphysical" theory of madness as a disordered time sense, whose two main forms are mania and melancholy (too fast and too slow a connection of ideas, respectively). In such works are found the stirrings of the modern notions of mind and of person.

Obviously such developments were under way when Kant wrote. They also appear in the structure—or more precisely, in the structural lapses—of a more influential treatise than any I have cited so far, Thomas Arnold's *Observations on the Nature, Kinds, Causes, and Prevention of Insanity*. Writing in 1782, Arnold acknowledged Locke as his philosophical master, and he divided insanity into two Lockean types, ideal and notional. Still, his title suggests that insanity has a single nature. His second volume is mainly concerned with the causes of insanity. These are divided into remote and proximate; the remote causes are subdivided into bodily and mental; while of the proximate causes, which lie in the brain, Arnold says that little can be known. His diagnostic procedure remains rigidly empiricist—he retails the physical causes organ by organ and likewise subdivides the mental causes into intense application, the various passions, imagination, and a catch-all, imbecility—and yet Arnold's radical separation of mind from brain inevitably increased the emphasis on "transcendental" factors in madness. Finally, Arnold's treatise is noteworthy for the absence of any account of cures for insanity; rather, almost a quarter of a century after the original publication he added a preface promising a discussion of cures at some time in the future. Thus Arnold creates the impression that madness is perhaps a condition rather than a pathology, or even an essence rather than an aberration. Cumulatively these structural imbalances create a climate in which some movement in a Kantian or transcendental direction must have occurred, all the more so given the combined impact of Hume's account of his "philosophical melancholy and delirium" at the crux of the *Treatise of Human Nature* (Conclusion to bk. 1; p. 243), the gothic novel, the current of sensibility, and the graveyard poets. In England those developments occurred largely without Kantian influence (though one should not underestimate the trickling of influence through the translation of authors who tend to escape notice). To be sure, one cannot say that Kant *merely* rode the crest of a wave. But the wave was there, and Kant did not make it.

The philosopher does not make currents of thought; he articulates them. Hume himself, picking up an image from Locke, writes of tempting the "boundless ocean" in the "leaky weather-beaten vessel" of his mind (*Treatise*, 237–38). Without philosophical articulation, it would be difficult, perhaps impossible, to identify the significant factors in works like Arnold's and to see how the factors cohere. Aphoristically, it might be said that the meaning of the gothic enterprise and of romantic psychology lies in Kant's philosophy. But then we must also reverse the aphorism. For Kant's works, too, are texts that have their own aura or contexts of significance. If the gothic signifies Kant—or, to be precise, a portion of Kant—then Kant likewise signifies the gothic. In the purity of the transcendental ego is something of what the gothic was searching for. But conversely, in the mysteries of the gothic is something of the meaning (the impulse, the intention) of the transcendental ego. Kant shows how to understand the difference between gothic credulity—"all old mansions are haunted" says Emily St. Aubert at one point (Radcliffe, *Mysteries of Udolpho* 3.12; p. 491)—and particular persecution by a "questionable shape" such as Hamlet's father (1.4.43); conversely, the gothic illuminates the difference between Kantian self-consciousness and Cartesian self-examination. Some portion of the meaning of any text is found outside it or at its limits.

Beyond the text there lies, for instance, a man. Somehow, the dry, forbidding prose not only promoted a critique of reason but aroused in Kant's readers the sensation of a passion outside the limits of reason. It was reading either Kant or "Kantian philosophy" (the documents are contradictory on this point) that drove the poet Heinrich von Kleist near to suicide in 1801. And after his mental deterioration and eventual death—like Samuel Johnson's Swift, Kant "expir'd a driveller and a show"—Kant the man acquired a powerful and long-lasting aura, which is perhaps best known from the moving homage in Thomas De Quincey's essay "The Last Days of Immanuel Kant" and from the persiflage in Heinrich Heine's "The Romantic School," and which Jean-Luc Nancy's *Logodaedalus* documents in remarkable detail. But even within Kant's own writings—indeed precisely at the limit of his writings, at the very moment when the self is dissolving into a state of mental alienation—there comes a point where the text of philosophy opens movingly onto the person of the philosopher. This limit text is the "Conclusion" of Kant's last significant essay, "The Quarrel of the Faculties." In a sense this is Kant's most wide-ranging single work, since it successively ponders the relations of philosophy with theology, jurisprudence, and medicine. Its thesis is that philosophy is the central, unifying science of mind that grounds all other intellectual enterprises. Yet it turns out that the unity of thought is threatened by the very act that purports to establish it, for as philosophy expands into the other fields the connections become increasingly tenuous. The phrase "unity of consciousness" can refer, of course, both to an intellectual and to a psychological phenomenon, both to the unity of the objects of thought and to the unity of the thinking subject. In the following representative extract, the intellectual yields to the psychological even as the perfection of the intellectual calls into question the very coherence of the psychological. Absolute, pure consciousness is the persona of madness.

> The sickly condition of the patient, which accompanies and encumbers thought insofar as the latter is a seizing of a concept (of the unity of the consciousness of connected representations), brings the feeling of a spastic condition of the organ of thought (the brain) as a pressure, which indeed does not actually enfeeble thought and reflection themselves, nor memory in respect of what has previously been thought, but in the delivery (oral or written) [that] should secure the coherence of the representations in their succession against distraction, itself effects an involuntary spastic condition of the brain, as an inability amid the flux of representations following one upon the other to maintain the unity of their consciousness.[12] Therefore it happens to me: that when I, as always in every discourse, first prepare (the listener or reader) for what I wish to say, point out to him the object *whither* I wish to go, in prospect, then back to that *whence* I started (without which twofold orientation no coherence of the discourse takes place) and now I am to connect the last with the first, I suddenly have to ask my listener (or silently myself): where was I? Where did I start from? which error is not so much an error of mind nor yet of memory alone, but of *presence of mind* (in connecting), that is, involuntary *distraction* and a very painful error; which in writings (especially philosophical ones; because there it is not always so easy to look back on the starting point) can with difficulty be circumvented, although with all possible effort can never be entirely prevented [variant: remedied].   ("Quarrel of the Faculties" A198–99)

I have quoted this pitiful, senile philosophical babble at length, respecting the original mispunctuation and textual corruptions, because the style so movingly confirms the argument. The more connections that are made, the more difficult connection becomes. The objective unity of consciousness—in formal Kantian terms the unity of the manifold of perceptions in the transcendental ego—exceeds the limits of the subjective unity of consciousness, or inner sense of self.

The end of thought and of life should be a gathering of all experiences and ideas into a network of simultaneous representation. In more concrete fields, such as mathematics, Kant says that such coherence is possible. But the "pure" philosopher works with visionary entities and "must keep his object floating in the air before him" (A200); ultimately he becomes disoriented, "disorganized" in his thought (A198). Kant acknowledges only a physical debility, an "epidemic catarrh accompanied by oppression in the head," perhaps "a gout that has partially passed to the brain" (A198), but the condition is precisely what the psychologists diagnose as dementia or dissociation. At the end of a life of thought, objectivity, terra firma, *presence* is lost. The unity of consciousness is a condition of mental alienation that lies outside of time.

The unity of consciousness is, for instance, a dream. Dreams are, like madness, a limit case of ordinary experience. As a result, Kant does not discuss them directly, and their fundamental importance must be inferred from shreds of evidence. In an essay cited in "Fantasia: Kant and the Demons of the Night" (Chapter 2 above), Lewis White Beck argues that Kant thought that dreams derive from ordinary, categorical experience. We first experience the world rationally, according to the categories, and then rational experience partially decomposes to produce dreams. All human experience, according to this argument, is fundamentally rational, and a dream is an objective event that "makes just as valid a claim on your credence" as any other empirical event, even if the contents of the dream are fantastic ("Did the Sage," 54).

There were, indeed, numerous contemporaries or near-contemporaries who did regard dreaming as deficient wakefulness.[13] But in fact Kant's allusions to dreaming press the limits harder than Beck's account recognizes.[14] There is, for instance, an incidental comment in the first version of the *Critique of Pure Reason* to the effect that sense "appearances" lacking a synthesizing rule or concept that arises in or proves the unity of consciousness would be "nothing but a blind play of representations, i.e., less than a dream" (A111–12). The concept of the self—the rule that all my perceptions are related to my singular mind—applies to my dream visions as well as to my waking experiences, and the quoted passage leaves open the possibility that the transcendental unity of apperception is like a dream (not "less than a dream" but also not more) until a second synthesis supervenes to give my perceptions that greater regularity to be found in waking experience. What is, after all, the difference between dream and waking? "When appearance is given to us, we still remain entirely free how we wish therefrom to judge the matter. . . . The difference between truth and dream is not ascertained by the constitution of the representations that are referred to objects [*Gegenstände*], for these are the same in both, but by their connection according to the rules that determine the coherence of the representations in the concept of an object [*Objekts*]" (*Prolegomena* A65–66). Representations precede the rules that connect one representation to another; they refer to a representing subject and to a represented content (*Gegenstände*) before the constitution of any regular object (*Objekt*) of empirical experience. Our initial freedom is thus progressively reduced as we move toward waking reality, but our starting point lies in representations that can be combined with all the freedom of a dream.[15] The sense of the self and of its representations anticipates the elaboration of a rational, knowable objective world.

Increasingly in his later works Kant uses the term "feeling" for the dreamlike self-consciousness that precedes cognitive thought. The word is introduced in a footnote to §46 of the *Prolegomena* (1783, A136): "the *ego* . . . is nothing more than the feeling of an existence without the slightest concept and only the representation of that to which all thought stands in relationship (relatione accidentis)." It is clarified at length in the important essay of 1786, "Was heißt: sich im Denken orientieren." And finally the true, transcendental feeling of self is elaborately distinguished from the merely subjective selfhood in a late, polemical essay, "Von einem neuerdings erhobenen vornehmen Ton in der Philosophie" (1796).[16] Of particular importance here, however, is the *Anthropology*, where Kant ascribes a distinct empirical reality to what might otherwise appear to be a merely theoretical condition. Elsewhere, Kant had written an anti-utilitarian essay decrying the separation of theory from practice ("Über den Gemeinspruch: Das mag in der Theorie richtig sein, taugt aber nicht für die

Praxis," 1794); here, at the limits of his philosophical enterprise, Kant inserts the theoretically constructed pure consciousness into a practical, real situation.[17] I say at the limits of his enterprise because the *Anthropology* is both the last book that Kant saw through the press and also not truly a philosophical treatise but a compilation of popularizing lecture notes. On the very first page of his text, Kant transgresses the limits of philosophy to do what properly belongs to a novelist, namely to *imagine* a state that can never actually be known or "experienced" (in the technical sense of the word); he says that there is a delightful period of infancy when the child does not know how to speak but nevertheless has already transcended the level of animals by having acquired "the unity of consciousness." Later the child will learn to say "I," but he already possesses the *I* "in thoughts" as "all languages, when they speak in the first person, must think it, even if they don't express this *I* by means of a particular word" (A3); or, as Kant finally says, "Previously it merely *felt* itself, now [after learning to speak] it *thinks* itself" (A5). Self-consciousness is a feeling before it is a thought, obscure before it becomes clear, "innocent and open" but also a "little tyrant" confronting the "caprice" of its tutors (A5). This appealing, inarticulate helplessness—Kant refers in particular to the "torture of words" (*das Radbrechen der Wörter*)—in a world without civilized order, lying amid female protectors ("mothers and nurses") and outside the male realm of human law and the lawyer, is, of course, precisely the condition in which the gothic hero is found or to which he or she is reduced. It is, for instance, perhaps no more than a redescription of this situation from the point of view of the struggling child rather than the adoring protectresses when Raymond de las Cisternas in Lewis's *The Monk* is subjected between the hours of one (unity?) and two (individuation?) to visitations by the ghost of a female ancestor who taunts his mastery of the first person pronoun ("Raymond! Raymond! Thou art mine! / Raymond! Raymond! I am thine . . . / Mine thy body! Mine thy soul!") until "my limbs were chained in second infancy" (170, 172).

Such threads within Kant's writings link pure or general consciousness and the ghostly world of the "something = X" with dream, with madness, and at last with the gothic mentality. In "Fantasia: Kant and the Demons of the Night" I have already suggested the links that many early readers of Kant forged. But by no means all followers of Kant treated him as an imaginative writer. Rather, his immediate heritage was divided. While eventually the greatest philosophical responses—Schopenhauer, say, or Hegel, or Heidegger—are loaded with affect, Kant's earliest professional adherents worked to restrict the meaning of his texts. On the other hand, an important medical controversy centering precisely on the practical significance of the concept of pure or general consciousness paved the way for the revolutionary new psychological understanding of the romantic poets and thinkers. I turn now to these early responses.

7

Kant's Disciples

A T ONE EXTREME AMONG post-Kantian philosophers of consciousness stands Salomon Maimon, third and last editor of the
Magazin zur Erfahrungsseelenkunde, the journal from which Karl
Philipp Moritz's characterization of Kant as a dreamer was quoted
above in "Fantasia: Kant and the Demons of the Night" (Chapter 2).
But Maimon was certainly no Moritz. On the road to elaborating his
own alternative logic of experience, Maimon distinguishes five different kinds of consciousness, each with its own type of object, and denies the very existence of any consciousness in general ("Einleitung,"
8–9). Maimon's critique is significant for its implicit recognition that
a consciousness in general would be an objectless consciousness (such
as a dream vision). Yet among Kant's avowed followers, consciousness in general really fares no better. The best known of them, Karl
Leonhard Reinhold, discusses consciousness in §§38–41 of his *Versuch einer neuen Theorie des menschlichen Vorstellungsvermögens*.
While Reinhold begins by stressing the importance of understanding
the concept of consciousness in general, it turns out that consciousness in general is merely a collective concept that synthesizes three
types of object consciousness: "The consciousness of the representation, the consciousness of the representer (self-consciousness), and
the consciousness of the represented object are related to conscious-

ness in general as species to genus" (325). For Kant self-consciousness is primary, mysterious ("a *thinking*, not an *intuiting* [i.e., perceiving], . . . far from a knowledge of oneself," *Critique of Pure Reason* B157–58), and equivalent to consciousness in general. For Reinhold self-consciousness follows upon object consciousness, it is "distinct consciousness" (in the neo-Cartesian sense of "distinct"), it is an empirical state; whereas consciousness in general is "only the *form* of consciousness" (322). Although Kant's essay "Was heißt: sich im Denken orientieren" had been published in 1786, three years earlier than Reinhold's book, feeling plays no role in Reinhold's discussion, nor in those of the other early philosophical commentators. Instead, feeling comes in for Reinhold's scorn: "'What consciousness is is self-evident; everyone must know it spontaneously; the feeling of self teaches it' were the refuges with which our *empiricists* contrived to ease or even to forego thinking about consciousness" (322). In actuality, the feeling of self is not the easiest of the alternatives to Kantianism but rather the most radical and difficult of Kant's own conceptions, and the one in which his closest, most literal disciples were unable to follow him.

The disciple who commented most extensively on self-consciousness was Carl Christian Erhard Schmid, whom I have already mentioned as the editor of the periodical *Psychologisches Magazin*. Schmid's *Wörterbuch zum leichteren Gebrauch der Kantischen Schriften* follows Kant more scrupulously than does Reinhard. According to Schmid (51), self-consciousness must be divided into the "empirical" and the "*transcendental, pure, original*, i.e., the consciousness of the identity of oneself." In the latter the ego is "bereft of all intuition [i.e., perception] of our self and solely a logical subject" (*Wörterbuch*, 51). This is a perfectly accurate paraphrase of the section entitled "Paralogisms of Pure Reason" in the *Critique of Pure Reason*. Yet that was one of the most troublesome sections of the whole *Critique*, one of the two that had been completely rewritten for the second edition the year before. What Schmid possessed in accuracy, then, he sacrificed in vision or foresight; he failed to recognize the "paralogisms" as an unstable point within Kant's system or to anticipate Kant's future development toward a reconciliation of the transcendental ego with a certain mysterious, poetic, gothic, mad, or childlike ego. According to Schmid, accurately paraphrasing Kant's doctrines, the empirical and transcendental egos are totally distinct; is it Schmid's fault if his poetic description of the *empirical* ego—"like perceptions themselves, variable, distracted in itself, and without relation to the identity of the subject"—also exactly describes Kant's *transcendental* ego in the "Quarrel of the Faculties" and the *Anthropology*? Meanwhile, Schmid's massive *Empirische Psychologie* moves in the opposite direction, continuing the pattern by which the deviations and omissions of Kant's philosophical disciples signal what is most original in Kant himself. Here, explicitly following Reinhold, Schmid effectively eliminates the "empty," pure consciousness and treats all three primary forms of consciousness—consciousness of the object, of representation, and of the represented—as transitive (202–3). For Kant the feeling of self is logically and even empirically prior to any of the contents of consciousness; for Reinhold self-consciousness derives from thinking about our perceptions or representations; and Schmid now further undermines the autonomy of consciousness by formulating as his special contribution a "*General Law*": "*Where representation is, there is consciousness. Where consciousness is, is representation*" (207). No space remains for a pure, unmodified selfhood; on the contrary, the soul has fragments and glimmerings of representations—what Leibniz had called "petites perceptions"—as the elements from which, for Schmid, consciousness is constituted (184). Dreams occur when the conscious links between perceptions chance to be impaired. "When for any reason representations disappear and are not *represented* in constant association with one another, then we lack memory, knowledge (recognition), definite judgment, as e.g. in sleep. Here consciousness is obscured" (217). Beck's theory that dreams are considered a deficient mode of consciousness thus reproduces Schmid's views and marks precisely the point at which Kant's immediate followers fell short of their master.

A final essay by Schmid, "Abriß der Metaphysik der innern Natur" (Synopsis of the Metaphysics of Inner Nature), will complete the negative side of the picture. The title is intriguing, and a certain amount of talk about *Gemüt* and *Geist* (two words meaning "mind"—but in the psychological context also suggesting mood and spirit) suggests that Schmid finally opened himself to the more mysterious sides of Kant's imagination. Indeed, on the model of Johann Gottlieb Fichte, most of the essay offers an analysis of the spontaneity of the "I think," "as [this proposition] is drawn indefinitely, in general, from inner experience" (295), and returns only at the end to an obviously neo-empiricist doctrine of different degrees of consciousness. Within a few years Schmid thus seems to have moved from eliding consciousness in general to emphasizing it. But underneath this apparent reversal there remains as the constant point of deviation from Kant the radical separation of transcendental and empirical consciousness. An empirical psychology has no place for consciousness in general; conversely, with complete consistency, an inner metaphysics allows for no bridge to an empirical ego. It would take a close reading of the whole devious and dreary argument to show this, but I believe it is accurate to say that pure consciousness remains as empty in this essay as it always had been for Schmid. Despite the phrase that I quoted from the essay, Schmid in fact envisions no "inner experience"; on the contrary, in the same essay he states, "an original, immediate consciousness . . . is a concept that permits no application for empirical psychology" (305), and curtly dismisses the gothic aberrations of the isolated fancy as "intimations, visions, and the correspondence of spirits" (321). Schmid distinguishes *Kraft* (power), which is "the predicate of substance," from *Vermögen* (capacity), "the predicate of a subject" (308). The difference here is more morphological than semantic, for *Vermögen* derives from a transitive verb, while *Kraft* is strictly nominal. Even though Schmid does not always maintain the distinction, the effect is clear: substance is not subject, subject is not substance, and only subject has a genuine predicate.[1] The substance, consciousness (in general) is active—even preternaturally active, since it acts with spontaneity and with a plethora of powers—but only the subjectivity, my consciousness, is effective. Thus Schmid cuts the link between the theoretical or transcendental substance and the practical or empirical subject; he writes, for instance, that "the mind [*das Gemüth*, here entirely lacking the emotive connotations of 'mood'] as simple, identical ego is, to be sure, the ultimate substratum of all those capacities, whereby however we cannot advance to a knowledge of the ultimate, fundamental powers" (342–43).[2] Finally, the transcendental ego that Schmid set out to analyze turns out to be just as much a phantasm in this essay as it was in Schmid's *Empirische Psychologie*.

The key issue that divides a disciple like Schmid from Kant, both philosophically and psychologically, is spontaneity. In the Kantian system the transcendental ego lies at the beginning of time; it engenders objective experience through what Kant calls "the *epigenesis* of pure reason" (*Critique of Pure Reason* B167).[3] For Kant himself, "beginning" is a limit concept. A beginning lies half within and half outside of time, leading Kant to prove (in the first of the "Antinomies of Pure Reason") both that "the world has a beginning in time" and that it has none (A426 and 427). Schmid's "Abriß" follows Fichte in trying to make the self a strictly active creator independent of the world it creates, and thus he dissolves the ambivalence of the limit. (Subsequently Hegel utterly changed the terms of the discussion by placing consciousness in the center of time, in the *here* and *now*.) And the failure of Schmid's attempt—indeed the general simplification of limits in Kant's philosophical commentators—points to what is most imaginative in Kant. For Kant's transcendental ego is by no means exclusively spontaneous and active; on the contrary, it must be passive as well. Pure spontaneity engenders nothing, or at most a name—"But this spontaneity does lead me to call myself an intelligence" (*Critique of Pure Reason* B158n)—unless the self is at the same time receptive. The epigenesis of pure reason demands that the self affect itself; it must be, so to speak, masculine and feminine at once. Its auto-affection takes place in a realm of generalized thought, without any specific objects, a thought that is not yet *Erkenntnis*, knowledge or recognition (B158). This is the realm that the first edition of the *Critique of Pure Reason* had broken down into a labyrinthine series of syntheses of apprehension, reproduction, and recognition, while other essays characterize it more simply as pure feeling.

Merely reviewing the terms begins to show what Kant's followers unconsciously colluded in repressing. Herder's barbed reference to "the onanism of pure-impure reason" is accurate: pure consciousness began (in the first edition of the *Critique of Pure Reason*) with a devious plot against things in themselves, and it was never so simple, so spontaneous (naive, childlike), or so pure as it seemed.[4] "I have no knowledge of myself, as *I am*, but only of how I *appear* to myself" (*Critique of Pure Reason* B158). What is this *I am*, this forbidden knowledge that is consequent upon thought (I think, therefore I am) but can never become an object of thought? What *is* the nature of consciousness in general?

We can never know the answer to that question. A hidden mystery of generation, something unnaturally, illicitly, even unspeakably erotic lurks at the borders of our understanding. If the capacity for generation within nature is incomprehensible for Kant (*Prolegomena* A161n, citing one of Ernst Platner's aphorisms), the capacity for engendering nature herself must be all the more so. "The occupation of reason merely with itself, and, while it [literally: *she*] broods over its own concepts, the acquaintance with objects presumably born [*entspringende*] immediately therefrom, without needing experience as a go-between [*der Vermittelung der Erfahrung*]" (*Prolegomena* A125) —is this an immaculate conception or a sordid imposition? If this were Rousseau, of course, we should know immediately because he tells us all about his dalliance with himself. But Kant refuses us the knowledge of ourselves, the secret of our inmost thoughts. We will never know the true confessions of pure reason.

Kant does not ignore the questions that I have asked. On the contrary, he journeys to the limits of his discourse and then draws the line so as to demarcate them. I have accused Kant's commentators of an unconscious repression, but in truth they are only repeating, without comprehending the implications, what is a conscious and explicit repression in Kant's text. When pushed to the limit, Kant withholds the fruit of the knowledge of the secret history of pure reason. *Prolegomena to Any Future Metaphysics* §33 reads:

> There is indeed [literally: *in the deed*] with our pure concepts of the understanding something ensnaring [*Verfängliches*], with respect to the seduction [*Anlockung*] to a transcendent use. . . . Therefore concepts of the understanding seem to have far more meaning and content than that the mere use in experience could exhaust their entire determination, and so the understanding builds itself unobserved next to the house of expe-

rience a yet far roomier recess [*Nebengebäude*], which it [literally: *he*]
fills up with mere creatures of thought, without once noting that with its
otherwise correct thoughts it has transgressed over the boundaries of
their use.   (A106)

What deeds does that seductive pimp transact with the bawd reason in its roomy yet hidden annex, filled with ghosts (creatures of
thought)? Kant seems not to say that we cannot answer this question,
but rather to say that we must draw the line and not ask. *Prolegomena*
§34 states: "Therefore two important, indeed entirely indispensable,
although extremely dry examinations were necessary, which were undertaken Crit. page 137 etc. and 235 etc." (A106). Why such a forbidding, curt, and cryptic reference here? And why were such *dry* investigations necessary? Something dangerous (fruity? juicy?) is being kept
out of sight.[5] The simple pure consciousness of self is in itself—in its
own house, which is not a genuine house, but a recess—neither simple
nor pure. Its simplicity and purity are the products of a repression at
the origin, and the transcendence of the transcendental ego is the sublimation that accompanies that repression. These are the ghosts that
haunt the edges of Kant's imagination.[6]

To sum up, then, the Kantian self consists of a collection of pure,
transcendental intuitions, such as time, that lie between, around, outside of all its empirical experiences. The Enlightenment problem of
personal identity is thereby circumvented. Selfhood is not subject to
the whims of empirical memory, as in Locke; our dreams are part of
our selves because they exist in temporal continuity with our waking
existence, even though in our dreams we may not remember who we
are. And selfhood is also not the fiction of an active intelligence as in
Hume; consequently we remain the same person even when we go
mad and lose the power to shape our life. But nothing more can be
said to specify what this "something" is, this third thing (neither phenomenon nor noumenon) designated by the sentence "I think." It is
an abstract existence, a space of possibility, beyond any conceivable
specification. The purity of the transcendental ego depends on its
intangibility.[7]

8

Kant and the Doctors

W HAT IS GAINED in the discovery of an empty space, a time without moments, an unknowable self? Kant's system is grounded on what looks like a purely negative intuition and an obscuring or forgetting of the meaning of the Cartesian cogito.[1] Yet in considering pure consciousness to be an intellectual or purely logical construct of no relevance to real experience, Kant's commentators overlook the message of one of the best-known of his earlier essays, the "Attempt to Introduce the Concept of Negative Quantities into Philosophy." This essay distinguishes between logical negation, which cancels out, and real negation, which corrects: "For negative quantities are not negations of quantities, as the similarity of the expression led [Crusius] to believe, but something truly positive in themselves, only opposed to the other" (A vi). The true inheritors of Kant's insights are not speculative philosophers but more empirical thinkers—psychologists, physicians, physiologists—who endeavored to recognize consciousness in general as something positive in itself. They elaborate what is implicit in Kant's system, namely that there is more to life than experience, more to personality than rational coherence, more to behavior than propriety, more to man than what he knows. Three topics can be distinguished here: the soul organ, the definition of life, and finally the evaluation of madness.

The search for a soul organ, the true site of thought and feeling, goes back to Greek times.[2] Descartes himself was responsible for one of the most systematic, empirically based hypotheses concerning the location of the soul; as is well known, he placed the focus of mental activity, the *sensorium commune*, at the center of the brain, in the pineal gland. Descartes's theory is basically epistemological—the pineal gland is the seat of ideas, not of feelings—and is founded on the geometrical principle of congruence and the mechanical principles of inertia and conservation of force:

> The gland H is composed of a material that is quite soft and is not completely joined and united to the substance of the brain, but only attached to small arteries (whose skins are rather loose and pliant) and supported as if in balance by the force of the blood that is impelled toward it by the warmth of the heart; so that very little is required to determine it to incline and bend more or less, now on one side, now on another, and to cause it in leaning to dispose the spirits leaving it to take their course toward certain spots in the brain rather than others.
>
> (*L'Homme*, in *Oeuvres*, 9: 179)

The line of mechanistic theories of the soul continued through the next century and a half, most influentially in Julien Offray de La Mettrie's *L'Homme-machine* (1748). In the 1790s the by-then-stale subject was briefly revived in a short treatise by a friend of Kant's, Samuel Thomas von Sömmerring, called *Über das Organ der Seele*. Sömmerring reflects the Kantian view that the mind cannot be limited to its knowable contents. Mind is not knowledge but the principle of knowledge, consciousness in general. The soul is not the organ that receives, retains, repeats, and transmits congruent images (which Descartes had called ideas) but the moving force that makes these mental activities possible. It is, in other words, the physiological correlative of the flux of time itself, "since primal life, primal movement or the beginning of movement is not even conceivable in fixed beings that are unchangeable in form; but these seem to demand a fluid" (41). The soul organ is thus not really an organ, but what Descartes called a spirit or humor, and its locus is not a Cartesian, limited and geometrical space, but a Kantian, open and empty space: it is "the fluid in the brain cavities" (36). And this in turn corresponds to a conception of man as, by nature or origin, a creature of pure potential, without any internal limits or prescribed character. "*What is a man*, in the first hours of his conception? . . . A small, clear, transparent droplet of a seemingly homogeneous moisture, containing to all appearance little that is firm, and on which no true physiologist has ever undertaken to show any trace of organization" (43, Sömmerring's suspension points). This is Locke's tabula rasa translated into the imagery of transcendental idealism.

The Kantians were not taken in by Sömmerring's essay. It remained too contrived an attempt to conciliate scientific empiricism with speculative philosophy. Schmid, for instance, while conceding that there must be a soul organ, objected to Sömmerring's localization of perception in the brain: we perceive through our whole body, and the soul must consequently be more widely diffused than Sömmerring would allow.[3] Kant himself was blunter; he compared Sömmerring's enterprise to a quest for the square root of -2, and he quoted the Latin comedian Terence to the effect that the project was a kind of rational insanity: "cum ratione insanias" ("Über das Organ der Seele" A86). Yet Kant was by no means hostile to Sömmerring's work. On the contrary, his remarks are contained in an appendix that he wrote to Sömmerring's treatise.[4] As a comic phrase, "rational insanity" designates not the antithesis of reason but its limits. Far from repudiating Sömmerring's entire endeavor, Kant's afterword redefines it; he uses Sömmerring's mechanistic and quantitative approach as the springboard to an alternative: a chemical and dynamic approach. Not at all averse to an empirical investigation of mind—what is good in theory must also be good in practice—he merely turns the investigation yet further inward: the mind is not the operations of the mental fluid on the surrounding physical structures but the chemical changes within the fluid itself. Twice Kant specifies that the empirical science of mind (*Gemüt*) is not a science of the soul and provides no information about the transcendental unity of consciousness. Yet even if the soul is not accessible to investigation by the senses, Kant's essay does not deny it a real existence. Though it cannot be localized in the outer, spatial world, it can still be known by its changes through time. Kant's logic thus leaves open a window to the empirical investigation of this transcendental object, the soul. And indeed, must the soul not also have at least a vague locale for its fluid reality? For, as Ernst Platner wrote in a Latin essay of 1796, even among Kantians ("etiam inter Kantianos") no one really thinks that his soul is just as likely to be in the tree from which he is plucking some fruit as somewhere close to his body.[5]

Where the study of the soul organ might lead after Kant is illustrated by *An Essay on Human Consciousness*, written nearly two decades later by the physician John Fearn. Fearn's philosophical training was entirely empiricist, primarily Locke, but his instincts were thoroughly romantic and transcendental. Thus typical concerns include demonstrating the continuity of identity even during dreams (234) and a distinction between brain, which is active, and mind, which is often passive—a suffering, as Fearn puts it (206). The mind is the seat of sensations and feelings, not of knowledge and action; it operates less by calculation than by a kind of instinct that manifests "ineffable wisdom" (55). It becomes a ghostly substance, the ethereal occupant of the spaces and pores between the points of physical matter: "*That thing*, then, which *divides* these parts, *cannot be matter*, yet it is *extended*" (9). It has a shape, but a perfectly rarified one, with no geometrical specificity and no mechanical inertia: "Main hypothesis: *The Human Mind is a flexible Spherule*" (89). And so the game continues for Fearn, as the genuine, transcendental empiricism of the Kantians yields to a fanciful, a priori realism:

> Prop. 1. The unconscious Mind is supposed *uniformly rotund* or *Spherule*, and its surface is perfectly equal during *Sleep*; in which state it may somewhat resemble an Egg.
>
> Prop. 2. Desire for *sensible* pleasure is occasioned by an *uneasy motion*, and in this state the Mind is inflexed by a Nervous impulse, under the Motions of which it also *distends* in a more *general* way. Thus it may in some sort resemble a *Turtle's Egg*.   (111)

I cite Fearn to illustrate not the productive side of the Kantian heritage but its reduction to self-parody; the embarrassed literalism of his imagination resembles that of William Beckford's *Vathek* more than that of Walpole and his descendants.

The true heritage of Kant is a science of mind conceived as the empirical study of the temporality of human existence. No matter how scrupulously modern scholars attend to Kant's arguments, failure to stratify the texts for their innovations and to attend to the intellectual contexts has falsified historical understanding. Thus, one important study claims: "Idealist analysis discovered long since that all consciousness implies an activity of the subject, but it used this discovery only as an instrument of war against materialism, . . . [refusing] to thematise *concrete human activity* as *objective reality becoming the subject*."[6] Kant's Sömmerring commentary demonstrates his interest in attempts to concretize subjectivity. He warned against it, to be sure, but the ensuing pages will demonstrate how wrong it is to say that idealist analysis warred against it.

One of the most intriguing collocations is that of Kant with Markus Herz. A prolific philosophical and medical author, Herz had been a student of Kant's and remained for almost four decades Kant's closest friend, at least among intellectuals. While Kant was writing and revising his Critiques, Herz was at work on his magnum opus, *Versuch über den Schwindel*, a lengthy treatise on vertigo. While Kant makes passing reference to vertigo in his brief essay on diseases of the head and in "The Quarrel of the Faculties," this hardly seems like a Kantian topic. And yet, in a letter to Kant, Herz acknowledges having received the idea for the study from discussions with Kant, which must have taken place just about when Kant was writing the *Critique of Pure Reason*. Herz pleads eloquently for an empirical psychology that will not be merely an enthusiastic, metaphysical, a priori, rational, and deductive construct (1: 28–33). Yet clearly he intends an empirical extension and application of metaphysics, not an empirical alternative to metaphysics. For Herz, man is by definition the *animal temporale*. The distinctive character of the soul is *Weile* ("whiling"), a word for which Herz recognizes no equivalent in other languages (1: 47). *Weile* is not the mind's acts of attention or dwelling on a sensation, for which he reserves the term *Verweilung* ("tarrying"), but rather the empty mental space *between* two points or acts of attention: *Weile* is "the designation of the distance between the point at which one representation is *completely grasped*, and the beginning of notice given to the following one" (1: 47). When not subject to an object of attention, the soul has its own temporal rhythm that can be identified as the normal state of the human mind. Two characteristics of the soul's "whiling" stand out in connection with the notion of a material subject of transcendental empiricism: the first is that the natural movement of the soul is as much physiological as psychological; the second is that when it is healthy, we do not feel it—except, presumably, as part of the feeling of self in general that Herz designates as comfort:

> When the train of representations in man passes by in the progression that is *natural* to him, the soul is in a free and comfortable [*behaglichen*] condition: the play of its activity goes along quietly and peacefully, like all affairs in the economy of the body when it is in its natural condition. The soul has as little particular feeling of this alternating tension and relaxation of its force as of the movement of the heart, the intestines, or even of such voluntary muscular movements as have become habitual.
> (*Versuch über den Schwindel*, 1: 153–54)

To be sure, the soul is not a physical object that can be localized in space, but it is a physical condition that manifests itself in the physiological pulse of life.

The soul is the rhythm of existence. As in Kant's *Prolegomena*, here, too, there may be a reflection of the fifth reverie from Rousseau's *Reveries of a Solitary Wanderer* (1782), with its evocation of the pure feeling of existence while the author bobs in a boat on a lake. Here, though, the soul has become empirical by definition, with its own nosology, diagnosis, and treatment. For Herz, as for John Haslam in the next decade, disorders of the soul arise from too slow or too fast a connection of ideas, *stasis* or *frenzy*; for Herz, in contrast to Thomas Arnold a few years earlier, these disorders are consequently treatable. An excessively slow progression of ideas (Haslam's melancholia) is designated *Langerweile* [*sic*], or boredom; an excessively fast and tumultuous progression is vertigo. Either of these conditions skews the relation of soul to body, even to the point where a man is "deprived of his identity [*seiner Ichheit entäussert*]" (*Versuch über den Schwindel*, 1: 13). Yet Herz observes "that in this mental condition even death is sometimes delayed for a time" (1: 14); and he anticipates Falconer in commenting, "it is astonishing how much the soul can influence the so heterogeneous seeming body" (1: 12). The complex term *Weilen* also approaches the meaning of "dwelling"; the body does not make a person if the soul does not dwell within it, and when there is no person, the person cannot die. As a practicing physician, Herz tried to keep such speculations about the empirical soul within the limits of what could be observed in nature. But if you were to exaggerate his pathologies into a myth, you would arrive at something like "The Vampyre" by Byron's physician John Polidori. The vampire is visibly set apart by the abnormal rhythm of life: he lives for months in a condition of lusterless inertia, followed at the proper moment by frenzied violence, apparent death, and startlingly rapid decomposition of the body. Yet he is immediately resurrected. The actions of his body are controlled by a supernatural power; no soul dwells within; and no true death occurs because he is never truly alive. Vampires neither dwell nor while their time away.[7]

According to Herz, the actions of the human soul most closely resemble invisible muscular actions such as those of the heart and the intestines, and secondarily certain unnoticed voluntary movements, by which Herz must be thinking of reflexive, self-directed actions like blinking. Life is the residence of the soul within the body and is independent of all visible, external bodily activity. This sounds like a strictly metaphysical definition of life. It certainly sounds metaphysical when Coleridge writes in *Dejection: An Ode*: "I may not hope from outward forms to win / The passion and the life, whose fountains are within." And while Coleridge proposes recovery of the "Natural Man" as the remedy for his melancholia, the means he envisions are not medication but "abstruse research." Thus does philosophy teach us of life.

Yet within Kantian circles the concept of a life within also led to distinct, practical reflections. The greatest examples lie in the work of Christoph Wilhelm Hufeland. An even more eminent medical man than Herz, Hufeland served as court physician in Weimar and for many years edited the voluminous *Journal der practischen Heilkunde*, one of the leading international medical periodicals of the time. Hufeland was strictly a practical researcher; his work shows no traces of philosophical speculation. Yet Kant was exceptionally interested in Hufeland; one of Kant's few reviews concerns a political essay by Hufeland, and the medical section of "The Quarrel of the Faculties" analyzes some of Hufeland's writings in detail. Naturally, Hufeland's views cannot be presumed to be identical with Kant's, anymore than are Sömmerring's; but they are contiguous with Kant's: Kant characteristically wrote in response to authors who stretched the limits of his system.

One of Hufeland's many pet ideas was a concept of *Lebenskraft* (life force), about which he wrote numerous essays. The essay that defines the term treats it as a limit concept, with a logic akin to Kant's. Life occupies the border between the material and the physical worlds; we cannot know just where to find it.[8] To reflect the antinomy, Hufeland says he prefers the more neutral term "force" to the more traditional term "spirit." Yet for Hufeland there follows on this uncertainty not inaction or speculation, but a practical science of life. The practical consequences are elaborated in a mortuarial essay of 1792, "Über die Ungewißheit des Todes und das einzige untrügliche Mittel sich von seiner Unmöglichkeit zu überzeugen und das Lebendigbegraben unmöglich zu machen" (On the Uncertainty of Death and the Sole Reliable Means of Reaching a Conclusion of Its Impossibility and of Rendering Live Burial Impossible).[9] If the fountains of life are within, then outward forms such as bodily movement cannot be identified with life: the life force gives no signs of itself. The life force sustains the integrity of the person, not his activity. A moribund state does not necessarily show that the person is dead, which is proved only by the actual decomposition of the body, and consequently interment should be delayed until decay has set in. Hufeland's essay comes complete with lurid newspaper accounts of people buried alive; here the outwaters of Kantianism begin to overflow one of the main thematic sources of the gothic novel.[10]

Beyond Kant's interest in Herz, Hufeland, and Sömmerring, a great deal of circumstantial evidence links Kant with a yearning somehow to find and investigate the recesses of the soul. It is well known that he was friendly with mystics such as Johann Georg Hamann and the physiognomist Johann Caspar Lavater. Less well known is the receptivity of the Berlin Enlightenment to such matters, which were anathema to more conservative rationalists. Kant's essay "Was heißt: sich im Denken orientieren?" was published in the *Berlinische Monatsschrift*, as were several of his essays a decade later. Now, Kant must have been aware of what was being featured in the journal where he published. But the *Monatsschrift*'s bread and butter in the mid-1780s was an interminable controversy about animal magnetism and somnambulism, occupying much of volumes 6–11, with contributions from the likes of Lavater and the Swiss Pietist Johann Georg Zimmermann, who is discussed below. To be sure, the Berlin rationalists reacted skeptically and were pleased to publish in their monthly an anonymous article proclaiming "that all wondrous things succeed more readily in Lavater's house than say in Kant's or in that of some other cold-blooded philosopher" ("Magnetische Desorganisation," 432). Still, proximity contaminates. Even Johann Heinrich Formey was given to suspiciously risqué effusions about sleep and death: "The sanest man passes through a kind of delirium, his ideas grow confused, the bonds that unite them are relaxed, and are separated at the end; and when this separation is complete, sleep begins."[11] Reading Kant against that background, an author in the *Deutsches Museum* in 1787 accused Kant's own orientation essay of *Schwärmerei* (enthusiasm).[12] Judged by his friends and their associates rather than by his avowed principles and by his commentators, Kant's philosophy starts to look very different.

Thus to many individuals in his day Kant did not look like a rationalist pure and simple, but rather like a rationalist superimposed upon a mystic. After all, as the empiricist J. D. Mauchart, trying to take account of Kant without being taken in by him, wrote, "even the madman *must* think according to the very same laws [i.e., the Kantian categories] by which the profoundest philosopher thinks in his most irrefutable deductions."[13] The madman's laws were investigated in Moritz's *Magazin zur Erfahrungsseelenkunde*. The first number contains an essay called "Stärke des Selbstbewußtseins" (The Strength of Self-Consciousness), about a series of haunted, seemingly supernatural awakenings that grow familiar and masterable with repetition. The author (whose name is given as Fischer) asks, where is the boundary between the normal and the abnormal, between mechanical disorders and higher forces? "Where is the boundary?" is, of course,

Kant's question. It is a question whose answer must be imagined, or dreamed, before it can be represented, or thought. Nor were all the accounts as good-natured as Moritz's praise of Kant's dreams, quoted in "Fantasia: Kant and the Demons of the Night" (Chapter 2 above). Here is the practical Hufeland, commenting on "how close insanity is to reason": "How can we still appeal to sound reason and expect to use it as a measuring rod, since many current philosophers themselves look down on it with pity and scorn, and one of them has even recently declared that nothing more vulgar exists than this honored sound reason.—And true it is, common human reason comprehends nothing of the speculations and deductions of that transcendental reason."[14] A serious and genuinely cold philosopher ascribed Kant's writings to a fever that cures "but does not thereby belong to health" and elsewhere declared Kantian "subjective certainty" to be no better than the delusions of lunatics.[15] And the lower end of this spectrum finds only scorn, not amusement or amazement at Kantian speculation. "Only enthusiasts or madmen take those medical teachings whose pillars are the reveries of today's so-called critical philosophy to be philosophical. . . . This metaphysical unphilosophical raving cannot last and will not at any rate have any influence on my medical doctrine, particularly since Kantianism and Vitus' dance are convulsive diseases that . . . attack only the young."[16]

Kant the vitalist, Kant the dreamer, Kant the enthusiast, Kant the physiologist of the soul, Kant the sponsor and friend of mystics and connoisseurs of arcana, Kant the lunatic.[17] It is, to say the least, a different picture of the Sage of Königsberg than the academic tradition bequeaths us. Its descendant is the romantic study of abnormal states of mind—those limit conditions at which humans alienate or transcend the body and reveal the transcendental ego to the observer's eye. The tireless theorist of this empirical transcendental, aiming to fuse Hufeland's practical vitalism with Kant's idealism, was the great German psychiatrist Johann Christian Reil. It is well known that Reil influenced the portrayal of daydreamers in Kleist and Hoffmann, but less well known how direct the influence of Kant was upon him, lasting from Reil's 1795 essay on the life force, "Ueber die Lebenskraft" (which includes a remarkable critique of Kant's conception of the organism), through the decades of Schelling-inspired *Naturphiloso-phie*. It is Reil who finally proposes a recipe for stripping away all externals until the naked self is at last revealed:

> This pure consciousness, separate from all contingent determinants, is the foundation of our whole knowledge, . . . the I, entirely empty in itself, . . . on which the whole infinity of the manifold depends. What abstraction presents to us as something merely thought, appears to us in reality just before the outbreak of a collapse in which first the surrounding world of the senses, then our own objectivity, and finally subjectivity or the consciousness of the consciousness of self is extinguished.
>
> ("Das Zerfallen," 551)

Kant had striven to draw the boundary so as to leave pure consciousness as a mere idea of reason, but here Reil terms it an observable reality. But where in fact is it to be found? As the passage proceeds, it turns out that the recipe for producing pure consciousness is precisely the same as the recipe for producing a gothic novel:

> The visible scene is wrapped in ever thicker fogs that finally remove it altogether from sight; sounds fade ever further away from us until they die off in the measureless distance. . . . Life has withdrawn from the boundary to the innermost focus of organization; absolute darkness and the stillness of death surround us. . . . Our whole prior existence seems but a dream to us. But at last our mental powers also vanish, even the memory of the past, the I hangs as but a single glimmering, but wholly empty spark in absolute night, of which naught but the consciousness remains, *that it still is and still thinks its empty being*, until even this passes into unconsciousness.[18]

Rethinking Kant (with the aid, to be sure, of Schelling and his school) taught Reil to conceive of himself as a soul doctor rather than a body doctor. His most influential work was the romantically titled *Rhapsodien über die Anwendung der psychischen Curmethode auf Geisteszerrüttungen* (Rhapsodies on the Application of the Psychic Method of Cure to Disrupted Spirits). Here Reil pleads at length for the establishment of a whole new branch of medicine, the psychic method, to stand beside the traditional chemical and physico-mechanical methods: sciences of the human machine and of the human organism need to be completed by a science of human consciousness in general. Within the new science insanity occupies the apparently paradoxical position of being an organic pathology and yet a metaphysical norm: it tears apart the human fabric, but puts us in touch with an essential part of ourselves.[19] Indeed, much that occurs in the madhouse resembles phenomena of the great world, as when madmen play at being kings and princes, though "more openly and harmlessly": "One fibre goes slack in our brain, and the divine spark that dwells within has become a fairytale" (*Rhapsodien*, 9). This is not the old topos of the world as madhouse but its complete inversion; what happens in the asylum obeys the laws of the world. Indeed, it reveals truths about ourselves that would otherwise remain hidden:

> Each man has an urge to yield to the play of his fancy, which spins out the thread according to the tuning (mood) of the temperament [i.e., sanguinary, melancholic, etc.]. Only in the head of men such as suffer from a sick and irritable nervous system do the above named hypotheses . . . unite with a drive toward executing them. . . . And the cause for this lies in the fact that their nervous illness brings them close to madness, in which alone such an action is possible—closer (and they feel it) than a healthy man, through whose head such fancies also course, but without drive or fear, because he feels himself too strong ever to allow them to come to execution within him.   ("Nachschrift," 592–93)

The healthy man represses his imagination in order to achieve a balance between internal and external needs, between the individual and the species. In madness the reality principle disappears and the genius is uncorked. Madness puts us in touch with the center of ourselves. But surrounding the center is a boundary, and to cross the boundary into the center of madness is to enter a region of fire. Purifying fire? Or destruction? How can we say, those of us who have never been there? This is the message that concludes the passage from which I have just quoted, the last outer (or inner) limit of Kantianism: "He who knows himself a hundred miles distant from a volcano will not be alarmed at the possibility of its eruption, but that other man well may be who lives on the edge of its crater."

Kant is on record as condemning the enthusiastic excesses of mesmerism (in a letter to L. E. Borowski, March 1790). But what would he have thought of the research of Reil, at once meticulous in its empiricism and sophisticated in its metaphysics? Seeing Kant through the eyes of his medical friends and antagonists completely changes the perception of where his philosophy led. What he says is that the depths of the soul and the inner essence of things are out of bounds. But what he shows is that they are mysterious challenges. They can't be penetrated by the empirical methods of the Enlightenment, not even using the sophisticated techniques of Sömmerring. But a new science of mind that is not a science of the brain could illuminate the structures of feeling, the impulses and drives that orient each of us in our common world of experience. The rational Kant tells us where we live. But the other Kant—and the other Kantians—have much to tell us about the mysterious vitality that helps us find our way in that world.

9

Meditative Interlude

AT THIS POINT a certain Pietist strain, deriving conjointly from Rousseau and from the mystic Lavater, may be considered. The movement of ideas keeps running into negatives: life is not in matter, not in measure, not in geometry, not in the punctual or momentary relation of man to the world, not in activity. Where then is Life, in itself, freed from its impurities? In the unburied, the not-yet-dead, the force that preserves the individual from decay after all externals have been stripped away, says Hufeland. In the eternal night of a shapeless, solitary dungeon, says the gothic novel. In "an inner cave, difficult of access, strange, and dangerous," says Beatrice, the guiding spirit of Mary Shelley's third published novel, *Valperga*, to the heroine Euthanasia. "This is the habitation of the madman," Beatrice explains, "when all the powers desert the vestibule, and he, finding no light, makes darkling, fantastic combination, and lives among them. From thence there is a short path to hell. . . . But it is here also that Poetry and Imagination live" (356–57). But these are obviously limit cases, not the norm. And so, before turning to gothic man, I will consider the Pietist, who finds life in the peaceful solitude of the picturesque Swiss hills.

> Solitude moves us in every one of its peaceful pictures. In sweet melancholy the soul collects itself to all feelings that lead aside from world and

men at the distant rustic tone of a monastery bell, at the quiet of nature in a beautiful night, on every high mountain, near each crumbling monument of old times, in every terrifying forest. But he who knows not what it is to be a friend, a companion to himself; who is never at home with his thought, never with himself, to him solitude and death is one and the same.

This is a representative passage from one of the genuinely popular works of the Kantian decade, Johann Georg Zimmermann's endless tract, *Ueber die Einsamkeit* (Solitude) (2: 105), published in 1784–85 and rapidly translated into the major European languages. Zimmermann offers a recipe for finding the self in a peace that is just this side of death. Nature facilitates the discovery, but it is a discovery of life in the person, not of life in nature; indeed, "with a fine imagination one would be happier in a dark dungeon than without imagination in the most splendid region" (4: 36). To the Pietist nature offers a space of abstraction from outer forms. Throughout Zimmermann's work it is notable that the immediacy of natural impressions is directly correlated to their remoteness. All these singulars—the bell, the night, the mountain, the monument, the wood—do not exist in a Cartesian, coordinate space but seem much more like isolated perceptions from nowhere. And they likewise exist in a time not subject to measurement, whether in the age-old ritual of the Church, the geologic age of the mountain, the vague prehistory of the monument, or the disembodied stillness of night and forest. To be collected, at home with oneself, is the opposite of the cogito: it is to live in a world of images that resist becoming cognitions. Zimmermann describes the landscape at enormous length, but he does so in order to remove us from all pressures of immediacy. Nature is not a sphere of activity or an object of possible knowledge; it orients us only in the Kantian sense of developing our feeling of self.

Contemplation trains the imagination by dissolving all practical relations to the point where we can live even in a prison; we study nature in order to turn inward. Despite appearances, *Ueber die Einsamkeit* is a school for the inner sense; it inculcates patience, passivity, *Weilen*. "Solitude naturally teaches, more than does the agitated life of affairs, the high value of time, which the idle man does not appreciate and which is never sufficiently valued without the appropriate activity of the soul [*Wirksamkeit der Seele*]" (2: 326). Zimmermann shows what he means and practices what he preaches by repeating this message unchanged for pages: life is time in and of itself, the activity of the soul, and not the activity of the body.

The threads of influence cannot be disentangled; nor, indeed, would I wish to. Kant and Zimmermann were both friends of Lavater, both avid readers of Rousseau. Can any one figure be designated as the originator of a new sensibility or a new anthropology? Is it not more reasonable to say that each work contributes its more or less modest share toward shaping man's self-image within a range of possibilities that are given by its historical context? The discovery of consciousness as an interior expanse, a world of qualitative feeling rather than quantitative knowledge, of open possibility rather than delimited action, mental dissociation rather than physical association —this discovery could, conceivably, have dispensed with its Swiss inflection or with its inflation into horror and madness, but was it not, in its general outlines, given as the goal for the groping of authors as early as Hume and Thomson?

It is certain, at any rate, that Zimmermann struck a responsive chord among those concerned with the practical experience and training of the soul. Herz, for instance, quotes two full pages of Zimmermann's description of boredom in his *Versuch über den Schwindel*. And Zimmermann's manner also illuminates that of Ann Radcliffe. Radcliffe's descriptive prose was widely admired in her own time, yet seems remarkably bloodless today. But it is a mistake to seek an impression of reality, for her posture is meditative, not responsive. Like Zimmermann, she discovered in nature not an objective external reality but a symbol of the life of the soul. Except as inspiration, indeed, nature may be said to be invisible to her; as the Count De Villefort says at one point in the *Mysteries of Udolpho*, "the landscape is not changed, but time has changed me; from my mind the illusion, which gave spirit to the colouring of nature, is fading fast" (3.11; p. 474).[1]

Radcliffe's fondness for obscure half-lights is notorious; they efface the reality of the external scene. It is true that her landscapes are typically more unified than Zimmermann's; she favors framed panoramas and ties the details into a composite picture. Yet on the whole the impression of detail prevails over the impression of totality, and the panoply of sounds, smells, and tactile sensations emanating from undefined sources contributes to the disembodiment of landscape. Nature lies beyond a window or a wall; it is not the concrete world of our physical activity but the embodiment of the inner sense, the moving picture of time in general. On occasion the apparently external landscape explicitly merges with what it really is, the immeasurable space of the soul and the music of time, as in the following passage, where the mythical sounds of the village function exactly as they do in Zimmermann:

> The windows, which were numerous and large, descended low, and afforded a very extensive, and what Blanche's fancy represented to be, a very lovely prospect; and she stood for some time, surveying the grey obscurity and depicturing imaginary woods and mountains, valleys and rivers, on this scene of night; her solemn sensations rather assisted, than interrupted, by the distant bark of a watch-dog, and by the breeze, as it trembled upon the light foliage of the shrubs. Now and then, appeared for a moment, among the woods, a cottage light; and, at length, was heard, afar off, the evening bell of a convent, dying on the air.
>
> (*Mysteries of Udolpho* 3.10; pp. 471–72)

More projected or imagined than seen, Blanche's landscape has little in common with the Burkean sublime: though large, dark, and punctuated by inarticulate noises, it elicits and does not overwhelm a human response. On the other hand, it does resemble the Kantian "sensible shining" of the idea of life. Its effect is produced, in part, by the frequent, almost instinctive personifications, which are, to be sure, more often passive metaphors of trembling and dying than active ones of working and forging. The movement is away from, not toward, transport and terror; the overwhelming impression of a powerful unity yields to the contemplation of evocative detail:

> When weary of sauntering among cliffs that seemed scarcely accessible but to the steps of the enthusiast, and where no track appeared on the vegetation, but what the foot of the izard had left; they would seek one of those green recesses, which so beautifully adorn the bosom of these mountains, where, under the shade of the lofty larch, or cedar, they en-

joyed their simple repast, made sweeter by the waters of the cool stream, that crept along the turf, and by the breath of wild flowers and aromatic plants, that fringed the rocks, and inlaid the grass.

(Mysteries of Udolpho 1.1; p. 3)

Diffusive effects are numerous: the generalizing plurals, the coordinates that undermine specificity ("larch, or cedar") or divide attention ("fringed the rocks and inlaid the grass"), the drag of the heavy punctuation. The entire thrust is to let contemplative immersion smother alertness.

Read in conjunction with Zimmermann, Radcliffe's landscapes remind us again of the inwardness that is a fundamental component of the gothic. Not everything in these novels is violent and turbulent; on the contrary, their essence is an alternation between *Schwindel* and *Langerweile*, vertigo and boredom, mania and melancholia. Their aim is to teach us to dwell with ourselves, to be at home in the bosom of Mother Nature. "The ruin . . . throws us back into the contemplation of Being itself. Its purpose becomes the creation of a space for thought" (A. Johnson, "Gaps and Gothic Sensibility," 18).

Solitude casts its moonlit shadow all across the genre. Radcliffe's early *Sicilian Romance* (1790), notably, takes the form of a quest for humanity that modulates into a discovery of the isolated individual. In this novel numerous groups of heroes and villains continually cross and recross the island in search of refuge or of revenge, that is, one form or another of human contact. (There is even an extra father-daughter pair thrown in with no other function than to create two scenes in which the wicked fathers mistakenly seize the wrong maiden in distress.) But contact is immediately broken or never made at all, because of the hairbreadth escapes that occur out of a series of ever more dangerous confinements: peasant's hut, monastery, wrecked ship, bandit's cave. At the end, the heroine stumbles into and immures herself in a dungeon, under her father's very own castle, where her mother has been confined for fifteen years. Her consciousness fades in this deadly spot of self-recognition; the novel contains the obligatory happy ending, but the release occurs by miraculous means not generated from the prior events. Mother Nature has its villages; the Mother

Church its priests; only underground does a realm exist from which the paternal Other has excluded itself and left the eternal feminine intact.[2]

The principle of solitude has a formal dimension as well. For gothic fictions are, almost without exception, "manuscripts found in a bottle." Typically, that is, they are cordoned off from real experience by a framing device, often a framing device so crude that you wonder why the author bothered. In the earliest instances, where the works were still masquerading as historical romances, plausibility is the pretext. But the fiction continues long after this pretext vanishes; its true purpose is evidently to insulate the narrative and to forestall comparison. The gothic novel is a *texte trouvé*, the pure play of mind discovering its own mad impulses, the artist's critique of judgment. Where the editorial fiction is absent, it is normally replaced by extended flashbacks and other encapsulated stories remote in time or place, often separately titled. (Structurally pertinent is the Pietist "Confessions of a Beautiful Soul," which constitutes book 6 of Goethe's part-gothic novel, *Wilhelm Meister's Apprenticeship*.) The mirroring of story within story serves the same function of suspending judgment as does the editorial fiction. Indeed, E. T. A. Hoffmann's *Devil's Elixirs* gives as many as three different versions of the same sequence of events. Since Hoffmann's first-person narrator is subject to fits of delirium, his confessions do not necessarily carry more authority than do reconstructions by those who were with him or those who were keeping guard from afar. The reader hardly has more tools for evaluation than the fictional librarian who writes the conclusion without having read the tale. The devil's elixirs are, in a sense, the author's intoxicants in a story that outruns thought. Creating a demand for new angles and new twists, narrative blind alleys and trap doors, the gothic novel is never far from frivolity; the demonic grin of the villain coalesces with the manipulative mirth of the author.

And yet are not gaming, narrative suspense, and readerly confusion all forms of absorption? Do they not share a deep structure with the meditative landscapes that leave the mind lost in thought? Cheap thrillers, which the romantic period produced in abundance, lack the expansiveness of the most characteristic gothic novels, whose pacing is as deliberate as it is (or seems) inexorable. Whiling is essential: we live while we are at peril. Almost without anyone's being aware of it, the *cogito* had become a *conscius sum* or even a *sentio*; from here it is a mere step to the gothic *patior, ergo sum*, "I suffer, therefore I am," or to the formula *cogitor, ergo sum*, "I am thought, therefore I am," beloved of the German romantic mystical idealist Franz von Baader. I suffer, I become a plaything, and thereby I prove myself. The gothic becomes an experiment in entrapment and manipulation, methodical in its procedures and often drawing magnetism, mesmerism, and other quasi-sciences of the day for its explanatory base. Game, passion, and system conjoin in the discovery of the self that lies hidden at the limits of pure reason.

PART III

Philosophy of the Gothic Novel

10

The Wild Ass's Skin

$\mathbf{F}$AITES LE JEU!—Le jeu est fait!" ("'Place your bets!' 'The bets are placed!'") The croupier's call resounds at the very beginning of Balzac's *Wild Ass's Skin*.[1] The protagonist Raphael, playing Russian roulette, has just wagered his last coin and laid his life on the line. He loses, but before he carries out the intended suicide, he stumbles into an old curiosity shop, where he acquires the magic shagreen that grants his every wish but also shrinks with each wish according to the measure of his remaining days.

The wager thus proves to be neither won nor lost but deferred for an indefinite time and subjected to an uncertain economy of voluptuousness and terror. For in truth, the wager is tantamount to Raphael's whole life, and life is not won or lost in a moment. As a child he first asserted his independence by robbing his father in order to enter a casino; at that time he won and returned the stolen money, thus ending the revolt but also acknowledging continued dependence. Later on his father failed, and Raphael was forced to be on his own in Paris while struggling to develop his *Theory of the Will*. Under these trying circumstances he has no other recourse than the gamble of living his own life: "it was as if I had made a wager with myself and were at once the player and the stake" (87; 105). He falls in love with the courtesan

Foedora, who instantly becomes both his despair and his only hope for salvation: "This woman's heart was the final lottery ticket on which my fortune depended" (106; 127). The subsequent acquisition of the magic skin changes the odds, though only with respect to Raphael's own assessment of them. So far as others know, life is as dubious as ever: "It's touch and go with him [*Chez lui, les chances de vie et de mort sont égales*]" (243; 279).

Within the croupier's cry, then, lies a homophonic formula: "Faites le je!—Le je est fait!," "Le Spiel, c'est l'homme même," as the Buffo(o)n of the nineteenth century might have said. Life perpetually forecloses options and imposes unalterable destinies, all the while recording the tally of a man upon his face: "The little old man, who no doubt had wallowed since his youth in the scalding pleasures of a gamester's life, gave him a lack-lustre, lukewarm glance, in which a philosopher would have seen the sufferings of doss-house inmates, the inquests held on innumerable charcoal-fume fatalities, sentences to penal servitude and transportation to overseas colonies" (12; 22). The individual resists such typing and struggles to preserve the meaning of life as *his* life by reserving a space for indeterminacy and risk. For Hume, society provided the individual with recreation. "Nature herself. . . . cures me of this philosophical melancholy and delirium, either by relaxing this bent of mind, or by some avocation, and lively impression of my senses, which obliterate all these chimeras. I dine, I play a game of backgammon, I converse, and am merry with my friends" (*Treatise*, 243, "Conclusion to Book I"). But now—meaning, for Balzac's heroes, after the Revolution—society has become the oppressor, and conviviality no longer relaxes. Rejoicing merely intoxicates; only revolt liberates, and the individual feels his pulse throb, glimpses his freedom among the litter of the antiquary, the residues of fallen civilizations.

> These works of art, under the favour of the half-light, and set dancing by the feverish turmoil fermenting in his stricken brain, stirred and whirled before his eyes. . . . It was a weird witches' sabbath worthy of the fantasies glimpsed by Dr Faust on the Brocken. . . . The terrors of life had no hold on a soul which had already become familiar with the terrors of death. He even favoured with a sort of mocking complicity the bizarre

elements in this moral galvanism, whose prodigious manifestations were coupled with the last thoughts which gave him the feeling that he still existed.   (30; 42)

The last phrase, "le sentiment de l'existence," echoes Rousseau (just as had Kant, and Wordsworth in his 1850 *Prelude* 2.401), except that now self-consciousness is explicitly gothic.

What is the relation between the feeling of existence and the feeling of terror? Normally criticism of gothic novels has recourse to the category of the sublime, but in Balzac the term "sublime" often seems parodistic, since any attempt to comprehend Raphael's predicament in terms of the sublime fails utterly for lack of an applicable standard of measurement. How large is the bric-a-brac in the back of the old merchant's attic? How strong are those last thoughts, how intense that feeling of existence? The predominant mood in the shop is not of transcendence but of perplexity—who is an accomplice to what, and why?—and of surfeit:

> He came to a Virgin by Raphael, but he was tired of Raphael [did Balzac really have to introduce this onomastic play on his hero's name?]. A face by Correggio demanded his attention but failed to obtain it. A priceless vase of ancient porphyry . . . drew scarcely a smile from him. He felt smothered under the debris of fifty vanished centuries, nauseated with this surfeit of human thought, crushed under the weight of luxury and arts.   (28; 39–40)

Byronism is outflanked; neither the self nor its antagonists (or are they its conspirators?) here appear at all large.

Beyond the confines of the shop the magic skin continues to display a certain pettiness. This rug has no personality and harbors no genie. And without a demonic presence there can be no dramatic agon. When Raphael throws the skin away, it obligingly stays lost for months, though it does contrive to get itself brought back on the day before his wedding. All it has is size. Hence Raphael develops a growing obsession with measurement, equating power with length, breadth, and thickness. As if this were not already a sufficient exposé of the vulgar notion of the supernatural, Balzac adds to it the skin's remarkable literalness. No penetrator of motives, the skin responds not to what Raphael wishes but to what he says he wishes, be it only a general expression of civility toward an ex-schoolmaster. What can you expect of a mere skin, after all? What is the lesson of such a shallow supernaturalism?

Indeed, where is the god in this particular machine? Like any good, enlightened deity, the magic skin works through secondary causes. "This music without dancers, this solitary old man with his surly profile, his rags and his few wisps of hair, hiding in the shadow of a lime-tree, looked to Raphael like a fantastic allegory of the wish he had made. . . . It was so natural an event that Raphael . . . did not bother to examine his magic skin" (241–42; 277). The events that happen to Raphael are actually less astonishing than those in *Le Père Goriot*, for the only occult forces are those that cause the skin to shrink. The supernatural acts on itself; it does not act directly on the world. In return, the skin's own condition is altogether beyond the reach of human forces. Not all the professors in Paris, with hammers and forges and hydraulic presses, avail to stretch it the twentieth part of an inch. If *The Castle of Otranto* employs the supernatural to divert interest from externals to internals, *The Wild Ass's Skin* separates the supernatural from the real world even more rigidly. The world of chance, of present limitation and future possibility, stands contrasted to the world of destiny, of unbounded present capacity and absolute future destruction.

To enter the realm of spirit, the world of the magic skin, one must therefore leave the world of experience. Raphael enters the spirit realm via a regression. He betrays first his father, by succumbing to the passion for play, then his mother, by selling the island where she lies buried. The shop itself resembles a time machine, and to browse among its relics of ancient civilizations is to experience a "retrogressive apocalypse" (29–30; 41). And accepting the magic skin puts Raphael in the position of a child whose every want is satisfied; indeed, his servant reports how the skin demands to be treated like a baby whose wants can and need never be uttered:

> "Jonathas, you'll look after me like a baby in his swaddling clothes." Yes, sir, that's how he put it: in his swaddling clothes! "You'll have to see to all my wants for me."
> I'm the master, you understand? And it's almost as if he were the servant. (169; 199)

Reversal of roles accompanies the regression into infancy. On the one hand, the skin confers its nearly unlimited power on Raphael: "I'm your Pope," as he cries out in the first flush of emotion (156; 185). On the other hand, Raphael concedes control of his own life force to the skin. Or perhaps not even to the skin, which is a measurable object that must die when Raphael dies—perhaps rather to some unknown Destiny in a world apart. In any case, he soon realizes that what he has conceded is the one thing that really matters. His power extends only to terrestrial vanities, and the reversal also almost immediately robs all terrestrial things of any interest. "That's my life. I'm vegetating, my good Jonathas" (169; 199).

Thus does pure spirit prove to be divided against itself: "This very human antithesis may be discovered wherever the soul reacts powerfully on itself" (14; 24).[2] The dilemma might be labeled a quasi-Kantian antinomy of consciousness in general: power is thwarted by its exercise; fatality is indistinguishable from contingency; knowledge confines and belittles the knower. The realm of spirit is gothic—mysterious, threatened, corrupt—because nothing can happen to a spirit without debasing it.

Thence arises the materialistic revenge of the gothic novels: "In the bosom of luxury, he led as mechanical a life as a steam-engine" (171; 201). If everything spiritual is, say, a papist conspiracy with the devil, then the heroine will be saved by recognizing the pettiness of the devil's means. It is all just a skin, just a potion, just the wind howling in the trees after all. Or if the supernatural is not unmasked as a mysterious materiality, out of touch with mind, then it is equally effectively subverted by being revealed as a personality, the demon in torment. It is always a manifestation of power, but by that very token never what it purports to be, namely, the very power itself (or one of the powers) that rules the universe.

Thus the antinomy gives rise to a dialectic. Pure consciousness is ungraspable because it is never *there*—it has no *Dasein*—but is always in the process of making itself matter. The supernatural in and of itself is the least material, the most indifferent substance in the universe. Power so vast is, to our perceptions, but a kind of whimsy or cosmic joke: the sublime is the ridiculous. By thus hollowing out power and purging knowledge of its attractions, the romantic gothic makes consciousness into a debased or indifferent mode of con-science. Here is Hegel's analysis of the supernatural sublime, from late in the *Phenomenology of Mind*:

> Just as that wise man of old searched in his own thought for what was good and beautiful, but left it to his "daemon" to know the petty contin-gent content of what he wanted to know—whether it would be good for him to keep company with this or that person, or good for one of his ac-quaintances to go on a journey, and similar unimportant things, in the same way the universal consciousness draws knowledge of the contin-gent from birds, or trees, or the yeasty earth, the vapour from which de-prives self-consciousness of its self-possession [*Besonnenheit*]. For the contingent is something that is not self-possessed and is alien, and there-fore the ethical consciousness lets itself settle such matters too, such as by a throw of the dice, in an unthinking and alien way.
>
> (*Phänomenologie*, 497–98; *Hegel's Phenomenology*, 431–32)

Balzac's fiction is a world of thresholds. His often theatrical vocab-ulary encourages us to regard them as proscenium arches, curtains that open onto the drama of existence. Yet the events that occur across the thresholds are typically startling and willful, beyond the bounds of natural causation, melodramatic rather than dramatic. Melo-drama in Balzac signifies an impulse toward an other world. He ven-tures into the realm of the self, governed by unconditioned drives and desires. Time stops as he routinely gives vast tracts of his fiction over to the narration of prior events influencing present actions; in his gothic fiction the freezing of time becomes obsessively literal. Almost like one of Poe's characters, Raphael condemns himself to a state of suspended animation. Here he is as seen from inside:

> I fashioned a woman for myself and pictured her in my thoughts, dreamed of her. During the night, I could not sleep: I became her lover; into the space of a few hours I crammed a whole lifetime, a lifetime of love. . . . The next morning, unable to endure the torture of waiting for evening to creep along, I went to a lending-library, took out a novel, and spent the day reading it, thus obviating the need to think or to measure the passage of time. (100; 120)

And here he is, later in his story, as seen, more brutally, from outside:

They looked like two old men reduced to equal decrepitude, the one by time, the other by thought. The age of the older man [the servant Jonathas] was written in his white hair, the young one [Raphael] no longer had an age. (228; 263)

From the opening tableau of the gamblers on, then, Balzac's novel draws the consequences of the gothic mode by functioning as a study in self-absorption. The oblivion of the players, the heartlessness of the courtesans, the thoughtless vanity of the young students are all modalities of the one central phenomenon; they constitute the book as what Raphael for years was absorbed in writing, a theory of the will. Even the scientists who troop in to demonstrate their mastery over the world by stretching the magic skin prove instead to be at the mercy of their desires and lost to the world. Rather than granting them power, their absorption in one consuming passion robs them of all power, not only over the world but even over their own material existence. Of the biologist Lavrille, the narrator observes:

This scientist, between two ages [i.e., of no age in particular], had a mild face. . . . But his obsession with science affected his whole appearance. His wig, which he was for ever scratching and pushing into fantastic positions, showed a fringe of white hair and revealed the single-minded search for truth which, like all passions when they dominate us, makes men quite oblivious of worldly matters, to the point where they lose all consciousness of *self*. (192; 224)

The professor of mechanics Planchette is described as follows: "Planchette was a tall, dry man, a genuine poet lost in perpetual contemplation, always looking into a bottomless abyss, MOTION. . . . Happy to live in the hope of making discoveries, he thought neither of fame, the world, nor himself; his life was devoted to science for science's sake" (197–98; 228). Raphael traces the same course. The antiques dealer sells him freedom from the categories and conditions of ordinary existence, that freedom whose other name, from Kant onwards, has been madness:

How could one prefer all the disasters of your frustrated desires to the sublime faculty of summoning the whole universe to the bar of one's mind, to the thrill of being able to move without being throttled by the thongs of time or the fetters of space. . . . Are not wisdom [*Sagesse*] and knowledge [*savoir*] almost synonymous terms? And what is dementia other than power or willpower carried to excess?   (41; 54)

Consequently Raphael's supernatural power alienates him from everything human. If the external effect of the magic skin is a ludic reduction of life to a materialistic spectacle, its psychological effect lies in the complementary alienation of spirit from everything real. The curse that lies on the skin makes Raphael afraid to exercise his power, and thus condemns him to dream of his existence as an embalmed corpse, a timeless creature of thought who is freed of his obligation to live:

> Suddenly he had a flash of illumination, in which the past appeared to him in a distinct vision; the reasons for the antipathy he inspired became suddenly apparent like the network of veins in a corpse which anatomists, by the injection of some chemical colouring, cause to spring into relief. He recognized himself in this fleeting vision, followed his own existence in it day by day and thought by thought. He realized—not without surprise—that he cut a sombre and distraught figure in this cheerful society; always brooding over his destiny, preoccupied with his illness.
>   (218–19; 252–53)

At the end, for Raphael as for the scientists, self-regard turns into self-oblivion as the master passion strips away all externals; all consciousness finally dissolves into the dreamlike animality of the madman:

> This man endowed with so violently active an imagination sank down to the level of those sloths that crouch in the depths of tropical forests, camouflaged to look like a lump of decaying vegetation, reluctant to shift an inch even to make sure of some easy prey. He had even shut out the sun, refusing to let daylight into his room. About eight in the evening he would get out of bed; without having any clear consciousness of his existence, he would satisfy his hunger and immediately go back to bed. The hours passed, like chilly, wrinkled beldames, bringing him nothing but blurred images, apparitions, bright shapes against a dark background. He had buried himself in deep silence in refusal of all activity and intelligence.   (243–44; 279)

Yet embedded within the harsh unmasking of Balzac's novel there remains a romantic nostalgia for the purer dreams of Kant and of

Rousseau. It is manifested first in the idyllic conservatory where Raphael and Pauline enjoy an artificial February spring before their abortive marriage. The episode begins when Raphael throws the skin down a well and terminates when the gardener fishes up "this strange sort of seaweed, . . . not either wet or damp [but] dry as a plank" (190; 222). The second such idyll takes place by Lake Bourget, immediately before Raphael's final breakdown:

> Above all it is the lake of memories; it enhances their charms by tinging them with the colour of its waves; it is a mirror in which past and present are reflected.
> Raphael felt his burden bearable only when he was in the midst of this lovely landscape; here he could remain indolent, meditative, free from desire. (224; 258–59)

And yet a third idyll prolongs the experience by the springs and the volcanic lake of Mont Dore. All these fantasy-regressions share the dream of a purified will, nondestructive and hence in truth inactive: "he resolved to settle there, where he could live undisturbed, as effortlessly as the fruit that ripens on the bough" (231; 266). These lakes combine the allure of an ocean without waves and of a well that never runs dry. The revenge of the skin is, to be sure, in part a "Freudian" thrust against the maternal bosom of Nature, in part an archetypal myth of the well as a reserve of power (supported by the buried pun on *puits*, which is homophonous with the present tense of *pouvoir*). But much more obviously it is a reminder that water, as the element of life, is inseparable from motion. There was no dry land that could harbor Rousseau from the turmoil of civic life, no dry logic that could free Kant from dreams of a purer existence, no dry science that could rescue Planchette ("little plank") from the vortex of motion, no dryness, that is, but the mortal desiccation of a magic skin that turns into Raphael's shroud. Such is the life-threatening antinomy of consciousness.

The doctrine of two consciousnesses is familiar from Wordsworth: "conscious of myself / And of some other being," "two natures, / The one that feels, the other that observes" (1805 *Prelude* 2.32–33, 14.331–32). It is true that Kant's philosophical project presupposed the transcendental unity of apperception. Nonetheless one could ar-

gue that the unity of apperception is not so much a given of Kantianism as a necessary defense against the glimmering recognition of a divided self. The gothic view of personality was implicit in Kant's
postulates, though incompatible with his aim of justifying the ways of
empirical reality to man. Such an interpretation would help account
both for the curious doubling of psychological processes (the so-
called transcendental and empirical syntheses) in the first version of
the *Critique of Pure Reason* and also for their elimination from the
sanitized second version. But above all there is the evidence of a note
to the *Anthropology*, which discusses at length the topic of two consciousnesses: a manuscript note says bluntly, "Doppelt Ich." "The
consciousness of self (apperceptio) can be divided into that of reflection and that of apprehension. The first is a consciousness of the understanding, the second the inner sense; the former *pure*, the latter
empirical apperception. . . . Here the self seems to us to be doubled."
To be sure, Kant immediately adds a defensive recantation—"(which
would be contradictory)." Yet the note continues to analyze the divisions within the self: "(1) the self, as *subject* of thought (in logic),
which means pure apperception (the merely reflective self)" and "(2)
the self, as the *object* of perception." This division, according to Kant,
must be a division *of something*: for man, he says, "can only become
conscious to himself of these changes by virtue of representing himself in the various conditions as one and the same subject, and the human self is, to be sure, doubled with respect to form (the manner of
representation), but not with respect to matter (the contents)" (*Anthropology* A15–16). Salomon Maimon had denied the existence of
consciousness in general, and I do not think that Kant successfully
reestablishes the concept here. He speaks deviously of "representing
himself . . . as one and the same subject" in lieu of claiming that we
are unified subjects; he locates unity inconsistently in the subject and
in the contents; finally, neither locus of consciousness in general is
compatible with the earlier designation of (1) the subject-self as reflective consciousness and (2) the object-self as the two partial selves.
Thus, despite its indispensable role in Kant's thought, pure or general
consciousness is an empty token or a ghost of the system. It is a reflex
of the empirical self and not its progenitor.

Put in other terms, the transcendental ego—pure or general consciousness—is generated not by an affirmation but by a denial. Indeed (to reiterate the claim made at the opening of "Kant and the Doctors," Chapter 8 above), the concept had originated through a suppression of the link that Descartes had instinctively assumed—and that Locke had explicitly formulated—between thought and experience. And despite all appearances in Kant's presentation, the true logic of the general in his thought is a logic of negation, such as is illustrated by one of the philosophical spokesmen in another one of the major gothic novels of the romantic period, E. T. A. Hoffmann's *Devil's Elixirs*: "It is very difficult to dress oneself so that the general character of one's clothes shall not provoke the thought that one's occupation is this or that trade. The costume of the man of the world is surely conditioned only by the negative" (*Elixiere*, 89; *Flixirs*, 93; the speaker is the character Peter Schönfeld). Hoffmann unmasks the general or transcendental as the dialectical negation of the particular or empirical. Independence can be manifest only as a denial of dependency: though the transcendental aspires to break free of time and space, it remains fettered to them, bound to acknowledge the empirical world if freedom from constraint is to have any determinate meaning. Here is Hegel's more abstract deconstruction of the idea of an autonomous, transcendent world, which in truth is opposed to empirical existence not prior to it:

> This world that has being in and for itself is also called the *supersensible world*, insofar as the existing world is determined as a sensory world, namely as one that, for intuition, is the immediate stance of consciousness.—The supersensible world likewise has immediacy, existence, but reflected, essential existence. The *essence* has as yet no presence; but it *is*, and in a deeper sense than being; the *thing* . . . is in truth not an *existing* immediacy. Things, as things of an other, supersensible world, are posited . . . as the true against that which has being.
>
> (Hegel, *Wissenschaft der Logik*, in *Schriften*, 6: 159)

The transcendental or supernatural world of things in themselves is pitted against the empirical world of everyday consciousness. Of the two worlds, the former possesses essential truth, but its existence is mediated and thus defined by contrast and marked by negativity. Precisely "because it is totality," Hegel observes, the world that has being in and for itself "is also only *one side* of totality and in this connection constitutes against the world of appearance a different self-sufficiency" (ibid.).

The opening development of the *Phenomenology*, in the chapter entitled "Sense Certainty," had unmasked empiricist immediacy as a hollow illusion; here the im-mediacy of transcendence is revealed as a double negation, the denial of a separation. A reflected immediacy may seem paradoxical. But the poetic imagination of romanticism easily resolves the paradox: it is when we peer into the bosom of a steady lake that we see our dreams and myths come alive. Yet so often in Wordsworth the water reflects a mortal trauma ("There Was a Boy," "The World Is Too Much with Us," the "slow-moving boat" episode in *The Prelude* [1850] 4.256–97, etc.), and Balzac's gothic versions of the same image plot reflection as a scene of haunting. The "I" may be made in the play of imagination, but only through immersion in the unruly or uncannily stilled waters of temporality. Consciousness is a game played unto death.

11

The Devil's Elixirs

O N HIS WAY TO ROME, where unwittingly and at great personal
cost he will help bring to light the despicable intrigues of the
Dominicans, Ernst Theodor Amadeus Hoffmann's protagonist,
Brother Medardus, goes mad. When he first begins to come to his
senses, he perceives his consciousness to be fragmented—"my self
seemed split into a thousand parts" (*Elixiere*, 209; *Elixirs*, 229)—and
only a lengthy convalescence partially restores his mental equipoise
and allows him to continue on his way. How is his madness to be interpreted? On the surface it would appear to be either another one in the
long series of evil effects of the devil's elixir that he has drunk, or another one of the divine punishments visited upon him for the sin of im-
bibing. But proposing these alternatives already signals the interpre-
tive dilemma. Sin results in both moral (or psychological) degradation
and physical torment, or, in other words, both crime and punishment.
And where the original sin is so trivial—sneaking a draught of some
old wine—and yet so much the product of preexisting hereditary and
psychological dispositions, then where lies the blame and whence
might come absolution?

An observer is better positioned to understand Medardus's torment, for an outsider would have noted not only the anxious perplexity of awakening but also the long period of oblivion that precedes it.

Psychologically the madness is a fragmentation, but behaviorally it is a regression to a situation of infantile dependence. "Food and drink had to be fed to you," says Medardus's caretaker. "You uttered only dull, unintelligible noises" (215; 236). Madness can then be seen as a pause and a new beginning capable of releasing Medardus from his psychological and moral servitude. In fact, Medardus goes mad because he has—or so he believes—desperately murdered his beloved fiancée, Aurelia, and his recovery from madness prepares for the one moment of true repentance before the closing tableau. Medardus's madness, then, is the whiling of a formerly frenzied spirit; his mental fragmentation separates him from the chain of evil actions that have fettered his spirit. "The atmosphere here in the madhouse," explains his interlocutor, the philosophical barber Peter Schönfeld—actually a spy who tails Medardus at the behest of the good Prior Leonard— "harmful to sane people, has had a beneficial effect on me. I am beginning to reason about myself, and that is not a bad sign. If I only exist by virtue of my own consciousness, then it is simply a matter of letting this consciousness remove the harlequin's dress from what is conscious, and I shall be able to present myself as a respectable gentleman" (215; 237). A small anthology of such assertions could easily be assembled from the novel, and a very large anthology if Hoffmann's remaining works and the writings of other German romantics were included. Let one further passage stand for many, this time Baroness Euphemia's description of her spurned lover Hermogenes: "It is a peculiar thing about madmen that, as if in closer contact with a mysterious spiritual force, they often pierce our hidden thoughts and express them in strange ways, so that the dreadful voice of a second self sends an unearthly shudder through us" (67; 68).

There can be few traditions so beset with second selves and doppelgängers as the gothic novel, and few gothic novels so obsessed with them as *The Devil's Elixirs*.[1] Personalities are split (Medardus-Leonard, Schönfeld-Belcampo); characters are doubled (true and false Medardus, true and false Victor, two Francescos); events repeat themselves (two visits to the Teufelsgrund, two murders of Aurelia); dream and waking coincide, as do sanity and madness; and even the most incidental attribute is potentially subject to doubling, such as the mysterious second key that Medardus finds to the reliquary where the devil's potion is kept. It would be perverse to regard so universal a phenomenon as a pathology; to be sure, Medardus and his family are diseased, but not the whole world in which they live. The doppelgänger figures in Hoffmann's novel are strikingly varied: they are real and imaginary, serious and ironic; they haunt and protect, bind and loose. Yet all share one characteristic: they break down the categories of ordinary experience. They are all figures of the supernatural, the supersensible, the transcendent. But as such, they function not to overwhelm the self but rather to reconstitute the self. The latter, I am arguing, is the function of the gothic in general. The doppelgängers' own constitutive category is not just repetition, but repetition with a difference and at a distance, and hence is, in all senses of the term, reflection. These elements can be observed in all the doubles of *The Devil's Elixirs*, indeed in all the forms of duplication that pervade the novel, but they are most schematically expressed in a pair of incidents from Hoffmann's later novel *Kater Murr*. The first is a warning vision of the lovesick musician Kreisler:

> Kreisler woke from his dream, and saw his dark figure in the water. Then it seemed to him as though Ettlinger, the mad painter, were looking up at him from the depths. "Oho," he called down, "oho, are you there, my dear doppelgänger, my dear companion?"
>
> (*Lebensansichten*, 436; *Life and Opinions*, 123)

The second incident repeats the vision but also, characteristically, reverses the roles; this time the reflection comes as a consolation to the love-crazed musician:

> The other day, when I was walking by the little lake in the middle of the Abbey's extensive grounds and saw my reflection walking beside me in the water, I said: "The man down there, walking by my side, he is a peaceful, circumspect man, no longer tossing wildly in vague, unbounded space, a man who keeps to the way he has found, and I am glad that man is none other than myself." A dreadful doppelgänger once looked up at me from another lake. (518; 196)

Variously evaluated by different characters at different times, the doubled selves always alert the reader to the division between a world of form or limitation and a world without limit. And at least on some occasions the characters, too, see them for what they are—images of absolute, productive consciousness—and use them accordingly:

> A higher spiritual principle [confers] the power to step outside of oneself and view oneself from without, and this then assumes the rôle of a servant of the superior will in the task of achieving the highest goals in life. Is there anything greater than to control life from within life itself, to dispose over all its manifestations, all its rich delights with the recklessness permitted to a ruler? *(Elixiere, 65; Elixirs, 65–66)*

What Kant did not yet acknowledge, except in a tissue of intimations, and what both the gothic and Hegel then showed, is that consciousness—even pure or general consciousness—is, like madness and dreams, a perspective on things as they are and an informing energy.

Like *The Wild Ass's Skin*, *The Devil's Elixirs* incorporates a theory of play. And like Balzac, Hoffmann introduces play both as a thematics of the theater—role, mask, caricature, the puppetry of fate—and also, in one programmatic episode, as gambling. Play combines the apogee of absorption with that of dispassionate calculation. Hence it brings the antinomies of consciousness to the fore. Play pits the actor's freedom against the determinism of his role, or the force of the gambler's will against the luck of the draw. To the casual gambler all is random, but the true card player—faro is the game in the novel—is the master of chances, and what happens to him appears not as contingency but as destiny. "It takes you out of yourself," says the Prince who established the gaming tables, closely echoing Euphemia's definition of consciousness, "or rather, it brings you to a point from which you are able to observe the strange webs and patterns woven by an invisible force that we name chance" (125; 133–34). Gambling, as the Prince describes it, creates the same bifurcations as in Balzac's novel. Will confronts caprice in a contest that establishes their radical opposition through their radical inseparability; the antitheses converge in a mutuality that the philosophers of the day termed "indifference." Without the power of will, there is only chance, not fate; without the provocation of the unforeseen, there is no room for will to exercise its power. In fact, the Prince upsets the equilibrium of the game by making up the losses of the players, and thereby vitiates the meaning of the spectacle and risks provoking retaliation by the forces he has unleashed. "But this very control you exercise, Sir," Medardus objects,

> takes the freedom out of the game and even erects barriers to those fateful entanglements of chance the observation of which makes the game so interesting to you. And will not this or that man who is in the inescapable grip of the game find, to his own peril, the means of escaping your supervision and thus cause in his life a state of tension that will bring about his eventual destruction?   (131; 141)

Play is the indifference of will and fate, or—because in the excitement of play even one's life may be at stake—of spirit and body, or finally of idealism and materialism. For if Balzac's Raphael leads the life of a steam engine, so too, in a sense, does every player: the gambler's life is a motor propelled by a spirit, "Win and lose are the twin poles round which revolves the mysterious machine which we set in motion and which is now driven on inexorably by the spirit dwelling within it" (125; 134). Play tells the story of human consciousness in general. In consciousness lies the sum total of human experience, but it is a sum made up of antithetical parts, bound to one another in perpetual struggle, with none of the icy clarity of an Alpine lake. In its ultimate significance play becomes an allegory of human life and of the conflict that rages from infancy right up to the moment of death. "This very struggle that seems to be the most daring act of bravado that man, with a childish faith in his own strength, undertakes; and once he has started, he cannot leave off, for he constantly hopes for victory, even in the throes of death" (131; 140).

But if play is consciousness and life, does this mean that life and consciousness are no more than a game? Here again appears the frivolity of the gothic mode. Like *The Monk*—and unlike most of the classic gothic novels—*The Devil's Elixirs* proves to have a tightly woven plot, with nearly every incident contributing essential pieces of the puzzling story that is finally assembled at the end. The frivolity of Hoffmann's novel is not like the playfulness of *The Wild Ass's Skin*, a matter of capricious construction and witty rhetoric. Rather, it takes the equally common and more troubling form of apparent moral frivolity. Again, as with Balzac's novel, there is a problem of proportion, but here the problem is spiritual, not physical, a matter of assessment, not of understanding. Given the multiplicity of disposing and causing factors—hereditary, psychological, and supernatural—how can we allocate blame for the exceptionally brutal events that occur? Is the elixir merely a novelist's contrivance to deflect attention away from Medardus's culpable egotism and thus to render tragedy palatable by distilling out its spiritual anguish? Given Medardus's numerous prior relapses into callous vainglory, how seriously can we take his final repentance? After all, his valedictory suspiciously obliterates the distinctions between body and soul, life and death, in a plea for heavenly compensation of his earthly suffering: for the final moment, he says, "is the moment when everything is fulfilled which Aurelia—Saint Rosalia herself—vouchsafed when she died" (288; 319). And how seriously can we take the implication that writing his own life functions as Medardus's penance? "If the spirit of evil has really departed from you," enjoins the Prior Leonard in assigning this task to Medardus, "if you have turned away from the temptations of the world, then you will rise above these things like a higher principle, and no trace of them will remain" (288; 319). Soaring above everything like a higher principle is, among other things, one of the canonical romantic descriptions of irony. Can we tolerate even the possibility, the accidental slip of the pen, that might lead us to regard good as nothing more than an ironization of evil?

None of the early classics of the gothic is altogether free of moral frivolity. By materializing evil they make it over into a pageant or a spectacle. Writing a gothic novel, as Medardus is enjoined to do by the Prior, does not illuminate evil but instead aestheticizes and anesthetizes the moral sense to the point where no trace remains of the original feelings. Hoffmann underscores the problem by attributing the devout fictional appendix that recounts Medardus's death to a scribe who has not read his papers, as if to suggest that piety is incompatible with consciousness or knowledge. Several passages within the novel address the moral dilemma directly, yet the most interesting of them suffers from a symptomatic confusion of terminology. In the course of a fateful interview between Medardus and a corrupt Pope, the latter comments on Medardus's personal narrative in the following terms:

"The spirit of God has created a giant, capable of subduing the wild beast within us. This giant is called Consciousness, and from its struggle with the beast emerges Spontaneity. The giant's victory is virtue, the beast's victory, Sin" (248; 273). This contorted utterance sounds like no more than a parody of romantic ethics. But whatever the intention, it is certain that the attempted bridge between philosophy—the learned philosophical term *Spontaneität* is unmistakable—and religion is possible only because the Pope uses the term "consciousness" (*Bewußtsein*) in the already obsolete sense of conscience. One more point of indifference can be added to the previous list of aestheticizing balances of the gothic novel: very often these works reduce the problem of rectifying conscience to one of rectifying consciousness through acquiring adequate knowledge about supernatural agencies. Only with the brilliant reversal consummated in *Frankenstein* does the gothic novel overcome its moral frivolity, rendering (as I shall argue) childishness as childlikeness. By making a human being, rather than some "eternal spirit," the author of the gothic creature, Mary Shelley reinstated the possibility of human accountability.

Yet frivolity is not insignificance. The moral frivolity of the romantic gothic was as productive in its way as the structural frivolity or dilettantism of *The Castle of Otranto*. Posing the indifference of apparently incommensurable factors may be the imagination's way of raising the question of their alignment or their relationship. The gothic may appear to trivialize the demonic by distancing it from ordinary experience; the author may appear to play irresponsibly with the vital boundaries between body and soul, matter and spirit. Yet the ironization of evil might prove to be a plausible moral stance after all: "Insofar as irony becomes conscious of the fact that existence has no reality, thereby expressing the same thesis as the pious disposition, it might seem that irony were a species of religious devotion."[2] Kant's conception of morality, meanwhile, had been strictly allegorical. The famous and unique apostrophe to a personified abstraction—"*Duty!* thou sublime great name" (*Critique of Practical Reason* A 154)—and the equally famous concluding designation of the two great objects of "admiration and reverence," "the starry heavens above me, and the moral law within me" (A 252), mark morality as an immeasurable quantity, a significance that may be intended by a good life, but never realized. The concept of duty became both the centerpiece for Fichte's extension of Kantianism in the 1790s and, later, a chief focus for attack by the romantics. Friedrich Schlegel, in particular, attacked the allegorical concept of duty as the desiccated nub of a system that he otherwise found full of inspired wit (!): "The duty of the Kantians is related to the commandment of honor, to the voice of calling and the divinity in us as a dried plant to the fresh flower on a living stem" (*Ideen*, no. 40). The very frivolity of romantic gothic helps bring morality down to earth; it counteracts Kant's self-abasement before his god by clothing the abstraction, however dubiously, in flesh and blood. In this respect as in so many others, the gothic is not sublime but countersublime. If the joint mission of the gothic and of idealist philosophy was a restitution of dignity to personality, then the particular mission of the romantic gothic was a restitution of personality (or of self-consciousness) to the one area that Kant had expressly excluded from his individualizing concern: the domain of conscience.

12

Melmoth the Wanderer

Nॏ㄀ONE OF THE ENGLISH OR FRENCH gothic novels is so explicitly epistemological as German romantic fiction. Nevertheless, their underlying concerns are much the same, as I wish to show from two British examples, the first being Charles Maturin's *Melmoth the Wanderer*. They are stories of sin and damnation, in which ultimately it is the soul, not the body, that is being tested: tormented, tortured, torn. Attacks on the body—by no means a universal feature of the gothic—serve merely to lay bare the fortress of the self. Whatever its physical horrors, the true end of imprisonment is to make the victim "writh[e] with all the impotent agony of an incarcerated mind" and to suffer "the agony of consciousness" (*Melmoth*, 56). Very often the itinerary of persecution follows that described in Reil's essay on self-consciousness: all connections with the physical world are broken until the victim is left only with the pinpoint illumination of consciousness itself, and then not even that. At the end looms the utter destruction of the self, "an invocation to the demon of insanity to come and take full possession of you from that moment for ever" (*Melmoth*, 57).

Yet madness is by no means the goal of Melmoth's persecutions. He wants to master the victim's soul, not to destroy it. "'Escape—escape for your life,' cried the tempter; 'break forth into life, liberty, and sanity'" (58). Just as in *The Devil's Elixirs*, madness here offers a respite for the soul to gather strength against a renewed onslaught. However nightmarish, madness is still a sleep followed by an awakening. "Perhaps the profound tranquility of my *last* abode contributed more than any thing else to the recovery of my reason. I distinctly remember awaking at once to the full exercise of my sense and reason" (*Melmoth*, 216). Herz had described how madness seems to suspend mortality and thus can delay death (*Versuch über den Schwindel* [1791], 1: 13–14), and the observation often seems borne out by the gothic novel.

Man's life is consciousness or reason, yet the force that sustains it emerges from an obscure realm beyond reason, a light out of the darkness. The attack on consciousness inevitably fails, because only the manifestations of life are exposed to attack and not life's source. An unfathomable reserve always remains, outside of space and time, the mystery that begets both the demon and his victims and then swallows them up again.

Melmoth, then, explores less the conflict between rational consciousness and the irrational demons that beset it than the border region inhabited by an informing force or energy where rational and irrational coalesce. Physical oppression and destruction come from external forces—Church, family, and, in one scene (the shipwreck witnessed by John Melmoth in chapter 4), nature—and often engender spectacular theatrics: "In Catholic countries, Sir, religion is the national drama" (165). But these are only the background for true psychomachia—a struggle of the soul rather than for the soul—that is intensely private. "The power of the Inquisition, like that of death, separates you, by its single touch, from all mortal relations" (250). But not even this extreme of isolation satisfies Maturin's purposes. Even the fetters worn by the victim chain him *to* something; the limbo of spacelessness and timelessness where the soul is most intimately tested lies beyond the boundaries of the prison: "Even in the Inquisition I belonged to some body,—I was watched and guarded;—now I was the outcast of the whole earth, and I wept with equal bitterness and depression at the hopeless vastness of the desert I had to traverse" (251). The desert of the soul toward which the novel drives is not a

Manichaean world of white good in the soul against black evil outside, but a shadow realm that effaces all distinctions.[1] Madness fuses
with sanity, dream merges into waking, temptation takes the form of
affability, friendship, even (in the story of Immalee) love. To be sure,
hostile forces exert their sublime terrors in order to drive the victims
of oppression into the limbo of pure consciousness, but the ultimate
threat of self-dissolution comes later in the form of a prospect of a
"discordant unison" (142) of one with all, good with evil, existence
with annihilation.[2]

Melmoth succeeds in driving his victims into the purgatorial
limbo of consciousness, but never beyond that into perdition. Life, it
seems, may be destroyed, but not spirit. Romantic psychology provides a general theoretical explanation for this indestructible resur-
gence of spirit. Life and material existence are entirely distinct essences that only come into accidental relationship to one another in
each determinate individual. Melmoth assaults the body and the
bond that links body and soul, but the soul itself remains unassail-
able. Life may be severed from the body to which it joins in order to
create a living being, but life cannot itself be destroyed. "Life cannot
be a state of the [living] natural being, any more than extension can be
a condition of the body, because without life no natural being can exist." There is no such thing as dead life. "The dead tree is not actually
a tree, but only a material that was a tree in an earlier state" (Hoffbauer, "Ueber den Begriff des Lebens," 471). The living individual is
generative and regenerative in its essence: "The self exists only when
it produces itself, e.g. acts; it is action itself" (Reil, "Zerfallen der Einheit," 583).

Such is the general principle of resilience that each of Melmoth's
victims discovers in the depths of torment. The romantic soul inevitably wills life just as the platonic soul inevitably wills the good. But
Maturin's thought-experiments with the life force go beyond this
merely general principle of vitalism. In seeking out and struggling
with the souls of his victims, Melmoth reveals the locus of the soul
and the nature of its activities. Reil says that the soul is essentially active and productive—"in madness and in dream the self analyzes itself, dramatizes its powers, is player and spectator alike" ("Zerfallen

der Einheit," 583)—but Maturin goes further, showing how it acts and what it produces. The theatrics of the gothic novel are this drama of consciousness.

Melmoth himself is pure disembodied spirit. He is subject to none of the laws of physical existence. He lives a life composed solely of thoughts and passions, with a ruthless disregard for all physical sensations. So, in his wake, one of his minions, the traitorous monk Guido, confides to Monçada, *"Emotions are my events"* (*Melmoth*, 204). Melmoth's strategy for enchaining his victims' souls depends on dissolving the bond between body and soul. As madness sets in, the ordinary categories of physical experience are overthrown: up is down, relaxation is constriction (249–50). As in other gothic novels, here, too, the victim becomes a marionette, the plaything of his destiny: "No automaton, constructed on the most exquisite principles of mechanism, and obeying those principles with a punctuality almost miraculous, could leave the artist less room for complaint or disappointment than I did the Superior and community" (99). In the depths of such alienation body and soul alike are plunged into total passivity. Monçada regresses to a primal malleability, becoming like a shapeless, nerveless fluid: "My life was a sea without a tide. . . . I neither thought, nor felt, nor lived,—if life depends on consciousness, and the motions of the will" (99–100). This ultimate passivity, however, is not the goal of torture: "My abstraction and calmness would not do for the Jesuits . . . ; my scrupulous, *wooden*, *jointless* exactness in its forms was only a mockery" (100). The true goal of the tormentors is not the dissociation of body and soul from their surroundings, but the dissociation of body and soul from each other, so that the soul can be directly attacked. The soul must be not merely destroyed but induced to will its own destruction. In the case of this novel, then, the frivolous "indifference" of body and soul serves to ward off the more threatening indifference of body to soul.

But indeed the soul cannot be subdued, for "the intellectual powers" always return, "like the waves of an advancing tide" (*Melmoth*, 217). Caught in the vault with Guido, Monçada for a moment does yearn to separate his mind from the punishment inflicted on his body: "burying my head between my knees, [I] tried to *forbear to think"* (203). The gesture symbolizes the ultimate abnegation of life, when the soul succumbs under the weight of bodily misery. "To inflict a suspension of the action on a being conscious of possessing the powers of action, and burning for their employment,—to forbid all interchange of mutual ideas, or acquirement of new ones to an intellectual being,—to do this, is to invent a torture that might make Phalaris blush for his impotence of cruelty" (203). Yet the gesture remains no more than a symbol, since only the head, not the soul, is brought to its knees. The very desire for annihilation remains a desire; the soul can never suspend action, because action is its essence. "Though sleep seems a necessity of nature, it always requires an act of the mind to concur in it" (203).

The isolation imposed by the demonic forces frees the soul to discover the oceanic roots of its own power. One activity continues even when all else is suppressed: if all power of motion is denied, there still remains the power of endurance In the depths of his dungeon Monçada discovers the essential activity of the soul, which is the production of time. He does not *while away* the hours but instead, to use Herz's term, *whiles* the hours. "So I sat and counted sixty; a doubt always occurred to me, that I *was counting them faster than the clock.* Then I wished to be the clock, that I might have no feeling, *no motive for hurrying on the approach of time.* Then I reckoned slower. . . . I oscillated, reckoned, and measured time on my mat" (146–47). Even when the soul crosses the limit into the frivolity of madness, its whiling continues: "Had I led this life much longer, I might have been converted into the idiot, who, as I have read, from the habit of watching a clock, imitated its mechanism so well, that when it was down, he sounded the hour as faithfully as car could desire" (147). The enslavement or destruction of the body plunges us into the realm of the soul, which is the inner sense, energy, time: "Without sense perceptions we would be merely in time, not in space, merely know about our own existence, but not about the existence of a world" (Reil, "Zerfallen der Einheit," 556).

In these depths the soul finds itself and its reserves of strength. It learns to generate out of its own inner light a kind of knowledge in the void. Externally, the "divisions of time, . . . by measuring our portions of suffering, appear to diminish them" (*Melmoth*, 144). Internally, in the absence of such external props, the soul produces its own surrogate for these divisions:

> These aeras by which we compute the hours of darkness and inanity are inconceivable to any but those who are situated as I was. You have heard, Sir, no doubt, that the eye which, on its being first immersed into darkness, appears deprived of the power of vision forever, acquires, imperceptibly, a power of accommodating itself to its darkened sphere, and even of distinguishing objects by a kind of conventional light. The mind certainly possesses the same power, otherwise, how could I have had the power to reflect, to summon some resolution, and even to indulge some hope, in this frightful abode? (145)

There is, of course, no real knowledge of present circumstances here, only hope, that is, the principle of knowledge as applied to some possible future world. The "conventional light" of the mind is the capacity to supply the distinctions or divisions that we normally appear to draw from without, to imagine a situation different from the present one. It is an originary reflection: to make distinctions is in itself not really to think but to have the power to think, and it is the inner sense that generates distinctions. What Maturin discovers or intuits in his character's misery thus corresponds in some sense to Kant's transcendental deduction of the categories of the understanding and in some sense even subtends it: it is a transcendental deduction of the categories of thought.

Reil observes:

> In the full force of life there is so complete a unity of the body and the soul that the beams from the indwelling spirit . . . occur as if in a transparent and immaterial body. . . . Even the world is one with us, it is our product, as it were, and we are in concrescence with it. In an uninterrupted flow and ebb our action passes over into the world, the action of the world into us. ("Zerfallen der Einheit," 559–60)

The soul, by its power of measuring (time) and distinguishing (places or bodies), not only constitutes reflection but, further, gives rise to the tides that flow between the mind and its world. Ann Radcliffe's landscapes, I have argued, are emblems of reflection; Maturin's, where they appear, are but reflexes of states of mind. There is a glow in the eyes—not just in Melmoth's—that irradiates the whole world, in the eyes of John Sandal, for instance, the hero of the last of the inserted narratives: "There was a mild, inoppressive, but most seductive light in the dark-blue eyes that fell so softly on hers, like moon-light floating over a fine landscape" (*Melmoth*, 465–66). The eyes, with "the sterling gold of a heart-minted look" (467), seem not just to color the landscape but even almost to create the picture that they see. Only at moments of greatly heightened sensibility does Maturin describe the landscape, as if nature were perfectly unconcerned except when the tide of feelings singles out details to incorporate into the observer's sphere. Something stronger than pathetic fallacy is at work here; it is not merely a sympathy with human emotion that is metaphorically imputed to a personified landscape, but rather a landscape conceived under the guise of pictures that exist only when they are flooded by the emotions of a human observer situated in space and in sentiment so as to make the most of them. Everywhere experience is governed by the category of time understood as pace—vertigo and boredom, restlessness and lethargy—and the external world is always an effluent of this inner sense.

Maturin deeply imbues his landscapes with the categories of thought and sensibility. His writing is verbose but functional, suggesting how the human subject gropingly organizes the external world into the picture of his emotions. We encounter the first landscape on the evening when Elinor Mortimer first beholds her cousin, John Sandal. According to the narrator, the scene exists independently of her feelings, yet it clearly does not exist *for her* except insofar as she has tuned it to the strings of her own heart. "Elinor took the path through the park, and, absorbed in new feelings, was for the first time insensible of its woodland beauty, at once gloomy and resplendent, mellowed by the tints of autumnal colouring, and glorious with the light of an autumnal evening" (*Melmoth*, 466). But then the miracle happens that makes the scene come alive as an extension of the soul: the brilliance of dawning love is transposed—seemingly projected—onto the forest.

> As they approached the Castle, the scene became glorious beyond the imagination of a painter. . . . Sometimes a gleam like gold trembled over the tufted foliage of their summits, and at length through a glade which opened among the dark and massive boles of the ancient trees, one last

rich and gorgeous flood of light burst in, turned every blade of grass it
touched into emerald for a moment,—paused on its lovely work—and
parted.   (466–67)

The moment Elinor clearly has been waiting and hoping for becomes
the transcription of her love without which, so far as she is concerned,
this setting would never have existed at all. It elicits an immediate reaction from her because for all intents and purposes it is a part of herself that she momentarily and memorably sees. "The effect was so in-
stantaneous, brilliant, and evanishing, that Elinor had scarce time for
a half uttered exclamation, as she extended her arm in the direction
where the light had fallen so brightly and so briefly" (467). The unspoken word designates not something external but an acknowledgment of something so personal that it does not need to be named, an
upwelling of inner feelings from which the landscape's golden glow
seemingly radiates. "She raised her eyes to her companion, in that
full consciousness of perfect sympathy that makes words seem like
counters, compared to the sterling gold of a heart-minted look" (467).
The interchange of emotions bathes Elinor, John, and the scene in a
light that comes from everywhere and nowhere, from the unseen sun,
from the eyes, from face meeting face. "He smiled, and his countenance was as that of an angel. It seemed to reflect and answer the last
bright farewell of day, as if friends had parted smiling at each other"
(467). Two friends—or three? One source of light, or two, or three? A
scene that is born pregnant with an inarticulate yet vital meaning.
Where the light comes from, ultimately, in some purely rational, Cartesian analysis, remains obscure in this long description that never directly mentions the sun, but where the meaning comes from is beyond
question: it comes from John's smile, an expression that impresses a
significance on the waiting landscape and on the human heart. "To
the last hour of her mortal existence, that smile and the scene where it
was *uttered*, were engraved on the heart of Elinor" (467).

A curious metalepsis—or collapse of the distance between cause
and effect—takes place with difficulty (and hence diffusely) in the description, where a barely articulate new epistemology of the human
heart is being forged within the grotesque violence of the gothic cauldron. John's smile, the passage continues, "announced at once a
spirit, that, like the ancient statue, answered every ray of light that fell
on it with a voice of melody, and blended the triumph of the glories of

nature with the profound and tender felicities of the heart" (467). The awkwardly invoked "ancient statue," a figure of Memnon, is decisive, but less because it suggests the gothic conflict between free will and ruling passion than because it is displaced: as Maturin elsewhere acknowledges (364), the statue of Memnon sang in the morning. The figure, then, perfectly collapses the birth and death of love into the one moment of unfettered (and unexpressed) feeling that is vouchsafed to the star-crossed lovers. And it puts the human emotions where they belong, at the dawn of light, and renders the landscape as a last glow of that inner radiance.

A repetition of this scene, some twenty pages and a year later, seems written expressly to confirm how wrong it is to speak of a discovery of nature in these romantic landscapes. Instead one discovers in them that the life of nature is part of the life of a man, that the outer sense depends on the inner sense, that the time of the world merely maps out the pace of the emotions. It is the same scene, the same time of day, with the same golden radiance, but now all is organized according to the categories of loss and melancholy, of which it speaks with the expressive silence of the heart. Even the effulgence on John's face now seems to come from without—confirming that in the earlier scene the gleam came from within, at least in Elinor's eyes—not because the visual scene has changed in any "objective" way, but because the informing love has been suppressed.

> It was a glorious autumnal evening, just like that on which they had first met,—the associations of nature were the same, those of the heart alone had suffered change. There is that light in the autumnal sky,—that shade in the autumnal woods,—that dim and hallowed glory in the evening of the year, which is indefinably combined with recollections. . . . They walked on together,—together they watched the last light on the purple hills, the deep repose of the woods, whose summits were still like 'feathers of gold,'—together they once more tasted the confidence of nature, and, amid the most perfect silence, there was a mutual and unutterable eloquence in their hearts. . . . The glow and the smile, that made it appear like a reflection of heaven, were there still,—but that glow was borrowed from the bright flush of the glorious west and that smile was for nature. (488–89)

All the other landscapes of the novel, indeed, show what Reil called the concrescence of man and nature that makes the world a product of the self. The demonism of the gothic expunges any lingering belief in objectivity or normality: all souls are driven, and their surroundings are organized according to a fundamentally irrational energy or life force welling up from within. Indeed the voice of nature echoes the stifled voice of the heart with monotonous regularity. Perhaps there is more dialectical vigor, more surprise and excitement, even in the uncertain gleams, forbidding yet seductive, of the Byronic landscape, and surely in the mystery and challenge that a certain blankness in nature presents to the Wordsworthian imagination. Yet what the gothic version of transcendental idealism lacks in subtlety it makes up for in its insistence on the absolute priority of subjectivity. And the gothic sensibility did give rise to at least one significant practical consequence: a dramatically altered psychiatric practice that assumes the ubiquity of demonic forces and sympathizes with the damned. It was a gothic poet, Thomas Penrose, who addressed the congenial powers of blackness in the unforgettable, if unforgivable, outburst "Hail! awful Madness, hail!"[3] The empiricist physician Thomas Arnold cited the line with derision (*Observations*, 1: 83), but Reil turned the poet's outburst into the watchword of his campaign to have the insane treated as human beings (*Rhapsodien*, 16).

Why does Melmoth subject only the pure at heart to temptation and torment? The minor characters in the novel include plenty of souls who are damned or damnable and who might more readily yield to his corrupting influence. And gothic narratives contain plenty of precedents for a destructive or a dubious outcome, quite the opposite of the release that comes at the end of *Melmoth*. To be sure, Melmoth's spectacular failure at winning converts reflects moralistic tendencies in the vein of Radcliffe. Yet the forms of tyranny are nearly as various in this novel as in *Caleb Williams*, and the downfall of Melmoth can hardly be taken to signify any lasting triumph of good over evil. And Maturin's theatricality may have preferred the most melodramatic possible encounters of pure evil with pure good—as if *The Monk* had not shown that the triumph of evil could be as sublime as its downfall. But a psychological answer is as possible as the moral and aesthetic answers. The yearning throughout *Melmoth*, and in much other gothic fiction as well, is for human communication: "the famished ear waited in vain for its sweetest banquet,—the voice of man"; "There is not so bitter a reproach on earth as silence" (217, 222). Even the landscape ultimately proves too much a mere projection of the self. Only in the answering voice that leaps from heart to heart does the self find true affirmation of its own reality and worth. Certainly, love often falls silent, but this book *requires* love to be silent, thus turning it into a perversion of itself: "Language is no longer necessary to those whose beating hearts converse audibly—whose eyes, even by moonlight, are more intelligible to each other's stolen and shadowed glances, than the broad converse of face to face in the brightest sunshine—to whom, in the exquisite inversion of earthly feeling and habit, darkness is light, and silence eloquence" (361). The true engine of Melmoth's seductions is not torture—which always ends in insanity, not in sin—but an affable eloquence that promises a way out of torture. I suggest, then, that what Melmoth is seeking, like the asylum inmates to whom Reil opened his heart, is a partner in discourse, a friend. Since those who are evil are, for that very reason, already within Melmoth's sphere, discourse with them would be solipsistic, like discourse with a part of oneself. For Melmoth to become real, he needs the influence of something external: communication with others who are genuine selves. In the end he never does become real. Just as the devil's pact that he offers can never be described aloud, so too Melmoth's death is indescribable: a night of inarticulate cries, a set of indecipherable traces ("a down-trodden track, over which no footsteps but those of one impelled by force had ever passed," 542), a "silent and unutterable horror" (542). At the end he disappears back into the sea, the home from which the daemon of energy that impels our lives strives to emerge into consciousness.

The most striking of the novel's several interlaced stories is that of the Indian maiden Immalee. A Spaniard by birth, but abandoned in infancy on a tropical island, Immalee grows up knowing nothing of humanity but only her paradise of birds and flowers. If it is possible to read the other portions of the novel as an allegory of transcendental psychology, it is inevitable to read the history of Immalee in this way. Seemingly Melmoth's polar opposite, she is nevertheless as much an outcast of the world as he, and she becomes linked to him in a bond of mutual love. They are the two faces of Herder's "pure-impure consciousness," the modalities of the transcendental ego yearning to become real.

Kant had written, "the *I think* must be able to accompany all my representations" (*Critique of Pure Reason* B131). For Immalee, however, the *I think* constitutes all her representations. Though Maturin has contrived to allow her knowledge of the Spanish language, her consciousness does not extend beyond the sphere of her own existence. "She told him that she was the daughter of a palm-tree, under whose shade she had been first conscious of existence, but that her poor father had been long withered and dead" (*Melmoth*, 283). Consciousness to her means only self-identity—"I live here alone, and other worlds must be like this" (283)—and reflection never transcends the narcissistic stage: "He found this innocent and lovely being bending over a stream that reflected her image, and wooing it with a thousand wild and graceful attitudes of joyful fondness" (285). Even much later, when she says, "I am *truth*" (348), she means that truth is nothing other than what is given by her unvarying identity. "I am Immalee when I speak to you," she continues, for she is incapable of recognizing any difference within herself, and she tells him: "in fact, everything had grown smaller latterly, for she was now able to reach the fruit which formerly she was compelled to wait for till it dropt on the ground" (283). This womblike consciousness takes "no note of time" (297); it knows no presence either before or after Melmoth's seduction: "My life was formerly all anticipation,—now it is a retrospection" (344). In her innocence she is like a Berkeleyan to whom objects are mere ideas: "Alive and more beautiful than ever!—all living, thinking things!—their *very walk thinks*. . . . *Thought should be a god*" (289). And in what ought to be her experience, the world gains no greater density or substance: "Alas! in the life that I now lead, dreams have become realities, and realities seem only like dreams" (345).

Immalee, then, represents the impotence of a consciousness so pure that it is incapable of ever emerging into existence. (It is no wonder that Immalee is the only one of Melmoth's victims who loses her life in the struggle to preserve her innocence.) Maturin insists on the allegory with tiresome repetitiveness, but he does unfold its significance when he develops the psychological dynamics of his transcendental ego. For despite the perfection of her earthly paradise, Immalee is incomplete. Nothing affects her; she has no *experience*. To enter into the life of things, she cannot be solely what Berkeley, in *Principles of Human Knowledge*, calls a "perceiving, active being" (*Writings*, 114), but must acquire the receptivity of a mind that is open to the world. The moment that Melmoth appears to Immalee he appeals to her philanthropic instincts by describing the world of suffering from which he comes. But Immalee seizes on his statements to learn an epistemological lesson that he has not taught: "I begin to comprehend what he said—to think, then, is to suffer" (*Melmoth*, 288). Her immediate passion for Melmoth is the spontaneous and unrequitable yearning of consciousness for what it is not. It has more than a tinge of madness, the frenzied recognition of a self whose life has never constructed or been given an orientation. Melmoth describes the state at length. "To love," he says, "is to live in an existence of perpetual contradictions—to feel that absence is insupportable, and yet be doomed to experience the presence of the object as almost equally so," and so on for over half a page (363–64).

The contradictions of the condition toward which Immalee yearns are the defining characteristics of romantic consciousness. It is both a preternatural energy and the dreamy inactivity of reverie, active and passive at once, creator of a world that it discovers outside of itself. Ultimately, then, consciousness is the principle of difference. It creates the primary distinctions that turn the mere flux known to Immalee into the measurable quality that we know as time, and that give the vast expanse of primal waters an orientation that makes them into a potential terrain. Consciousness in this basic sense is not yet understanding—just as these differences are not yet the categories of the understanding—but it is the ground of understanding: it is the fundamental imagination that has not yet become reality (obviously, no gothic novel is concerned with real experience), but that nevertheless makes the construction of reality possible. "Those who love . . . have but two eras in their delicious but visionary existence,—and those are thus marked in the heart's calendar—*presence*—*absence*" (*Mel-*

moth, 364). The gothic demon is an inescapable presence that is never there. The importance of *Melmoth the Wanderer* lies in its insistence on the insatiable drive of the heart to divide its sensations into the agonizing yet essential categories of now and then, here and there, within and without.

13

Caleb Williams

THE STARK CONTRASTS of the gothic novel play with the antinomies of pure consciousness, staging them for the benefit of even the least attentive reader. As the gothic or romantic sensibility diffuses beyond the bounds of supernatural fiction, the issues remain recognizably the same even while the delineation of contexts and determinants becomes ever more complex. Thus such heroines as Amy Dorrit and Sue Fawley are of the tribe of Immalee, not in the narrow sense that they are specifically modeled on her or any other particular gothic heroine, but in the broader sense that they continue to dramatize the conflicts between purity and engagement, timeless sensibility and timely action, selfhood and love that the gothic novels bring to the fore. To be sure, the shift from a supernatural to a natural setting is decisive in many respects, for, like the shift from a Kantian to a Hegelian dialectic, it implies the hope for a natural (historical, social, or psychological), rather than a strictly transcendental (moral) resolution of the antinomies of existence. No magic curtain is required to discover the torment of self-realization; every doorway is liable to lead into a prison-house of the self. Yet transcendental and empirical psychology remain in contact.

William Godwin's *Caleb Williams* is one of the works that most obviously carries over gothic concerns into a comparatively realistic social setting. Undoubtedly, *Caleb Williams* is primarily a critique of political and social conditions; Godwin's brief preface tells us this, and any reading of the novel will surely confirm it. Yet the "general review of the modes of domestic and unrecorded despotism" produces an indictment so sweeping that it must be fueled by more than merely political considerations. Godwin himself opens the preface by saying, "The following narrative is intended to answer a purpose more general and important than immediately appears upon the face of it." Its concern is not just with political justice, but with (as the original title has it) "Things as They Are." The problems are radical, and the implicit stance is concomitantly revolutionary. If the thrust of the novel is not merely metaphysical—Godwin says that it "is no refined and abstract speculation"—it is also not merely pragmatic. Instead, the logic of its critique is transcendental. Godwin calls it "a study and delineation of things passing in the moral world," and the last phrase carries a meaning close to Kant: the "moral world" is the world of spirit, of the ideals and categories governing the operations of reason, not the concrete manifestations of society but "the spirit and character of the government." The ills that Godwin attacks rest in the constitution of the social fabric, but the causes reside in the constitution of the human mind.[1]

In his very first sentence, Caleb Williams calls his life history a "theatre of calamity." More than the obvious epithets and attributes —haunting demons, basilisk eyes, and the like—it is perhaps the melodramatic form that most clearly links Godwin's novel to the gothic tradition. Like many gothic novels, *Caleb Williams* never altogether escapes the conventions of the picaresque—it even has a wicked robber with the Cervantine name Gines. Yet the disparate incidents relentlessly converge, as they do not in the true picaresque, on the revelation of character. "Hitherto I have spoken only of preliminary matters," says the narrator at one point, "seemingly unconnected with each other, though *leading to that state of mind* in both parties which had such fatal effects. But all that remains is rapid and tremendous" (1.6; p. 37, my italics).

Who narrates the last sentence: the author Godwin, the fictional memorialist Williams, or the putative source of information, Falkland's steward, Mr. Collins? A novel like *Melmoth* regales us with a vertiginously complicated embedding of narratives, but at least the third-person narrator sorts out the narrative line with scrupulous precision: it is always possible to know, if rarely easy to remember, who is reporting what to whom. Thus Melmoth tells Immalee's father "The Tale of Guzman's Family" and "The Lover's Tale," which then become part of the story of Immalee that Monçada transcribes for Adonijah the Jew and then later relates to the young John Melmoth. The sequence of transmission is never so intricate in *Caleb Williams*, but the uncertainties of self-reference and fictional reflexivity work toward the same end of abstracting the story, and the effect of a suspended or "aestheticized" narrative is reinforced at the close by uncertainties about Williams's motivation and sanity and by the stress on his new-found vocation as a writer. All these factors render mechanical models of cause and effect as spurious or as irrelevant to Godwin's novel as to more typical gothic novels. There is no accounting for things as they are, no explanation for motives or for the sequence of events. To be sure, supernatural forces do not palpably intervene, but neither are mundane forces—the oppressive mechanics of physical torment and material persecution—detailed to the extent found in most gothic novels. Instead, in this unaccountable narrative, an accidental error acts like "a kind of instant insanity," and in a moment all is lost: "Alas, my offence was short, not aggravated by any sinister intention: but the reprisals I was to suffer, are long, and can terminate only with my life!" (2.6; pp. 133–34). In a world of destiny, caprice reigns supreme.

The very permanence of things as they are renders them inexplicable.[2] They are essences remote from or even inimical to experience, establishing a reticulated space (shall we call it Britain?) resistant to the impact of time (change, revolution). But in consequence, things as they are—the material and social environment—are irrelevant in the end. Like Zimmermann, Williams learns the art of being happy even in prison:

> My fare was coarse; but I was in health. My dungeon was noisome; but I felt no inconvenience. I was shut up from the usual means of exercise and air; but I found the method of exercising myself even to perspiration

in my dungeon. I had no power of withdrawing my person from a dis-
gustful society in the most chearful and valuable part of the day; but I
soon brought to perfection the art of withdrawing my thoughts, and saw
and heard the people about me for just as short a time and as seldom as
I pleased.

    Such is man in himself considered; so simple his nature; so few his
wants.   (2.12; pp. 186–87)

Like the novels previously examined, *Caleb Williams* is a study in
regression. Orphaned at eighteen, Caleb spends his life striving to return to the condition of sonship. He calls himself "new to the world,"
knowing "nothing of its affairs but what has reached me by rumour,
or is recorded in books" (2.10; p. 173). He describes himself to Falkland as having been "a raw and inexperienced boy, capable of being
moulded to any form you pleased" (3.12; p. 282), and his most urgent
desire is to remain untouched, inviolate in the face of experience, to
leave no material "trace of my existence" on the face of the earth (2.8;
p. 155). The novel is one long paean to the primal, transcendent power
of the human mind. "The mind is master of itself" (2.12; p. 188); "You
may imprison my body, but you cannot conquer my mind" (1.8; p.
57). And yearnings for a Rousseauistic purity and innocence that
punctuate the narrative reinforce the repeated assertions of the dependence of matter on mind.

    The specifically gothic dimension of *Caleb Williams* goes beyond
merely asserting the power of mind, a stance that in itself is hardly
unique to gothic fiction. The real spectacle of *Caleb Williams* is the insistence with which the novel represents the conflicts of existence as
the "tragedy of the incorrigible division in the human mind" (Kiely,
Romantic Novel, 95). Abstraction from the material conditions of life
leads to a focus on the interaction of mind with itself. What is mem-
orable in the novel—and romantic and gothic as well—is not the
power of the mind but the demonstration that the exertion of the
mind's power is inseparable from the mind's defeat, either by external
tyranny or by internal degeneration and insanity. *Caleb Williams*'s
"theatre of calamity" is perhaps the purest novelistic representation
of the antinomy of pure consciousness.

    Mind asserts its innocence in the face of accusation, its power in the face of oppression. Initially, therefore, the power of mind appears as a negation. It is the individual's rebellion against an external consensus, the seemingly irrational defiance hurled by the free will against a systematic order established from outside. Without these negations, individuality and freedom would have no meaning or would be absorbed into the isolation and capriciousness of the gothic demon. And indeed, neither of Godwin's two conclusions to the novel allows mind to escape from the inevitable negations at the end: in the original version Caleb goes mad, in the published version he internalizes all the accusations of guilt after vindicating his innocence. Between the initial and the terminal negations, however, the play of mind's dialectic is graphically set out. Hostility and sympathy arise together and tempestuously condition one another. "The instant I had uttered these words, I felt what it was that I had done. There was a magnetical sympathy between me and my patron, so that their effect was not sooner produced upon him, than my own mind reproached me with the inhumanity of the allusion. Our confusion was mutual" (*Caleb Williams*, 2.1; p. 112). Here, in a notable foreshadowing of Hegel's master-slave dialectic, ruler and ruled exchange roles:

> Palaces are built for his reception, a thousand vehicles provided for his exercise, provinces are ransacked for the gratification of his appetite, and the whole world traversed to supply him with apparel and furniture. Thus vast is his expenditure, and the purchase slavery. He is dependent on a thousand accidents for tranquillity and health, and his body and soul are at the devotion of whoever will satisfy his imperious cravings.
>
> (2.12; p. 187)

Likewise, as the power of mind makes the servant into the master, so it makes the pursued into the pursuer:

> Why should I be harassed by the pursuit of this Gines; why, man to man, may I not by the powers of my mind attain the ascendancy over him? at present he appears to be the persecutor and I the persecuted: is not this difference the mere creature of the imagination? may I not employ my ingenuity to vex him with difficulties and laugh at the endless labour to which he will be condemned?
>
> (3.14; p. 306)

At the end, to be sure, Caleb learns that if slavery is freedom, so on the other hand freedom can be slavery; for Gines (the criminal become bailiff) announces to him the terrifying sentence that he is to be a "prisoner at large," free to roam, yet denied what Caleb clearly perceives to be the element of life, "the salt seas" (3.15; p. 313).

The dominant metaphor throughout is the chain, and over and over it appears that chains are tied at both ends and that the manacles are both forged and shattered by the mind. Even in less explicit moments the logic of Godwin's analysis remains the same. An example is the Welsh idyll, where, for the last time before the concluding debacles, mind and nature seem to harmonize. Caleb sets himself up as a watchmaker and "an instructor in mathematics and its practical application, geography, astronomy, land-surveying and navigation" (3.13; p. 289)—in other words as a master of time and space—and attaches himself with filial devotion to the poetically named matron Laura. The town proves, however, to be within Falkland's sphere of influence, so Caleb's story gets disseminated, and he is ostracized. In a vertiginous moment of recognition Caleb learns again that the very tie that makes men sociable is also a tie that binds and a barrier that excludes. The confined freeman is a perverted externalization of the categorical imperative (you should freely choose what the structure of rationality imposes on you) and thereby validates Kant's warnings against trying to bring creatures of reason to light. Godwin finds no escape from this insanity, no end point or resolution of the dialectic of pure-impure reason, short of a revolution in our ways of thinking.

A revolution in thought is, of course, just what Kant had proclaimed—a revolution that might even end the *bellum omnium contra omnes* and lead to eternal peace. Even the evil tendencies of man, Kant rhapsodizes in "On Eternal Peace," attest to the ultimately benevolent purposes of nature. Punctuated by numerous ironic sallies against political pragmatists, Kant's argument, such as it is, envisions an inevitable harmonization of the antitheses of nature and mind, mechanism and teleology. Yet his poetical chimera touchingly omits human responsibility, whose problematic nature his earlier works had partly explored, partly hinted at. It is *nature's* mechanisms that prove concordant with *nature's* purposes, *nature's* mechanisms that triumph over man's purposes, *nature's* purposes that triumph over man's mechanisms. Man's destiny is peace, but man—that mad savage—has no role in his destiny. "What offers this *assurance* (guarantee) is nothing less than the great artist Nature (natura daedala rerum), from whose mechanical course purposiveness visibly shines forth, causing unity to arise through the disunity of men, even against their will" (B47). "Things as they are" are of no account (see, for instance, B75, opposing those who draw their political morality "from the way things happen in their world [*aus der Art, wie es in der Welt zugeht*]"). As Balzac was later to do in his sequel to Melmoth, Kant reconciles the demonic forces in the human breast by objectifying them in the form of cash: "For because, among all the powers (means) subordinate to the power of the state, the *power of money* must surely be the most reliable, so states see themselves (not, indeed, by the springs of morality) compelled to further the noble cause of peace" (B65). It is indeed a noble yearning, yet full of the pathos of a lost cause.

Throughout this long confrontation of Kantian and gothic psychology, it has become apparent how the authors and texts express an imaginative vision that nevertheless exceeds the comprehension of any one of them. At stake is nothing less than a difficult, even dangerous rethinking of the relation of man to his world. The novels often seem to have some of the fleshless, abstract quality often attributed to allegory because the underlying issues are cosmic ones, larger than the characters. The philosopher defines the issues and the terms for analyzing the vital statements implicit in the novels; the novelists put on display the energy that brings the philosopher's rigors to life. It would be tempting to say that novelists open questions and philosophers close them, but more than just chronology prohibits this simplified picture: the philosopher's answers often prove only to defend against his own psychological intuitions, and the novelists' explorations just as often prove only to serve pat moral conclusions. Nothing, indeed, allows us to distinguish sharply between philosophers and novelists: philosophers (even Kant) also tell stories, novelists (even gothic novelists) also reason about higher issues. If anything, the philosopher is the greater fabulist, driving his premises to the neatest, most organic denouement; if anything, the novelists are the greater dialecticians, working out the dynamics of their premises in the free play of forces acting on their characters. These distinctions are, of course, in no sense absolute. What I do wish to have established for "philosophical" and "poetical" texts alike is that both insights and intuitions—is the difference between philosophy and poetry no greater after all than the difference between a Germanic word and its nearest Romance counterpart?—come trailing bright clouds of intellectual ferment. The metaphor favored by Michel Serres seems apposite here: definitive formulations are but nodal points, eddies in the turbulent flow of human consciousness. Major texts stir up such eddies, or more precisely, they juxtapose points of condensation with expanses of sublimation. (Or at least, we always read in this fashion, although I know of no hermeneutic theorist apart from Roland Barthes who has taken into account the selectivity and intermittence of our reading process, and he did so only intermittently.)[3] While the proportions may differ, we ought to see in any major text a conjuncture of binding with loosing, terminating with initiating, looking backward with looking ahead.

Whether in the idylls of Rousseau or the melancholic anti-idyll that concludes *The Castle of Otranto*, consciousness once appeared to be a pure, undefined, empty condition. As I have written elsewhere, the eighteenth century found it difficult to "become conscious of consciousness" because it was groping toward the negation of the very empirical, relational, and comparative judgment that was conducting the search ("Romanticism and Enlightenment"). From the earlier perspective, the later conception could only appear as a zero-point, a negation of all that had hitherto been meant by selfhood. And the earlier conception appears similarly empty or invisible to the later perspective: those to whom the self is a temporally expansive unity are unable to imagine the earlier conception of the self as a punctual reflex of its spatial environment. Consciousness is discovered as a sublime cipher, "mere" Being.

Yet with the hindsight of history, it becomes possible to ask about the content of that discovery. Consciousness as pure Being proves to be a differential concept. It entails an external differentiation or isolation of self from its surrounding world—whereas, to repeat, the self had earlier been seen only in relation to its world ("no man is an island"). And it engenders a variety of internal differentiations, conceptual distinctions that respond to questions about the mode of selfhood or Being. These are formulated in terms such as sleep and waking, insanity and reason, freedom and mechanism, mind and body, subject and object, being and existence. They are represented in pervasive metaphors of water and dry land, of feminine and masculine. They seem to be subtended—but not (or not equally) in all texts—by fundamental distinctions between now and not-now, or less prominently, here and not-here; consequently it becomes possible to speak in connection with some texts of a deduction of the categories of time and space analogous and logically prior to Kant's deduction of the categories of the understanding. To complicate matters further, the generation of distinctions is not a simple process, because they are generated within the one undivided self in the process of inquiring after and coming to know itself. I found it useful to employ the terminology of post-Kantian philosophy to describe the results, since very often in the novels the self both posits and suspends distinctions. In the language of the philosophers, it posits the indifference of, say, fate and freedom, or permanence and change. The language of the poets, of course, often seems handier; in that language we say that the self plays with distinctions, tries them out, experiments with them prior to fixing them in relation to one another and to itself. In any case, the romantic self is productive. In prospect it appeared that Being must be inert, a "mere" space of time through which identity is maintained. But in retrospect the self turns out to be active, though with a curious kind of mental activity that retains a passive or reflexive component: it acts in response, shaping and sorting experiences.

I have not attempted to describe an end point to the romantic dialectic of self. History flows on unceasingly; end points are only apparent, at best. We cannot rest in them; they look too simple in advance, and they turn out to be too complex after all. Yet it is clear what such an end point—or, better, nodal point—would be. It would be the point that Hegel calls "definite simplicity," the point where all differences have been posited and have then been suspended or returned to unity. It often finds an echo in romantic pantheism, the doctrine of the one life. But I would rather cite an image than a name. So I shall conclude this chapter with the blank stone face that the gothic personality turns toward us when it has perfectly encompassed and grown indifferent to all differences:

> I had no thought, no feeling—none—
> Among the stones I stood a stone,
> And was, scarce conscious what I wist,
> As shrubless crags within the mist;
> For all was blank, and bleak, and grey;
> It was not night, it was not day;
> It was not even the dungeon-light,
> O hateful to my heavy sight,
> But vacancy absorbing space,
> And fixedness without a place;
> There were no stars, no earth, no time,
> No check, no change, no good, no crime,
> But silence, and a stirless breath
> Which neither was of life nor death;
> A sea of stagnant idleness,
> Blind, boundless, mute, and motionless!
>
> . . .
>
> It was at length the same to me
> Fettered or fetterless to be.[4]

PART IV

Consequences

14

In Defense of Cliché

Radcliffe's Landscapes

Whatever lacks interest as act or significance for language is without value. There is speech because language maintains itself only in the continuity of repetition. But anything that repeats only what is at hand from the past is in itself nothing. Weather talk. But this null is not absolute nothingness, but rather only a minimum. For significance unfolds in relation to it.
—Schleiermacher, *Hermeneutik*, 82–83

All writing is a campaign against cliché.
—Martin Amis, *The War Against Cliché*, xv

A CERTAIN "LITERARINESS" seems inseparable from gothic narration. None of us, after all, has ever seen a ghost, but we have all seen ghost stories. Pictorial realism defines a certain variety of fantasy writing from more recent decades, but gothic ghosts come alive in the shadows. Gothic narratives that strive to break this barrier all too often burst it: the devil becomes inescapably manifest only at the cost of a spectacular collapse, as at the end of *The Monk*. What keeps the stories going is ambiguity, be it a flickering hope of escaping the inevitable or an uncertainty about whether the ghosts are really there at all. They set us thinking, wondering. Indeed, as Ann Radcliffe's novels made clear right from the start, they don't even need ghosts to be gothic, just the appearance of ghosts, or the appearance of the appearance of ghosts, or, since "apparition" can be a synonym for a ghost, the appearance of the appearance of appearances. As Marc Redfield has sagely written, "to be or to see a ghost is precisely not to know whether or not one is or has seen a ghost" (*Phantom Formations*, 85). Ghosts are defined less by their contents than by the manner that the expected contents prescribe. We recognize them because they resemble what we have read about.

"Literariness" is, of course, a jargon term.[1] When I used it above, I put it in scare quotes, as we gothically call them, to signal its dubious value. For while literariness takes its name from literature, it is in the nature of literature to strive for uniqueness. To be sure, in earlier periods imitation had more positive connotations, but by the later eighteenth century, when literature came to be identified as a distinctive category of writing, the creative genius became the new standard. Literariness names a recognizable type, which consequently is only a facsimile, not an authentic individual. If gothic writing doesn't positively define such second-rateness, it certainly exemplifies it: it is apprentice writing; you grow out of being a gothic novelist, rarely if ever into it. The "literary" is unqualified to be literature.

Since gothic prose depends on being recognizably uncanny, it manifests a kind of self-consciousness. Often, indeed, it seems self-conscious in the negative sense—awkward, slightly embarrassed, even unintentionally funny. Self-consciousness is a hallmark of literary romanticism as well, but the primary self-consciousness or romantic irony of a Schlegel or a Byron is fundamentally different from the parasitic character of the gothic. Romantic irony rises above its models, relativizing and judging them; it laughs serenely at its world, not nervously at itself. It is a disjunctive or synthetic awareness, whereas the self-consciousness of gothic facsimiles is edgy. Ghosts are like real beings without quite being real, and gothic prose wants to participate in a familiar mode without quite being overshadowed by it. Above all in Radcliffe's explained supernatural, it seeks a chimerical individuality that will be strange enough yet remain respectable enough.

The obvious rhetorical manifestation of gothic's marginal self-consciousness is its similes. "She seemed like a spectre," with its stylistically slack double qualifier "seemed like," is the best possible mark of spectrality, a transparent idiom for a transparent body, whereas "she was a ghost" would be too hard-edged. Terry Castle has written memorably about the permeability of substance in Radcliffe and about how the dissolution of bodies turns gothic experience into a mental spectrum. But she still has not taken full account of this writing through the body. For the workings of gothic formulae are more complexly self-conscious than even her discussion acknowledges. The phrase I have instanced comes from the scene in Radcliffe's *The Italian*, where Ellena di Vivaldi is abducted into an evil convent, and it refers to the nearly silent nun who guides her way. "As [Ellena's conductress] glided forward with soundless step, her white drapery, floating along these solemn avenues, and her hollow features touched with the mingled light and shadow which the partial rays of a taper she held occasioned, she seemed like a spectre newly risen from the grave, rather than a living being" (1.6; p. 67). Reports of consciousness characterize the gothic from the very beginning, but in Radcliffe in particular the boundary between narrator and character becomes as fluid as that between mind and body. The language of feeling belongs to the character, but the language of analysis belongs to the narrator: "these solemn avenues" is a deictic close-up that cannot be attributed to the bewildered Ellena. Though Vivaldi earlier resists becoming "an unsuspected observer of [Ellena's] secret thoughts" (1.2; p. 27), the narrator knows no such restraint; she is not a reporter but an over-consciousness who elaborates the primitive reactions of the characters. The similes mark a self-consciousness without a defined self, in a world of floating and disembodied impressions.

Understood as a derivative mode or facsimile, the gothic has traditionally seemed to lack rigor and invention; a ghost after all is nothing very definite and was nothing very new. The general stylistic term we use to belittle the crudeness of the gothic mode is cliché. But cliché, too, has value. It is precisely the power of the gothic to put cliché to use that fascinates me in Radcliffe. ("Cliché" originated as the French term for "stereotype," a new printing process invented in 1797, coincidentally the year *The Italian* was published. In both English and French, "cliché" acquired its colloquial sense in the second half of the nineteenth century. Only then, one might say, did cliché become clichéd.)[2] No one could argue that Radcliffe is a fine writer—at least not without putting "fine writer," too, in scare quotes. For when it comes to speaking about the unspeakable, careful distinctions, the province of fine writers, lose their meaning. It seems to make little difference to

Radcliffe's narratives whether they revel in horror or instead in terror, or whether they explain the supernatural or instead leave it mysterious. To be sure, the Inquisition as Radcliffe imagines it metes out surprisingly calibrated punishments, but as storytellers gothic novelists know no such refinement; their endings are all overkill. Yet the writing accomplishes something remarkable through its struggle for expression, its very failure or refusal to come to life. The following analyses mostly expatiate on various shopworn clichés that—some readers may think—hardly warrant more expansion than Radcliffe already gives them. But only through such close-ups is it possible to seize the methods in the madness of gothic cliché.

I open my account of Radcliffe's clichés with the cluster around the voice of feeling and its spooky correlative, unspeakable horrors. Love at first sight is an old story, which Radcliffe's novel varies to love at first hearing. *The Italian* begins with a murmur of voices. The first epigraph in the novel is from Walpole: "What is this secret sin; this untold tale, / That art cannot extract, nor penance cleanse?" (1.1; p. 5). (The story is also dated to 1765, the nominal year of publication of *The Castle of Otranto*, and the first great climax comes in a beach hut in a town called Manfredonia, as if in homage to Walpole's protagonist. *The Monk* is not the only book Radcliffe seems to want to copycat.) As the story opens, Vivaldi is transfixed by Ellena's voice before he ever sees her face, and their early exchanges are songs and sighs and silent glances.[3] From glimpses of her features, which are hardly described, Vivaldi acquires an unshakable conviction of the fineness of her intellect even though, as the narrator tells us, he manages not to learn how she earns a living. They do not exchange words in the first chapter, and the dialogues that the chapter does quote lead nowhere: Vivaldi ignores mysterious warnings to stay away from Ellena and conducts aimless exchanges with a companion named Bonarmo, who then disappears from the narrative. The sounds of the volcano, the ocean, the mountains, the leaves and trees; of singing and cheering and whispering voices from near and far; a rustle of garments; and Bonarmo's echoing cries create a cocoon of noises that enraptured sense will never break through. It continues unabated—and is even enhanced in the dungeon by a rather pointless display of ventriloquism from a secondary character, Brother Nicola—to the very end, where it sustains the fragile threads of recognition upon which the plot is spun. "The voice, indeed, the voice of the penitent, I think I shall never forget; I should know it again at any distance of time," Father Ansaldo brags to the Inquisition, yet when he hears it shortly afterwards, he can only hesitantly affirm, "I think it was [the voice of the penitent], . . . but I cannot swear to that" (3.7; p. 338, 341). Such thinking is how we qualify our failure at voice recognition when we cannot confidently utter our stories; it is reason decayed into the colloquial and the clichéd.

Still, whereas portrait likenesses may deceive, voices don't. When Vivaldi challenges Schedoni at Nicola's abrupt prompting, Nicola proves correct in his outspokenness, and so does Olivia when she recognizes the speech patterns of an old servant: "'I certainly ought to know that voice,' said [Olivia] with great emotion, 'though I dare not judge from your features'" (3.9; p. 377). The gothic is a world of inarticulate expression, of voices seeking recognition, stories seeking utterance, thoughts seeking substance. Peter Brooks's book about romantic drama, *The Melodramatic Imagination*, titles contiguous chapters "The Aesthetics of Astonishment" and "The Text of Muteness," but the novels show that inarticulacy rather than silence is the crucial issue. In the ponderous formality of silent reading in books that are often long, we may forget that characters like Frankenstein's monster are desperately trying to speak up and to be acknowledged. But that dilemma is the very crux and atmosphere of gothic books. *The Italian* itself opens with a prelude concerning a secret confession that remains unheard as a pretext for unveiling the ensuing story of Schedoni's confession. To write the utterance, to fix the voice, to publish the story—that is the initial challenge for Radcliffe or her narrator, and one that the main narrative noisily solves and the frame hauntingly evades.

Through its imagery the novel offers two models for bringing speech to fulfillment by penetrating its veil of cliché. The first model is topical decoding: translating visual pointers as signs in order to discern character. Neither fully self-aware nor unconsciously looming, lacking the density of an ego or the raw power of an id, both character and author lapse into commonplace when they try to decode personality. Schedoni is one instance: living in "unconquerable silence" and throwing "an impenetrable veil over his origin," he grasps "artificial perplexities" but "seldom perceived truth when it lay on the surface" (1.2; p. 34). Here is how the first meeting of Vivaldi and Schedoni continues: "[Schedoni's] eyes were so piercing that they seemed to penetrate, at a single glance, into the hearts of men, and to read their most secret thoughts. . . . Vivaldi, as [Schedoni] eyed him with a penetrating glance, now recoiled with involuntary emotion" (1.2; p. 35). Scrutinized too closely, that utterance baffles with a look that simultaneously penetrates and bounces, though there is a kind of perverse precision that literalizes piercing eyes into seeming penetration and that prefers the mobile term "glance" to the more static alternatives, "gaze" or "stare." Still, none of the signs has more than a highly conventional meaning, and the yield is vague or circular: "there was something terrible in [Schedoni's] air; something almost superhuman." Faces reveal character, but not very interesting character. Readers sometimes praise Radcliffe's depiction of Schedoni, yet his character is clearly only skin deep.

The other model of reading is dynamic. Noting reactions rather than corporeal inscriptions, it takes utterances, descriptions, and appearances to outline the inhibitions and resistances confronting consciousness. Properly realized, cliché is transmuted from a shallow possession into a deep problem. The cover-up of convention remains: neither narrator nor character truly penetrates personality, and so they lapse readily back into cliché. But their very failure creates an impression of depth.[4] Here, for instance, is Vivaldi as character reader: "The keen dart of suspicion, . . . sharpened as it was by love and by despair, pierced beyond the veil of her duplicity; and Vivaldi as quickly detected [his mother's] hypocrisy as he had yielded his conviction to the sincerity of [his father]." Vivaldi thinks well of himself. But the narrator deflates him with the ensuing comment: "But his power rested here" (1.9; p. 101). In fact Vivaldi appears rather imperceptive. His father proves not sincere, merely uxorious, and the novel is rife with hints of sexual duplicity in the mother that neither Vivaldi nor the narrator ever acknowledges. The yield is not a penetration that would plumb psychic depths, but merely gestures seeking fulfillment. Underrealized as a study in insight, the gothic novel becomes that much more effective as a study in frustration.[5]

A later incident similarly displaces topical decoding with dynamic allure. Vivaldi and Ellena are trying to escape the dungeon beneath the convent where she has been imprisoned, but their guide, Father Jeronimo, can't open the door. In the gloom, her eyes anxiously seize on a mattress, which, as the narrative superconscious says, "seemed a dreadful hieroglyphic"; and "a hollow sigh" appears, undecidably, either to deepen the mystery or to confirm that it's all just a travesty of *The Monk*. "Be not alarmed," observes the valiant hero, "I have a sword," as if that would help when what they desperately need is a key. As for his feebly flickering lamp, "he held it high, endeavouring to penetrate the farthest gloom of the chamber" (2.1; pp. 140–41). The emptiness of the gesture becomes its realization: once Vivaldi and Ellena have experienced the trauma of not knowing, the pressure comes off, and a stranger they encounter in the catacombs unlocks the exit. Like so many incidents in Radcliffe's novels, this one is more artificial than artful: neither Jeronimo nor the unnamed second monk ever reappears, the happily reunited lovers are soon unhappily separated again, and it seems most inconsequential. In the many episodes like this, it is easy to condemn as trumpery both what is said and how it is said, but not much would be left to admire. Rather, style cliché resonates with plot cliché to model the dynamic that makes the novel worth reading. It is not out of place here to invoke the Lacanian *manque-à-être* as the generative moment of supernatural novels with such hollow hearts. To penetrate is to enter, to comprehend, and to wound; Vivaldi's abortive gesture with the lamp irradiates the lovers' pointless success with a reminder of the pains of knowledge.

If, then, the voice of feeling and the unspeakable horrors that beset it were my first pair of clichés, implied by the novel though not verbally invoked within it,[6] the impenetrable veil and the penetrating glance make a second cluster, all too obsessively reiterated in Radcliffe's novels. These clichés are situationally or topically weak; they hardly seem well motivated and distinctive where they occur. But as tenacious gestures toward an unrealized structure, they can come to seem compelling in a different way, particularly if we, as readers, stay alert to the various shifts and turns in their usage. The weakly self-conscious narrator encounters the task of separating from the characters, like the self that struggles to emerge from the confused surge of primitive, unbound and unbounded desire that Freud describes in "The Ego and the Id." And while the tremors of the characters often manifest what Freud calls real anxiety (by which he means well-defined fears, not necessarily well-grounded ones), the tics and atmospherics of the writing in which character and narrator are linked convey the free-floating, so-called neurotic anxiety aroused when desires fail to take shape and reach a goal. Hence, though the real dilemmas of escaping from dungeons and tormentors verge on the ludicrous, perhaps intentionally so in *The Italian*, the neuroses about conveying the truths of a self are genuine. The narrator is not a transparent double of the author but a genuine protagonist, groping toward a shape for her plot.

The once much admired landscape descriptions, for instance, are remarkably impoverished semantically: they tell us little either about the vistas or about the psychology of the characters.[7] Yet through their cumulative reiteration they compellingly enact the labors of description. Often viewed through a window, they are spare and itemized, frequently with lists of species complemented by the most formulaic of emotive adjectives, giving them much the character of painted stage decor. They are not observations or plein-air writing. Rather, "scenery" in Radcliffe never entirely sheds its older, theatrical sense of stage flats with depth projected onto them.[8] One passage in *The Mysteries of Udolpho* particularly reveals the effort to distill a living landscape out of a static nature. The Count de Villefort is speaking with his daughter Blanche about the varying impressions of the enduring landscape. "Though the grand features of the scenery admit of no change, they impress me with sensations very different from those I formerly experienced." She asks, "Did these scenes, sir, . . . ever appear more lovely than they do now?" And he responds: "They once were as delightful to me, as they are now to you; the landscape is not changed, but time has changed me; from my mind the illusion, which gave spirit to the colouring of nature, is fading fast" (3.10; p. 474). Considered as scenery, the landscape at this moment in the development of pictorial description is a decor whose life is a dubious projection from within the unstable spirits of the human observer. The affect is floating and ghostly; on a single page of *The Mysteries of Udolpho* Blanche passes from actual "scenery" to observing "scenes" on a "faded tapestry," then back again to "the face of living nature" (3.10; p. 475), with little sense of the difference between storied images and observed ones. As in other manifestations of gothic cliché, here the seer and the thing seen are too fused for either landscape or character to be fully realized. The narrator needs to get a life of her own in order to see into the life of things.

Human activity appears necessary to the scenic backdrop, and almost all the landscapes in *The Italian* incorporate it. I'll quote the very first, brief view, since it appears to be an exception, but only proves the rule. "The house," we read, "stood on an eminence, surrounded by a garden and vineyards, which commanded the city and bay of Naples . . . and was canopied by a thick grove of pines and majestic date-trees" (1.1; p. 6). Not a prepossessing depiction, but what distinguishes it is the phrase I have omitted: "an ever-moving picture." The moving picture was an early-eighteenth-century invention, particularly associated with theatrical decor: the 1782 citation in the *OED* praises the stage designer Loutherbourg, and its next quote (from 1822) is explicitly theatrical. Nature becomes describable when it is converted into spectacle, and the power that converts it is more or less explicitly magical; hence this description concludes with "the bay below, and a prospect of the whole scope of its enchanting shores." The diction is a little watery, perhaps, but we can't really escape from its ramifications, since the mysterious Ellena is lurking in the garden and the very next paragraph reminds us of "the beauty of her countenance haunting his imagination, . . . the touching accents of her voice still vibrating on his heart, . . . [and] the enchantment of her smile" (1.1; p. 7). The life in the scene comes from one mystery reinforcing another.

In the scenic clichés one senses the discomfort of the narrator, who is trying to get on top of things. Three tendencies may be observed. The first, which I have just reported, is to import life into the scene.

The following paragraph from *The Mysteries of Udolpho* is worth quoting in full as perhaps the most fully developed instance:

> The market people, passing with their boats to Venice, now formed a moving picture on the Brenta. Most of these had little painted awnings, to shelter their owners from the sun-beams, which, together with the piles of fruit and flowers, displayed beneath, and the tasteful simplicity of the peasant girls, who watched the rural treasures, rendered them gay and striking objects. The swift movement of the boats down the current, the quick glance of oars in the water, and now and then the passing chorus of peasants, who reclined under the sail of their little bark, or the tones of some rustic instrument, played by a girl, as she sat near her sylvan cargo, heightened the animation and festivity of the scene.
>
> (*Mysteries of Udolpho* 2.4; p. 212)

A second tendency recognizes the mysteries of the life: in a landscape with dancing peasants, "such magic scenes of beauty unfolded . . . as no pencil could do justice to" (*The Italian* 1.3; p. 37). And, third, there is a continuing urge to shape the scenes as total impressions composed of emblematic parts, such as (in this particularly fully elaborated scene) beautiful land, picturesque mountains, and sublime ocean. It is not necessary to trace in detail the gradual, and somewhat fitful, narrative conquest of the living landscape through the two dozen or so landscape descriptions in the novel. They culminate in the remarkable depiction that opens the last chapter. I'm going to quote parts of it out of order. First, the composed middle:

> The marble porticoes and arcades of the villa were shadowed by groves of the beautiful magnolia, flowering ash, cedrati, camellias, and majestic palms; and the cool and airy halls, opening on two opposite sides to a colonade, admitted beyond the rich foliage all the seas and shores of Naples, from the west; and to the east, views of the valley of the domain, withdrawing among winding hills, wooded to their summits, except where cliffs of various-coloured granites, yellow, green, and purple, lifted their tall heads, and threw gay gleams of light amidst the umbrageous landscape.
>
> (*The Italian* 3.12; p. 412)

Here is landscape as embodied scene—not a formalized allegorical body like that of Milton's Paradise, but still a formally differentiated setting, beginning in pictorial balance (architecture vs. nature, beautiful magnolia vs. sublime palms, modulated by the remaining flowering species [cedrates are a variety of citrus], land vs. sea, east vs. west, valley vs. mountain) and rising to organic fulfillment with the emergent "tall heads" of the cliffs. While the schematism never attempts to escape from stereotype, it fulfills the cliché by replacing superimposed human activities with the inner vitalism of the "gay gleams of light" that are juxtaposed to the shadowy depths. Landscape grows out of the heavy nostalgia with which Radcliffe tends to invest it[9] into a majestic self-animation that defines the scene from the start—or nearly the start:

> The pleasure-grounds extended over a valley, which opened to the bay, and the house stood at the entrance of this valley, upon a gentle slope that margined the water, and commanded the whole extent of its luxuriant shores, from the lofty cape of Miseno to the bold mountains of the south, which, stretching across the distance, appeared to rise out of the sea, and divided the gulf of Naples from that of Salerno.

The pale personifications ("stood," "gentle," "commanded," and so forth) are admirable in their way, though the way is no sort of freedom from conventionality. Rather, these figures are apotheoses of "literariness," most quintessentially so the "bold mountains," which, with typically spectral narrative timidity, merely "appeared to rise." The lead-in links the narrator's mastery of the form to its gothic sources, with the most wonderfully puzzling display of self-assurance in the entire novel: "It was, in truth, a scene of fairy-land." "In truth," indeed. Here, if anywhere, is the gothic version of truth: the moment when all the pieces finally fall into place to form a scene at once perfectly familiar and yet perfectly adapted to its mysterious occasion.

Yet the coinciding of truth and fairy magic strains the composure toward which the gothic novel yearns.[10] And so, a different figure glimmers at the end. For the description continues by leaving its exotic setting altogether: "The style of the gardens, where lawns and groves, and woods varied the undulating surface, was that of England, and of the present day, rather than of Italy; except 'Where a long alley peeping on the main,' exhibited such gigantic loftiness of shade, and grandeur of perspective, as characterize the Italian taste." Here the narrator abandons all pretense that this is the characters' vista. Indeed, even where the narrator characterizes it as Italian, she quotes a line of English poetry in witness. Perhaps Radcliffe was still an amateur in her fifth work of fiction and simply forgot that her introduction says the story comes from a manuscript written by "a student of Padua" (p. 4). But even if she did forget, I prefer to regard this as motivated rather than crude forgetting. Throughout the novel, a narrator has been struggling to emerge as a knowing subject. By the third volume the judgments of the narrator start to break free from the blending or contamination by individual subjectivities. In particular, when the Inquisition becomes more rational, so does the narration; for example: "The suspicions of the tribunal, augmenting with their perplexity, seemed to fluctuate equally over every point of the subject before them"—this is a conclusion too measured to be attributed to any of the participants in the proceedings, such as Vivaldi, who is "silent, thoughtful, and amazed" (3.6; p. 332). A brief paragraph in the next chapter provides another example: "The penitentiary Ansaldo was next called upon. Vivaldi observed that he faultered as he advanced. . . . Vivaldi himself was then summoned; his air was calm and dignified, and his countenance expressed the solemn energy of his feelings" (3.7; p. 336). Vivaldi's perception of Ansaldo yields to a more impersonal perception of Vivaldi. In such passages, and most notably at the end, the narrator has found her own voice at last, as the story has finally broken through to the light of day.

Another cliché, "speechless with astonishment," manifests the resistance generated by the style and the reactions that ensue. "Astonish" is a remarkable word. Together with its nephew, "stun," it appears to derive from the French *étonné* and the Latin *attonitus* and to mean the state of being thunderstruck. Yet, at least according to the *OED*, its ancestry bears the stain of a Germanic root that has *staunen* as its modern representative and that means to stare in wonder. Finally, in gothic contexts the word "astonished" leans toward a false etymological association with "turned to stone, petrified." Semantic overdetermination gives the word some of its strength, but also, I suspect, some of its lability. While dictionaries do not adequately document semantic degradation, I hazard a guess that at the time Radcliffe was writing, "astonishment" was losing its semantic moorings and consequently its punch. *OED* citations from before her time normally invoke a life-and-death context or a state of lasting bafflement. By contrast, colloquialisms like "astonishing vitality," "astonishingly numerous," or "a moment of astonishment" all date from the nineteenth century. This evidence suggests that gothic astonishment is a serious, if helpless, attempt to hold onto powerful sensations that were felt to be slipping away into the everyday. Radcliffe's clichés invoke a lost knowledge, a vanished consciousness. It's the sublime gone nostalgic.

In its more violent manifestations, astonishment represses speech. One is too stunned to talk. But in its more modern, subtle, or transitory forms, astonishment relates to repression more intricately. One must bring to the surprise a predisposition to wonder. Speechlessness precedes its occasion and latches onto it—anaclitically, in Freudian parlance—in order to gain time for reflection. In this condition one is less preoccupied with the thing that astonishes than with one's own state of astonishment. Gothic astonishment naturally wonders about itself—what it is doing in its terrified situation, what it is after—rather than remaining transfixed by the inexplicable Other. The unknown unleashes an image of self even if not a voice; passions that had been nothing more than vague or instinctual drives and aversions gain a direction. That is why speechless astonishment takes time, and why it lends itself to rational analysis even though it cannot be narrated. The moment that endures despite its stunned ineffability confronts the writer with an insuperable obstacle: how to give authentic voice to the unutterable and personality to a stony fate superintended by a demonic agent or (in the subgenre to which *The Italian* belongs) by a shadowy secret society. From Walpole on, one recourse to the problem of narrating astonishment lay in chattering servants—to one of whom I will turn presently—who add volume, though little density. But especially in Radcliffe, the servants are only one manifestation of the general assault from below that crystallizes as cliché. To retain its mysterious power, a story seeks access to consciousness without taking form.

Life is short and art—in this case—is very long. With apologies for some unavoidably verbose quotation, I will limit my commentary to two of the many instances of speechless astonishment in the novel. Here is one:

> Had it been possible to have shut out all consciousness of himself, also, how willingly would [Schedoni] have done so! He threw himself into a chair, and remained for a considerable time motionless, and lost in thought, yet the emotions of his mind were violent and contradictory. At the very instant when his heart reproached him with the crime he had meditated, he regretted the ambitious views he must relinquish if he failed to perpetrate it, and regarded himself with some degree of contempt for having hitherto hesitated on the subject. He considered the character of his own mind with astonishment, for circumstances had drawn forth traits, of which, till now, he had no suspicion. He knew not by what doctrine to explain the inconsistencies, the contradictions, he experienced, and, perhaps, it was not one of the least that in these moments of direful and conflicting passions, his reason could still look down upon their operations, and lead him to a cool, though brief examination of his own nature. But the subtlety of self-love still eluded his enquiries, and he did not detect that pride was even at this instant of self-examination, and of critical import, the master-spring of his mind. In the earliest dawn of his character this passion had displayed its predominancy. (2.9; p. 225)

Note how motionlessness liberates emotion: while gothic astonishment stuns physically, it sets the mind running. But what kind of consciousness does this astonishment liberate? It is oriented toward the self, methodical, yet baffled. Mental processes continue unabated, indeed intensified. The itinerary progressively steers consciousness from its feelings toward a thought that tries to order the feelings by revealing their source. First "his heart reproached him," then "he regretted," then he "regarded himself with . . . contempt," then "he considered." And finally, though "he knew not," still "his reason could . . . lead him to . . . [an] examination of his own nature." In the end, this consciousness knows and can know only itself, for it is a reflexive process that comes to the surface exactly when it would be burrowing into the depths. The cooler the examination, the more it severs itself from its violent foundations. Schedoni's astonishment thus reveals how resourceful the mind is at concealing its true impulses.

"Lost in thought" is a precise idiom, since the thought screens from view the primitive wellsprings of passion.

Later in the same chapter comes another moment of wordless astonishment, this time a mutual one:

> Another deep pause succeeded, during which Schedoni continued to pace the room, sometimes stopping for an instant, to fix his eyes on Ellena, and regarding her with an earnestness that seemed to partake of frenzy, and then gloomily withdrawing his regards, and sighing heavily, as he turned away to a distant part of the room. She, meanwhile, agitated with astonishment at his conduct, as well as at her own circumstances, and with the fear of offending him by further questions, endeavoured to summon courage to solicit the explanation which was so important to her tranquillity. At length she asked . . .   (2.9; pp. 238–39)

The typical features of wordless astonishment here are these. First, a "deep pause" suggests a prolonged moment, a moment with depth, a glimpse of eternity on a different plane of existence. Second, the subdivision of that moment into instants and of the powerful emotions into conflicting feelings reflects how ungraspable that eternal moment is in its essence. It is no surprise that when Ellena "at length" asks her question—in the sentences following the quoted passage— she merely fritters away her feelings into circumstantiality. For, third, what puts us in touch with our hidden truth is a wordless knowledge, what my colleague Raimonda Modiano once called "languageless meanings." The questions cannot be answered because they cannot even be asked without removing us from the realm of primitive passions they would direct us toward: reflection swathes trauma instead of probing it.

The prolonged moment of speechless and agitated astonishment occurs at the boundary between the unconscious and the preconscious. Regarded topically, in the Freudian map of the psyche, the unconscious is the realm of pictures, the preconscious the realm of words, and consciousness the realm of stories. Dynamically, primitive drives are subject to what Freud calls an originary repression (*Urverdrängung*). They are unexpressed because they fluctuate too vaguely to be expressible. They must first be "fixed," or attached to particular representations, as here, where the surging feelings of love and hatred between Schedoni and Ellena condense onto the mistaken belief that he is her father. But at this point, where needs become desires, "actual repression" intervenes, which Freud also calls a "supplementary repression" (*Nachdrängen*, elsewhere *Nachverdrängung*), as when Schedoni deflects Ellena's anxious questions. There is no "transcription" (*Niederschrift*), no writing down and conscious formulating of the meaning of the drives, but only "an alteration of the condition, a change in the cathexis," which Freud also calls a "countercathexis" (*Gegenbesetzung*). The speechless astonishment for which no adequate language is possible, but only a wordy cliché, reflects a mechanism to redirect the drives without physically satisfying them.[11]

Freud is the only writer I have encountered who theorizes the expressive function of cliché.[12] He develops his theory in two related sections of *The Interpretation of Dreams*. The earlier and simpler section concludes the chapter on dream-work. Here Freud discusses "secondary revision," the process by which the fragmented, elusive dream thoughts are patched together into the unrevealing whole familiar to us as a dream. Dreams express drives that are too strong to ignore but too dangerous to acknowledge; by means of secondary revision the mind veils what it is seeking to express so as to make the dream thoughts appear palatable. Secondary revision "serves to lull [the censorship] to sleep" by working "to reduce the significance of what has just been experienced [in the substance of the dream] and to enable us to tolerate what is to come."[13] Freud's imagery in this section is partly architectural and even gothic, as when he compares the process to the construction of Roman baroque palaces on top of ancient ruins (*Studienausgabe*, 2: 473; *Interpretation*, 492), and partly literary, as when he speaks of one very fully elaborated fantasy as a "dreamed novel" (2: 477; 496). (*Verdichtung*—"condensation" in English—is a second technique used by the mind in dream-work that inevitably recalls poetic composition, *Dichtung*.) Weaving buried desires and their symbolic representations—dream symbolism is another form of Freudian cliché—into seemingly harmless stories, secondary revision is the poetic filler that allows unconscious desires to be expressed.

Near the end of *The Interpretation of Dreams* Freud reformulates his theory of cliché in a second and much more abstract account of dream-work. His subject here is secondary process. The earlier chapter had discussed the different mechanisms of the dream-work and the methods for decoding each kind of dream strategy. In other words, it had considered dream-work topically: what is going on at each point and what depth lies below any given surface? The discussion of secondary process reexamines dream cliché in a dynamic perspective. It asks, in other words, not how dreams work, but what they accomplish and why. "Primary process" is Freud's name here for the construction of dream thoughts in the unconscious, "secondary process" for the means by which they are expressed. Secondary process aims to tone down or diffuse libidinal cathexes—desires—until they can be tolerably confronted; its rationalizations allow our impulses to find indirect satisfaction by concealing their true nature. As the imagination's cliché machine, secondary process "succeeds in transforming the cathexis into a quiescent one" (*Studienausgabe*, 2: 569; *Interpretation*, 599). Freud therefore calls it an "ostrich policy" (2: 570; 600) that pretends all is well when it isn't in order to free itself "more and more from exclusive regulation by the unpleasure principle" (2: 572; 602). Consequently, while secondary process reassures us by such ruses as converting passions into feelings, it inhibits understanding and control of "the core of our being" (2: 572–73; 603). In successful cases the "*transformation of affect . . .* serve[s] a useful purpose" (2: 573; 604); in other cases there "follows a defensive struggle" that leads to "the production of a symptom" or to "open, hallucinatory revival of the desired perceptual identity" (2: 574; 605). Freud says, "The mechanics of these processes are quite unknown to me" (2: 569; 599), but I think we can see them at work in fiction—more remotely in realistic fiction, where uncanny affects are successfully transformed into useful intentions, more directly in gothic works, which are indeed the kind of novels to which Freud implicitly and sometimes explicitly refers.[14]

A little-noted episode in *The Italian* contains the most elaborate fictional treatment I have found of the dynamic motives and topical resources of secondary dream-work.[15] It is a transient episode in which Schedoni leads Ellena away from the seaside hut where he had planned to have her murdered and where he has discovered her supposed identity as his daughter. The very chatty guide, who is never named, first begins a tale of the Barone di Cambrusco that is never continued, then is pumped for information about Spalatro, Ellena's imprisoner and the murderer of her real father, Schedoni's brother. This story, too, is abandoned in midstream, but it gives the first shadowy inkling of the long-concealed events of Schedoni's tormented history.

Schedoni's aim here is to find out how much the guide knows without letting on why it matters. His role is similar to that of a dream censor. And the wily guide reflects the ruses of the unconscious, seeking a way to vent its repressed and guilty self-knowledge, the "censored wishes" that "appear to rise up out of a positive Hell," as Freud writes in the chapter on censorship in his *Introductory Lectures on Psychoanalysis* (*Studienausgabe*, 1: 154; *Complete Introductory Lectures*, 143). This episode, in other words, while superfluous from the point of view of the surface story, richly exemplifies the motivations for telling. It fills out the last cliché that I want to note in my chapter, the Bulwer-Lytton Prize sentence, "It was a dark and stormy night." The episode is all banter between the guide and the monk, who would like to be on top of things but is being led by the nose. One by one, the countless conditions of storytelling pass in review—all the obstacles that intervene between the deep truth and its surface presentations. The extension of the episode marks all the elements repressed by a successful cliché.

Going in order, in volume 3, chapter 2, the jockeying begins with a notation of interest whose casualness conceals the real passion at issue: "I have now a few moments of leisure, and you may relate, if you will, something of the wonderful history you talked of." But a story has a pace: "It is a long story, Signor, and you would be tired before I got to the end of it." Next comes locale—"there is a strange history belonging to that house"—and then the question of the Marchese's identity. Gathering up all the pieces requires a kind of self-possession that the interest of the story continually undermines and that secondary revision continually needs to reestablish: "I left off there, I think." Identities must be confirmed—"This Spalatro was connected with the Baróne di Cambrusco?"—and reasons given. The jockeying tests the emotional involvements: Schedoni presses for reasons when the guide pursues the story, then for the story when the guide holds him up with reasons. Finally, after interjecting an observation about listeners, the guide begins "at the beginning," with the inevitable cliché, "Now the story goes, that one stormy night—."

No sooner does the story start than Schedoni jumps the gun, inferring a murder where none had been mentioned. The story that was meant to clarify the situation or—Schedoni hoped—exoncrate him instead entraps him, and he wants it to end quickly, "in two words." But the cat is out of the bag, lured by the persistent cliché—now amplified to "It was one stormy night in December"—that allows the truth to emerge without ever quite being told. The guide seeks a name; Schedoni leaps to judgment ("Well, what happened to this old dotard?"); and cliché reasserts its right to regulate the ventilation of the story: "It was a stormy night. . . . It was quite dark, as dark, Signor, as I suppose it was last night." Marco, who witnessed the trauma, becomes like the story of the trauma: "He wandered about a long while, and could see no light." And then, if the tale has become like the teller, the teller in return projects his feelings into the tale— "I suppose," "I warrant." A projective identification becomes the ground for an analytical anatomization, "and it comes nearer and nearer . . . and then he saw . . . and then spied." Identity is the dissolving focus, "a little moving light . . . just opposite to him," and then, shadow upon shadow, in the dark of night, "the shadow of a man." The story is gathering force without gathering clarity, for it is the dynamics of storytelling that count, the attachment to a moment and a motive, and not the resolving name that is too dangerous to reveal. "Old Marco, Signor, my father"—in this wonderful adnominatio all possible suspects are aligned, with no one to witness the final truth. The guide becomes circumspective, inconsequential, meandering, evasive, all to find opportunities to tell the story by not coming to the point. Schedoni now wants answers—"Who was this man?"— when the guide provides only circumstances. It becomes a narrative of nonrevelation: "but Marco took care not to tell." By dangling his clichés, the guide entraps his inquisitor, who blurts out the name of Spalatro, the perpetrator of the evil deed: "How well you have guessed it, Signor! though to say truth, I have been expecting you to find it out this half hour." The guide grows more eager as Schedoni grows more possessed, but neither will acknowledge what, manifestly, each covertly knows about the other. Instead, averting what eventually proves inevitable, Schedoni names the episode for what it has really been: "the narrative resembles a delirious dream, more than a reality."

It is an extraordinary moment in an extraordinary, perhaps unique episode, full of reminders of the intricacy of assembling and narrating a story. And the moment alerts us to the function of story in ventilating unconscious desires. By a *"displacement of psychical intensities to the point of a transvaluation of all psychical values,"* as Freud says in the chapter on secondary revision (*Studienausgabe*, 2: 486; *Interpretation*, 507), dreams tell stories through an ostrich policy of deflection and indirection. The pervasive anxiety of the gothic is the symptom of the seismic forces it registers. As has been written about the clichés of a fictional character from Freud's era, "The words don't have to make sense so long as they make noise: what he cannot stand is the silence in which his real topic might articulate itself."[16] The very awkwardness of the dreamlike stories is the sign of their power.

Readers commonly comment on the tightness or looseness of gothic novels. *The Italian* is supposedly well composed in comparison with other gothic novels that are less consistent or coherent. But it would be disingenuous for any reader of Fielding, Austen, or Dickens to praise the autotelism of *The Italian*. It is too rife with idle incidents like the guide's tale, with nonce characters like Bonarmo and Margaritone, and with untold stories at its margins. Even central incidents like the suspicious death of Ellena's aunt, Signora Bianchi, remain unresolved to the end. Vivaldi traces Ellena when a chance listener to his tale chances to wonder if she might have been the concealed passenger in a passing carriage (1.9; p. 108). He contacts her when his servant Paolo bribes a gardener who "had sometimes seen Ellena at the window," and he proceeds to plan their escape by a long-distance conversation from a "dangerous" perch beneath her window (1.11; p. 124). Stories can be rescued from oblivion in the nick of time just as characters are; they belong to the realm of buried truths, like the identity of Schedoni and the long-lost Marinella, barely "discovered" through a "faint resemblance" (2.9; p. 226). These contrivances are transparently irrational and reflect the traces left by repressed origins. From the canonical perspective, the proliferation of such untold and badly told stories is unforgivable—and has recently led David Richter to write a book called *The Incoherence of Gothic Conventions*.[17] But from a Freudian perspective it is unforgettable. The value of stories is inseparable from the difficulty there is in getting them told.

The last word in *The Italian* belongs to Vivaldi's servant Paolo and to the chorus of his companions, who repeatedly exclaim, in a foreign tongue, "O! giorno felice!" It is not insignificant that the novel ends with these stereotyped, imported, and inexpressive words. The social order resists the seismic threat of a Neapolitan narrative. In realist novels, as Bruce Robbins eloquently documents, "servant volubility [is] a means of floating submerged perceptions of social inequality over the reefs of censorship . . . and of depositing them before the common view" (*Servant's Hand*, 72). Radcliffe's seeming complacency keeps the social lid on. Thus, in a fine discussion, David Kaufmann calls the novel "blind to questions of class," and it is true that the book is blind to questions of labor (*Business*, 72). But how many eighteenth-century novels apart from *Tristram Shandy*, with its doctors and midwives, depict the work of honest laboring men and women? In the psychological sense, on the other hand, *The Italian* is finely differentiated, and far from condescendingly so; its volubility does succeed in venting the psychic turbulence of real experience.[18] There are no workers in *The Italian*, but there are those on high who know secrets they will not tell and those in the depths who tell secrets they do not know. The whole is pieced together at the end, painfully and perilously, out of bits and pieces that barely escape oblivion time and again. The story the novel tells is not all that complicated, but getting it told is a heroic labor in which the battle between knowledge and narration is brilliantly engaged.[19]

My itinerary has proceeded from literariness through cliché and its concealments to the dynamics of Freud's dream-work. It has concerned the gothic surface throughout—the shellac of style and the evasiveness of the narratives whose "literariness," as one critic has written, offers "a model of the unconscious that eschews naturalised depths in favour of narrative surfaces" (Botting, "Gothic Production," 32, 22). Bad writing is good for the genre—that is as true of romantic gothic as it is of contemporary romance. It gives time for the story to unfold and acceptable means for its messages to make themselves felt. The crucial parts of the books are thus precisely those that seem least in touch with their sensational undercurrents. The successful gothics do their most characteristic work when they seem merely symptomatic, repetitious, or bland. More than any other literary form, these works should be taken at face value, not because the face is "the marble index of a mind" (*Prelude* [1850] 3.62), but because their job is to save face, and to let us know how much saving face costs, and why it is worth the effort.

15

Frankenstein
A Child's Tale

Only inaction is innocent, such as the being
of a stone, not even that of a child.
—Hegel, *Phänomenologie*

MARY SHELLEY WAS UNLUCKY from the moment of her birth. Young as this passionate author was when she wrote *Frankenstein*, she had led a profoundly disrupted life. Perhaps that explains why her wildly excited novel resists settling into any neat pattern of individual or group meanings. It was written with head and heart inseparably, and its turbulent energies overwhelm any ideology we may discern in it. Critics have found it a more or less direct representation of Shelley's biography, a reckoning with the ideas of her parents, a fable of the role of women, an allegory of the unconscious, a critique of family or social structures, an indictment of political turmoil, or of scientific discovery, colonialism, economic theory, capitalist enterprise, or literary production. Their accounts succeed, for Frankenstein's monster spells trouble in almost any imaginable sphere of life. But they do not satisfy.[1]

The present chapter begins by confronting the novel's unruliness head on and continues by linking its form not to the author's beliefs but to her situation. Expression more than representation, *Frankenstein*, like its monster, grips by virtue of its ungraspability. The novel was prompted by the unhappy yearnings of an author who was barely more than a girl when she conceived it. One surmises that it embodies the only form she knew—the unformed, inchoate existence of child-

hood. I undertake to demonstrate the prescient if unthematized intuition of early experience that Shelley's adolescent masterpiece be-
queathed to its readers.

What Is Gothic About *Frankenstein*?
The Question of Form

My operating premise is that thematic readings must give way to formal readings if we are to break the logjam of successful accounts of
the novel's message. Much of the criticism reads like a course in applied Frankensteinics. In linking the novel to concerns familiar from
other romantic writers, critics tend (in varying degrees, of course) to
gloss over what is unique about the book or what links it in particular
with its nominal peer group, the gothic novels. Many essays about
Frankenstein never hint that it is a fantastic tale, and indeed was one
by design. I start, then, where many critics leave off.

For whatever light gothic novels and their ilk might shed on real-
life questions, the world they portray is not like the real world. Critics
who "allegorize" fantastic fiction, as Tzvetan Todorov charges (*Fantastic*, 63–79), reduce it to the mundane. He responds that its very
meaninglessness, or radical uncertainty, produces a triumph of pure
form. Hence for him the fantastic *is* the literary—meaning distilled
into sheer wonder. In a related approach, David Kaufmann has argued that *Frankenstein* undoes definitions: in its "deconstruction of
exemplary readings and stable allegorizations," it offers a utopian
promise of happiness in a Nietzschean realm beyond any definable
truths (*Business*, 63). Aestheticizing critics are unfazed by monsters;
they delight in a world that is "unfinalizable" (Howard, *Reading
Gothic Fiction*, 284). But in steering clear of the Scylla of looming lit-
eralizations, these critics tumble into a dark Charybdis of overgener-
alization. Gothic novels are not the universe, nor pure anything other
than themselves. Todorov confuses the gothic novel's remoteness
from real experience with great generality, as if the gothic were a quin-
tessence rather than a distinctive literary kind.

We cannot escape *Frankenstein*'s grip so easily. "Unfinalizable"
has too ready a ring of Kant's purposeless purpose. However es-
tranged from everyday experience, the gothic is not irrelevant to it.

Pure fantasy is represented by Walton's embarkation on a "wind of promise" (9) toward an imagined "region of beauty and delight" (10). But he at once acknowledges these Kantian formalisms as "day dreams" (9) like those of "a child . . . in a little boat" (10), and bitter cold soon unmasks them as a delusion. Perfection is unattainable. Like the monster, the novel is misshapen; its strength lies in its revelation of its own disabilities, not in their transformation or redemption. The mode of *Frankenstein* is not aesthetic but metaphysical; that is, it characterizes in specific (not generalized) ways the ultimate factors conditioning human experience. Without undue technicality, my account of *Frankenstein* aims to shift from both thematic-particularizing and aesthetic-generalizing discourses toward an abstracting one.

Gothic novels were often produced by apprentice writers. There is typically a struggle either to exploit or to master an unruly surface. Partly because it is shorter than other gothic classics, *Frankenstein* is singularly jolted between violence and reflection. The open-ended novel's exploding frames unsettle its meaning, and neither the turbulent nature imagery nor the angry sociopolitical content can be sublated into pure play. With sublimities too pervasive for Burkean psychologizing and too intensely felt for Kantian moralization, no mere exhortation can tame its adolescent extravagance. In the same landscape, Percy's "Mont Blanc" imagines a "voice . . . to repeal / Large codes of fraud and woe," but Mary's novel does not. It is a diagnosis, not a cure, and for lack of catharsis has never resided comfortably within the aesthetic, high-art canon. Consequently the monster can easily seem more contemporary to twenty-first-century, posthuman sensibilities than to the classics of high romanticism. Like Jean-François Lyotard's "inhuman," Shelley's monster is "*the Thing*" (Lyotard, *Inhuman*, 142), disfigured by a residue of unformed matter that resists our domination. Form and its pathologies are the key to *Frankenstein*'s significance, which must be examined not in order to instill wondering admiration but to acknowledge what the novel's irrationalities open up.

The decisive question is so obvious that it hasn't much troubled critics, namely, what is special about the plot of *Frankenstein*? Probably most readers sense the problem: the book is not as creepy as the movie. The back cover of one cheap paperback describes some of the book's departures from conventional expectations: "Many readers, familiar with the Hollywood movies of *Frankenstein*, and opening the book for the first time, may be surprised not to find themselves transported at once to a remote castle, complete with galvanic flashes and the inarticulate grunts of Boris Karloff" (Airmont ed.). A representative critic, David Richter, expresses the same reaction more formulaically: "Tradition may identify a particular text with a genre even when there are relatively few formal features in common, as Shelley's *Frankenstein* has been identified with the gothic novel" (*Progress of Romance*, 17). Yet *Frankenstein* contains an eeriness beyond mere flamboyance or terror.

For in fact *Frankenstein* is not what it was meant to be. Both Percy's 1818 preface and Mary's 1831 introduction describe the occasion of its composition: the Shelleys had been reading German ghost stories with two friends, Byron and Polidori, and the group had agreed they would each write one of their own.[2] The reports are very explicit: the preface speaks of "a story, founded on some supernatural occurrence"; the introduction relates how frustrated Mary became in trying to conceive "my ghost story,—my tiresome unlucky ghost story!" (*Frankenstein*, 8 and 180; page references here and below are to Crook's edition). The story, beginning with the most tiresome cliché in the books ("It was on a dreary night of November"), was the "short tale" of the monster's creation that became chapter 5 in the final version of the novel. The way the rest of the novel shapes its core tale, however, is something else—something more connected and less amazing. Mary describes a process of composition aimed at constructing a plausible chain of events preceding and succeeding the central nightmare: "Every thing must have a beginning," she says, "and that beginning must be linked to something that went before" (178). Her three narrators—the explorer Walton, who seeks a passage to the North Pole despite all physical and human resistance; the scientist Frankenstein, who irresponsibly creates a living being, then dishonors his solemn promise to create a partner; and the monster, who lacks nurture and self-control—are emotionally disordered, but they are not mad. No grunts and galvanic flashes here.

Rather, in a spirit of logical and psychological plausibility the text repeatedly sidelines gothic models. It resists the form it was meant to exemplify. In the novel it is not Frankenstein but his childhood friend Henry Clerval who "began to write many a tale of enchantment and knightly adventure" (193; in the earlier texts he merely "wrote a fairy tale," 24), whereas Frankenstein enjoyed a more rational upbringing: his father spared him "supernatural horrors," and he never "trembled at a tale of superstition [nor] feared the apparition of a spirit" (35).[3] In boyhood, Frankenstein confesses, he had envisioned "the raising of ghosts or devils" and aspired to "search [for] the philosopher's stone and the elixir of life" (26), which are the subjects of Godwin's supernatural novel *St Leon*. But by the age of fifteen Frankenstein had abandoned such "ardent imagination and childish reasoning" (196; the 1818 text is different, but to similar effect) in favor of electricity and, in the 1818 text, hydraulic and steam engines. Even the "almost supernatural enthusiasm" of his quest to create life is but a methodical intensity, "not . . . the vision of a madman" (36) nor "like a magic scene" (36). When he plans to create a female monster, he prudently consults specialists to get "the information necessary for the completion of my promise" (121); and, in any case, unlike the movie versions, very little of the novel is given over to the processes or the moments of creation. Much later, after destroying the almost completed female companion, Frankenstein "walked about the isle like a restless spectre" (131), but even this figure of speech lacks the pervasive resonance of similar similes that Terry Castle has examined in Radcliffe. Finally, near the end, when a skeptical magistrate in Geneva "heard my story with that half kind of belief that is given to a tale of spirits and supernatural events" (153), Frankenstein and Walton both insist on its truth and—more importantly for what I shall have to say later on— its consistency: Frankenstein says that it "is too connected to be mistaken for a dream" (152); Walton that it "is connected, and told with an appearance of the simplest truth" (159). Arguably these characters protest too much; the novel is, for sure, unusual. Still, whatever one may say about *Frankenstein*, its monster is assuredly no ghost.[4]

What, then, is supernatural about the plot of *Frankenstein*? Originally "supernatural" was a religious term referring to god and angels.

Sometimes in *Frankenstein* "supernatural" does mean magical, as it regularly does in Radcliffe and Godwin, but this was still probably not the commonest sense of the term. The earliest unambiguous instance of this sense recorded in the *OED* comes from Walter Scott in 1830. Before then, the word seems typically to have implied exceeding rather than violating nature—in Kantian terminology, a mathematical rather than a dynamic sublime. So, at first appearance the monster is said to be "of gigantic stature" (16). But at eight feet (indeed, "7 or eight feet" in the original manuscript; *Notebooks*, 85), it would deserve to be called impressive but not titanic.[5] The monster does leap across vast chasms of ice and is "capable of scaling the overhanging sides of Mont Salêve" (55), and it runs "with greater speed than the flight of an eagle" (110), as Frankenstein says at one place, or "with more than mortal speed" (155), as he says at another. Yet it's hard to know how much to credit these phrases: when wrestling with Felix De Lacey, the monster reports being grabbed "with supernatural force," yet remains confident that it could tear Felix "limb from limb" (101). Here "supernatural" clearly just means "a lot." The monster's physical accomplishments seem disproportionate even to its unusual stature, but still they are supernatural only in the older and weaker sense also used for Felix's wrestling: they are quantitatively impressive, not qualitatively alien.

Other aspects of the plot, however, are harder to explain, even if less flamboyant. How does the monster so infallibly track Frankenstein? Though rarely seen, it appears always to be close at hand and never at a loss for means of locomotion and transport. If a single glimpse of it at a great distance leaves Walton awestruck, how is it able to remain unnoticed as it follows Frankenstein to "one of the remotest" of the Orkney Islands—"a place" that is "hardly more than a rock"—and then watches over him for an extended period (126)? Similarly, at the end, the monster passes out of sight before Frankenstein is rescued by Walton's boat: how does it know when it is being amateurishly tracked and where Frankenstein has left off? Nothing in the novel is presumed to violate the laws of nature, but there is much like this in the plotting that remains unaccountable. Food is always to be found, and weather is not a problem. Though early in its existence the monster sometimes suffers from the cold, later it promises to live easily in the wilds of South America, saying that its "food is not that of man" (109), and according to Frankenstein it can "exist in the ice caves of the glaciers" and possesses "faculties it would be vain to cope with" (110). A mental prodigy as well as a physical one, the monster apparently learns to manage fire without trial and error and to speak without active practice: it says it acquired French pronunciation "with tolerable ease" (86)—which is not true of babies who must practice sounds for years—and within a few months it becomes so fluent that the blind De Lacey takes it for a native. To a great extent the monster's supernatural facility is shared by other characters. While slower than the monster, Frankenstein still claims, in the 1818 text, to have mastered English and German "perfectly," along with Latin, and to have begun to read Greek by the age of 17 (28). Shelley's humans, like her monster, learn with astonishing ease, surmount incredible hardships, arrive at their destinations (Safie), accomplish their goals (Frankenstein), travel beyond the limits of everyday possibility (Walton), communicate across linguistic boundaries, and generally conclude their labors on time and on budget. Mundane normality is represented by Walton's sister, to whom his letters are addressed, and she is not heard from in the novel.

In short, *Frankenstein* is supernatural to the extent that it takes the form of a charmed world. Its representative landscapes—the far North, the high altitudes, the remotest corners of Europe—lie beyond ordinary human experience. Humans are subject to limits, as Walton perhaps is in the Arctic, even though his name means "the powerful one." But Frankenstein and his monster are different. Whereas picaresque novels travel roads, and realist novels (as Stendhal famously said) learned to mirror highways, *Frankenstein*'s journeys are incipient or terminated, not in process. Even Walton's adventure proceeds by seven-league boots, with the epistolary form encouraging a record of finished accomplishments. His first letter, from St. Petersburg, says, "I arrived here yesterday" (9); the second, from Archangel, "a second step is taken. . . . I have hired a vessel, and am occupied in collecting my sailors" (12); the third, "I am safe, and well advanced on my voyage" (15). He thinks his power is unbounded, "the very stars themselves being witnesses and testimonies of my triumph" (185; not in 1818). Eight feet tall is nothing. Here, in line with Walton's initial irresponsibility, megalomania meets child's play. The novel consists of situations and dramatic encounters, eliding labor and process.

The gothic of *Frankenstein* is thus defined by its disjunctness. Whatever the "consistency" of its internal narrative, the story as a whole lacks continuity. Its characters favor dark and enclosed spaces, or they exist with a kind of sacred invisibility behind visible nature, as does the monster much of the time, and as does Frankenstein in the Orkneys, where he is "ungazed at and unmolested" (127). *Frankenstein*'s gothic is *in* our world and yet not *of* it.[6] And its temporality is likewise disjunctive—intermittent or repetitious, without growth and gradual change. The long months that Frankenstein spends in his library are as if out of time. To him they are "like a hurricane," in "a resistless, and almost frantic impulse," like "a passing trance" (37–38). Yet he remains incommunicado—dead to the world even in the middle of Ingolstadt. Presumably Frankenstein must eat while at work, but all we learn is that his consuming passion ate him: it "swallowed up every habit of my nature" (38). The materials in Frankenstein's "workshop of filthy creation" (38) are a kind of antimatter, stealthily collected from the refuse of ordinary life. This world lacks what Kant calls "reciprocity" with the ordinary world; that is, while it may follow natural laws in their own right, it does not participate in an exchange of qualities with ordinary matter. The monster is forced to rove at night and skulk by day, for, as Frankenstein says to it on behalf of all humans, "There can be no community between you and me" (74). Matter and antimatter do not interact; there is no inertia or resistance governing their encounters. Either actions misfire totally, or causes work their effects with unregulated intensity. Frankenstein describes the monster's powers in terms of strength, but a strength that cannot be resisted really reflects an absolutism of the will; hence, the monster isn't pure physicality, as Frankenstein insinuates, but pure volition.[7] Alien to the material world, it takes no captives. Either it is reduced to blubber at the first encounter—which is what happens to it emotionally—or it is condemned to annihilate what it meets.

The book's effective axis is matter-spirit, shunning any potential pun on *Geist* and lying perpendicular to the nature-magic axis.

The physical world observes quantitative laws; the supernatural appears when its nature changes. Quantity (the right number of bones, a measurable height) is converted to quality (a living soul, superhuman strength).[8] One of the book's commonest turns of phrase reflects the way a mass or heap can abruptly become an uncanny enemy. For both Frankenstein and his author have a counting problem. "Fear overcame me; I dared not advance, dreading a thousand nameless evils that made me tremble, although I was unable to define them" (53). Frankenstein's "thousand" here is his futile attempt to pretend that the nameless could somehow be computed. But it cannot. The book is obsessed with failed enumeration. Here is Walton: "When my guest was a little recovered, I had great trouble to keep off the men, who wished to ask him a thousand questions; but I would not allow him to be tormented by their idle curiosity" (17). Here is Frankenstein on the teacher who stimulated his inhuman passion: "In a thousand ways he smoothed for me the path of knowledge, and made the most abstruse enquiries clear and facile to my apprehension" (201; not in 1818). Here is the monster, in a sentimental vein: "If any being felt emotions of benevolence towards me, I should return them an hundred and an hundred fold; for that one creature's sake, I would make peace with the whole kind!" (108). Frankenstein on the female monster: "she might become ten thousand times more malignant than her mate" (128). And in reaction to the monster's death threat: "my imagination conjured up a thousand images to torment and sting me" (131). And the delirium only increases as the book proceeds. "This suspense is a thousand times worse than the most horrible event" (139); "a thousand feelings pressed upon me. . . . my dreams presented a thousand objects that scared me" (141); "a thousand times would I have shed my own blood, drop by drop, to have saved their lives; but I could not, my father, indeed, I could not sacrifice the whole human race" (143). The totality exceeds definition—not that the monster is measurably too big, but that it is somehow, unaccountably, too much to grasp. It can be made, perhaps even in a sense born, but it cannot be conceived.[9]

The monster has no name because it has no one to give it a name. No one, that is, stands in a natural relationship to it. Since (as part of the novel's anti-gothic struggle toward consistency) the monster yearns for its creator, it normally calls itself Frankenstein's "creature." Yet it repeatedly calls humans "creatures," not because it shares an identity with them but only because it sees in them an alliance with a creator and desires the same for itself. Meanwhile, except in moments of creation, Frankenstein and the other humans variously call it "monster," "fiend," "dæmon," and "devil." Perhaps it is best just called a "being" (16, 107).[10] Or perhaps the most appropriate term is "thing"; Frankenstein uses that word next to "creature" as he is destroying the female monster (129), and his own creatureliness is destroyed in return, as he later says: "no creature had ever been so miserable as I was" (151). "No creature," not "no other creature"—at this point Frankenstein has lost his creatureliness altogether. He has become set apart, plagued.[11] That is the fate of a monster, as Mary Shelley could have learned from her father:

> How unhappy the wretch, the monster rather let me say, who is without an equal; who looks through the world, and in the world cannot find a brother; who is endowed with attributes which no living being participates with him; and who is therefore cut off for ever from all cordiality and confidence, can never unbend himself, but lives the solitary, joyless tenant of a prison, the materials of which are emeralds and rubies.
>
> (Godwin, *St Leon*, 211)

Disjunct, unregulated, unbounded. No wonder the monster's skin doesn't fit. It lacks a properly positioned selfhood. Romantic philosophers taught that identities require a boundary. For Kant the issue was a boundary *between*—between consciousness and matter, subject and object, empirical and transcendent. For Fichte, perhaps more relevantly, it was an outer boundary. For him, to posit a self means to limit a will. Thoughts are free, but only the existence of an outside world confronting and limiting the thoughts can make them real. Pure self-consciousness is like a solipsistic dream verging on a life-denying nightmare. Without a proper determination, the self can *do* anything but can *accomplish* nothing, and that is precisely the dilemma of the monster at the heart of Shelley's novel. Its gothic is a disorder in the relationship of the self to the not-self (that is Fichte's terminology), of mind to body, of cause to effect.

The control of causality is a crucial problem in worlds where magic reigns or where, as in *Frankenstein*, the intellect can accomplish impossible goals. The inscrutability of magic precipitates the final catastrophe of Godwin's *St Leon*, where the corrupted title character is confronted by his virtuous son: "When I consider the mystery and inscrutableness of your character, I am lost in conjecture. You are said to be a magician, a dealer in the unhallowed secrets of alchymy and the *elixir vitae*. In cases like this, all the ordinary rules of human sagacity and prudence are superseded" (473). And the more general problem governs, for instance, Charlotte Dacre's *Zofloya*, which opens as follows: "The historian who would wish his lessons to sink deep into the heart, thereby essaying to render mankind virtuous and more happy, must not content himself with simply detailing a series of events—he must ascertain causes, and follow progressively their effects; he must draw deductions from incidents as they arise, and ever revert to the actuating principle" (39).[12] Shelley takes Dacre's injunction to heart. From the start, Walton attributes to Frankenstein "a penetration into the causes of things, unequalled for clearness and precision" (187; the 1818 text already speaks of "causes," though more casually [19]). In preparation for creating a monster, Frankenstein says he had to "examine the causes of life" and "analys[e] all the minutiæ of causation" (35–36), and in his "fervent longing to penetrate the secrets of nature" he blames "the most learned philosopher" because, "not to speak of a final cause, causes in their secondary and tertiary grades were utterly unknown to him" (195; not in 1818). And a manuscript passage in the first chapter that Mary eventually canceled contrasts Frankenstein's desire "to analyze the causes" of lightning with Henry's fancy "that the Fairies and giants were at war" (*Notebooks*, 31). The highest conviction arises, as we have seen, from a narrative that is "connected."

But of course gothic narratives cannot thus perspicuously connect. They must be utterly remarkable, produced by the most surprising and inexplicable occurrences. Even in Radcliffe's novels, where the supposedly supernatural incidents are eventually explained, contingencies and frayed ends of stories abound. In *Frankenstein*, too, the marvelous is by no means limited to the monster's creation. The very next day Frankenstein uncannily prognosticates the arrival of his friend Henry Clerval, who has come searching for him: "Here I paused, I knew not why," says Frankenstein, "but I remained some minutes with my eyes fixed on a coach that was coming towards me"—the very coach carrying his friend, just past the nick of time (41). It may not be entirely a "strange chance" (155), as Frankenstein claims, when he later glimpses the monster he is pursuing, for the monster may want to tantalize him, but it is surely a product of "strange coincidences" (136) when the storm-tossed boat he has taken from the Orkneys lands precisely at the Irish village where Henry has been murdered. The monster's narrative features even more incidents of providential character that seem incompatible with the predictability of efficient causality: when it is cold it finds a fire "through accident" (78); when it has food to store it finds a wallet (79); as a reward for its good deeds it finds clothes and books (95); it learns its origin through "some papers in the pocket of the dress which I had taken from your laboratory" (97); when it seeks vengeance, a sudden "impulse" (106) leads it to the doomed William Frankenstein, who gives himself away by blurting out his surname and who chances to be wearing the picture of his mother that the monster deposits on an innocent woman he stumbles upon, who proves to be Justine, from the same household, and who is convicted after she falls ill and a servant "happen[s] to examine the apparel she had worn on the night of the murder" (56). No wonder, after such an accumulation of improbabilities, that she is "confused" (56)! Safie locates her lover through "some papers of her father's, which fell into her hands" (94); Felix De Lacey meets Safie after having "accidentally been present" at her father's trial (214; "accidentally" is an 1823 addition). Indeed, between these coincidences and numerous other incidents there are differences more of degree than of kind.[13] Consider, for instance, the stormy weather on the disrupted wedding night and the foundling Elizabeth's fairytale-like origin (in the 1831 text), not to mention the happenstance of Walton's framing encounters with Frankenstein and the monster. Such accidents are hardly the stuff of a seamlessly connected and probable narrative.

Coincidence can be understood in two seemingly opposing ways. On the one hand, a coincidence is something that happens by chance: the figures who happen to meet have no reason to be in the same place together. On the other hand, where coincidences accumulate, they suggest a guiding hand that leaves nothing to chance. The improbable becomes the inevitable, and contingency takes on the coloration of fate: "The bizarre coincidences that are produced to explain the supernatural are . . . evidence of a higher supernaturalism that ensures that every 'accident' has its rightful place in the schema of Divine Justice" (Clery, *Rise*, 112, writing about Radcliffe). Hence Freud takes the superabundance of coincidence to be one of the defining characteristics of the uncanny.[14] The terror of *Frankenstein* lies in the collapse of the antinomial categories of reason into a grotesque deformation of the order of experience. The narrative is perfectly connected with a ring of inevitability, but not with a logic humans can live by. The normal and the pathological can scarcely be distinguished. "Noble and godlike in ruin" (160), Frankenstein acquires the same Satanic tinge as the Milton-echoing monster, who "sit[s] among the ruins, and lament[s] the fall" (168). If critics cannot agree on the morality of the novel, cannot decide whose side, if any, Shelley is on, that is because of an epistemological collapse inherent in the conception of monstrosity. What is gothic about *Frankenstein* is the fact that it is—not just that it is about—a monster.

A Monster's Tale

Discussions of the monster almost always focus on its meaning for the human characters in the novel or for the book's human author, Mary Shelley. They treat the monster, that is, as one character among many. The monster does, after all, represent itself as filled with human thoughts and emotions, and the tendency to treat it as one more personage in the drama is encouraged by some critics' preference to refer to it by its self-chosen name of "creature" rather than by the novel's preferred, more inhuman designations, such as "monster." But their respectful acknowledgment of the monster casts the book as precisely what it can never be. If we ask instead what the monster means for the book, what it means to write a book around a monster, we focus the questions differently and, as I have been suggesting, with more specific bearing on the novel's form.[15]

By definition (and common usage in Shelley's day), a monster is a being without a place in the cosmic order. A book about a monster lacks a stable ground for experience. In *Frankenstein* none of the usual candidates for an ordering principle holds against the monster's onslaughts. Confronting a monster, religion proves witless. Religious *institutions* are represented only by the minister who coerces the innocent servant girl Justine Moritz into a false confession. Religious *mores* are manifested in Islam's abhorrent treatment of women, the imprisoning harem from which the half-Turkish Safie De Lacey runs away—into the arms of the monster, as it were. And even the genuinely admirable Christian *tenets* that Safie adopts from her mother and the "brotherly love and charity" offered by the blind elder De Lacey collapse in the revulsion aroused by the sight of the monster. One glimpse of it and their life lies in ruins, while the monster appropriates the language of religion, via Milton, to utter its self-recriminations: "I, like the arch fiend, bore a hell within me" (102). Nor is the social order any more dependable. Families are dysfunctional throughout the novel, and the larger social groupings cohere via denial, including locked city gates and the inhospitable Irish villagers' suspicions of English inhospitality.[16] Critics differ as to whether the monster disrupts the scheme of things or brings out the monstrosity inherent within them, but either way its story cannot be rightly told. Otherwise it would be not a monster but merely a freak.

For, as Peter Brooks has made especially vivid ("What Is a Monster?" 83), the question "What is a monster?" becomes equivalent to this other question: What language is adequate to a monster? The novel's problems of form are echoed by its problems of expression. When it first encounters language, the monster calls it a "godlike science," but "godlike" is the word later used for Frankenstein's miscreative activity (160) and for the monster's obviously undependable judgment that humans are "all that can be conceived of noble and godlike" when they aren't "a mere scion of the evil principle" (89). The weakness of Walton, the injustice that befalls Justine, and the black ballots that erroneously attest to her "blackest ingratitude" (60) all point to the proclivity of names and of language to mislead in dealing with unfathomable things. Frankenstein warns that speaking too loudly can precipitate an avalanche (72; and see Ferguson, *Solitude*, 105), and, as if in verification, his ensuing exclamation brings on the monster (*Frankenstein*, 73). Walton, who has to communicate through the defective medium of writing despite calling himself almost "illiterate" (13), is bowled over first by the eloquence of the "divine wanderer" Frankenstein (19; also see 160) and then, at the end, by the monster's "powers of eloquence and persuasion" (168). But while Frankenstein, despite hating the sight of the monster, resists the monster's covering his eyes (75), Walton has to shut his eyes in order to listen to it (167), and its best listener—or true dupe—is the blind old De Lacey. Not that the monster lies. Far from it, for it speaks with the profoundest sincerity. But it speaks from a position beyond identity and hence beyond determinations of truth or falsity. Language is undone by its transcendence.

Throughout the book the monster is identified with the glaring sun. According to Frankenstein's narrative, the monster's conception is "a light so brilliant and wondrous" that "the sun does not more surely shine in the heavens, than that which I now affirm is true" (36). There can be no doubt that this is the monster's light, for Frankenstein himself works in the dark, "aided only by one glimmering, and seemingly ineffectual, light" (36). Hence Frankenstein curses the light of day (75) and swears by earth and Night (154), whereas the monster swears by the sun and heaven (110) and invokes earth when cursing "the cause of my being" (104). The monster tells its story from midday to sundown (75, 110), in a hut that protects Frankenstein from the cold glare and by a fire that the monster has lighted. Frankenstein's story, while told by day, is written down at night (20). He begins his confidences "in dark gloom" and with his hands shading his eyes (186; not in 1818, but the tonalities are similar), though "the starry sky" and other beauties of nature "have the power of elevating his soul from the earth" (28). Men seek to conquer the vast unknown by exploring the secrets of nature as Walton does or the secrets of the intellectual world as Frankenstein does, but a man's reflections are "gloomy and narrow" (25) and depend upon the safety of dark and confined spaces—drifting boats or feminine domesticity. A light that cannot be faced, the monster reflects back to humans their buried drives and obsessions. The monster is thus merely encouraging Frankenstein's native darkness when it vows to make him hate "the light of day" and "curse the sun" (130). For the scientist, for the book, and for readers, the monster is a figure of an impossible truth.

Truth (in the definition used by Kant) is the coincidence of a perception with a judgment. But the monster cannot be properly perceived because it cannot be looked at without panic, and it cannot be properly judged because it has no name with which to formulate an objective statement about it. The conflicting versions of its story, all of them disturbed, reflect the antinomy at the heart of the genre: what we know about the monster and what it knows (or feels) about itself are irreconcilable. That is the pathos of the sympathetic demon in a great many gothic novels. Nor can monstrosity be localized; it pops up in the most out-of-the-way places. Linguists might call the monster on the ice floes a floating signifier, a lexeme whose meaning varies contextually. For the monster exists beyond or before language, not within it. Uncannily precocial, it hardly stirs before it walks, feeds, and clothes itself, and within days it has begun to think (naturally, about cause and effect, the precipitating topic of the gothic), long before it learns about speech.[17] Thought without speech is the mental equivalent of existence without a proper body or identity without a name. In all facets of its being, the monster instantiates the limits of the thinkable. Thus does the gothic irrationality of the novel's form prove commutative with an ideological quandary. No matter how intensely the narrators desire coherence, the story refuses to take a distinct shape. The problem is not that it fails to get told; indeed, this work, like many other gothic novels from *The Castle of Otranto* on, includes a plethora of tellers. Yet the monster's story defies comprehension. It becomes a threshold or limit case—an exception of dubious value in proving any rules.

The disturbance affects the moral arena most of all. The meticulous Kantian formulations of the moral imperative illuminate the problem. The moral imperative applies the golden rule to all like creatures, but how much likeness is requisite? Sometimes Kant extends the principle to rational beings, sometimes to humanity, sometimes to nature in general. And sometimes he hedges, notably in the cardinal seventh section of the *Critique of Practical Reason*, containing the "Fundamental Law of Pure Practical Reason." The law states, "Act so that the maxim of your will could always count simultaneously as the principle of a general legislation" (A54), while the corollary adds a parenthetical specification to humans: "Pure reason is practical in and of itself, and gives (to men) a general law which we call the *moral law*" (A56). Are men always rational beings? Are they the only rational beings? Are they the proper subject of the moral law, contingent subjects, or mere examples of a greater good? And how is the moral law given—as an order is given, or as a gift? Kant's recourse to parenthetical qualification here and elsewhere points up the problem of human identity, and hence that of coexistence with a monster.[18] How specific is the moral species? Is the monster one of us? What do we owe it, and what does it owe us?

Therefore, instead of a final dispensation, the story of a monster at the limit of the tellable concludes irresolutely, even incoherently. The legitimating epistolary frame is not only forgotten but positively dissolved into legend. As Walton says, hardly seeming to think any longer of the sister to whom his narrative is purportedly addressed, "the tale which I have detailed would be incomplete without this final and wonderful catastrophe" (166). Like all other auditors of the monster, Walton cannot look at it; he declares, "I shut my eyes involuntarily," and insists, "I dared not again raise my looks upon his face" (167). How is it, then, that between these two denials he can pretend to describe the monster's appearance and gestures: "He paused, looking on me with wonder . . . , and every feature and gesture seemed instigated by the wildest rage of some uncontrollable passion" (167)? The narrative loses its bearings; it ends with an unresolved dissonance when the monster imagines a glorious fiery death on a funeral pyre and then jumping onto the ice that carries it into "darkness and distance" (170). The monster's vision of glorious extinction is self-evidently grandiose and hallucinatory. The monster cannot transcend its nature through physical destruction, let alone through mere flight, so it continues to besiege the reader's imagination even after it has floated away. In a novel striking for its lack of an epilogue, out of sight is not out of mind. The novel's mysteries, willfully irrational plotting, and broken form constitute a psychic rift that cannot be overcome. Monstrosity haunts the novel from within. Silly ghost stories are otherworldly dalliances, whereas *Frankenstein* projects dilemmas of coherence and comprehension that are a permanent challenge for narration. Could we be confident that the monster had left the world, we could write off the novel as escapist. But it is not. For a monster always lurking to bring home justice or revenge remains a universal terror. That is why *Frankenstein* is so easily but mistakenly allegorized into one or another material or situational problem. It implies all the cases to which critics reduce it, but remains more pervasive than any of them.

The Monster and the Child

As befits a work of imagination, *Frankenstein* follows instinct rather than demonstration in its diagnosis of the human condition; it has no explicit name for its fears. It is characteristic of literary insight to intuit an issue of which there was as yet no conceptual grasp. Literature is forever untimely in this sense; indeed, it loses its aura when it falls too comfortably within the horizon of understanding. Its meaning is a legacy for us to hunt.

Frankenstein is too anticipatory an achievement and too enduring a legend, too quick and too slow at once. The gothic novel seems perpetually out of time in this way. Here the impossible funeral pyre remains an unquenchable flash in the pan. The monster's terminal gesture eternizes adolescent delusions of glory, as, throughout, its self-congratulatory defiance perpetuates the juvenile air of all the characters. Bratty to the end, the monster will not distinguish vindication from vindictiveness. Romantic gothic novels always contain elements of childish thrill, wonder, or fear. *Frankenstein* began as a game—Percy's preface speaks of "a playful desire of imitation" (8), and Mary's introduction abounds with allusions both to her birth and to her childhood. Her narrator Walton, physically mature but less educated than "many school-boys of fifteen," was raised on "day dreams" and occasional adventure tales (13), and from the start his Arctic is a fairytale land where "snow and frost are banished" (10). Frankenstein and his monster both idealize childhood, describe it at length and in infatuated terms, imagine themselves and others in the guise of children. They speak with childish bravado (130: "I am fearless, and therefore powerful"); they dream of children, yearn for children, and appear infantile to others, like the Genevan magistrate who "endeavoured to soothe me as a nurse does a child" (173). Birth fantasies and womblike retreats figure prominently, as all readers recognize, but the entire perspective of the helpless mortal confronting a large and powerful figure with a poor complexion itself also reproduces in distorted form infantile experiences and neuroses.

Finally, what can corroborate the book's untimeliness, though rarely if ever noticed by critics, is the infantile character of the monster's desire for a female companion. It makes its demand on Frankenstein immediately after confessing to two passionate and jealous crimes: first, the murder of William, who is portrayed as "a beautiful child, who came running into the recess I had chosen with all the sportiveness of infancy" (106); second, the betrayal of the servant girl Justine by planting false evidence on her. The 1831 text adds an erotic coloration to the second crime, but even then only a fairytale variety, evoking Prince Charming coming to his child-bride: "Awake, fairest, thy lover is near" (216; not in 1818). When the monster demands a female monster, Frankenstein presumes that it desires a bride and offspring, "sexual satisfaction" in the words of one critic, "monogamous wedlock with a complementary mate" according to another.[19] Yet what the monster actually says is this: "Shall each man . . . find a wife for his bosom, and each beast have his mate, and I be alone?" (130). Since it is neither man nor beast, the only literal content of the complaint here is the deprivation of companionship. (Indeed, might not the sailor Walton understand "mate" to mean a shipmate, and a child understand it as a playmate?) But the monster's first model of a blissful existence is the threesome of blind father, son, and daughter, who is called the "companion" of both her father and her mother (81, 82); and in William the monster had fantasized and then lost a playmate, "my companion and friend" (106). From its new female "companion" (the same word used for William), it seeks "sympathy"—a

word that often characterizes same-sex friendship—and "the affections of a sensitive being" (110), echoing language that Walton's second letter uses to address and to describe his sister Margaret. Sharing
a begetter, the two monsters would be siblings, and nothing in Percy's
ideology of love allows a neat separation of sexual from fraternal
emotions. Frankenstein, after all, is the one who conceives of marrying Elizabeth, his playmate and "sister," as his father calls her (117)
—his "more than sister" in his own words (192, not in 1818)—and
only he imagines the two monsters proceeding to have children. It is
notable that at the very moment when the monster demands a "creature of another sex," it repeatedly insists that it is nothing like "man"
(109). Sexual feelings are often evoked, according to the language of
men that the monster has learned, but attenuated throughout; hence
the homosexual overtones often found within the heterosexual discourse. For while the monster is large, its skin is "shrivelled" (40): it
remains emotionally stunted, neither growing up, successfully separating itself from its daddy, nor finding a home. Even if it desires a
bride, in short, the incestuous passion would preserve its infantile
character.

The infantile and primitive character of the gothic seems to me its
most distinctive contribution to the history of the human imagination.[20] Roughly contemporaneous with the development of the literary fairytale, gothic narratives differ from them in being written not
for children but as if from within a child's sensibility. What distinguishes the gothic, thus understood, has little to do with the marvelous. Swift's Gulliver, after all, explores reaches as remote as Walton's;
encounters physical, moral, emotional, and scientific monsters; finds
himself in situations of immense power and utter weakness; has a vision of the end of the human race; and goes mad—yet the experience
of reading *Gulliver's Travels* is totally unlike that of reading *Frankenstein*. Rather, the sensibility of the gothic arises from its exceptionally
undirected and unregulated emotions. Adults play by the rules, but
children allow games to get out of hand, with an intensity of involve-
ment that puts them, in Hogg's fine phrase, "beyond sport" (*Private
Memoirs*, 22). In the gothic, fathers and other authority figures conduct themselves with the peremptoriness of little children, yet they remain as futile as any neighborhood bully. And if Frankenstein roves,

so too do William, Justine, Safie, and Walton, all under the sign of the monster, who becomes an all-embracing figure for the childishly un-regulated spirit. Characters are alternately babyish and babied, mag-isterial, manipulative, and furtive.[21]

The childish feelings portrayed in gothic novels are the determi-nants of behavior, yet they lack determinacy, with love being insepa-rable from hate, need from desire. (That is why the fixing of blame can become such an endless sport for critics.) Childishly, the gothic sub-lime confuses the self with the objects of its perceptions. In "the glori-ous presence-chamber of imperial Nature," as the 1831 text calls it (212), the grandeur of the landscape simultaneously overwhelms and consoles; it is alien yet allied and even subject to the self. In a dream, Frankenstein sees the Alps "congregated round me," as if to serve him, yet when he awakes they are covered in mist, "so that I even saw not the faces of those mighty friends" (212–13). As duplicitous as Kirwin or as Alphonse Frankenstein, the landscape is both near and remote, enveloping and forbidding, projection and boundary of the self.

The mind that cannot disentangle (Freud's term is *entmischen*, "de-fuse") either its perceptions or its emotions is the slave of the world it dreams of mastering. The terror of the monster is that of a calculation gone awry. As multiplication turns exponential, and as the more-than-natural proves transcendental, the child confronts the powerlessness of a supposedly all-powerful imagination. Heading off for the university with a child's ardor to prove himself and "enter the world" (31), Frankenstein stakes his fortune on conquering nature through mastering scientific rationality. But he loses control of mate-rial causality when greater purposes combine to overwhelm him, as wind and weather cooperate with the monster to work Frankenstein's demise. The external world becomes a reserve of energy almost as nameless as the monster itself. An inexplicable teleology subjugates the freedom we feel within us to a controlling fate, rendering what seemed malleable as hard as ice and what seemed predictable as capri-cious as a mountain storm. At the height of his mountain ecstasy, just before the monster appears, Frankenstein quotes the last eight lines of Percy Shelley's sonnet "Mutability," which in this setting portrays what the world feels like to the uncomprehending child:

> We rest; a dream has power to poison sleep.
> We rise; one wand'ring thought pollutes the day.
>   . . .
> Man's yesterday may ne'er be like his morrow;
> Nought may endure but mutability.
>
> (*Frankenstein*, 73)

Frankenstein, then, is just as horrible as it seems. Like a child's game described from the loser's perspective, it toys with our sensibilities. To reduce the gothic to the status of imaginative fantasy is not an adequate response to the complexity of the novel.

On the other hand, *Frankenstein* is not horrible in the ways that it often seems. While it does not forecast a Nietzschean extravagance, it does lie beyond good and evil in the negative sense that it trumps the moral questioning supporting ideological readings. The monster is inescapable because it emerges from within all of us. *Frankenstein* portrays an essential even though invisible reality, the monstrosity that Mary Shelley intuits at the core of childhood.

All the passions in *Frankenstein* are unregulated. Parental figures are either brutal or inconceivably tender, fraternal relations loving in impulse and suffocating in outcome, loves doomed, social institutions a perversion of reason, justice, and hospitality. The tellers—guilty victims all—cannot possibly make sense of a world so far out of control, subject to both natural and cultural forces of the utmost pervasiveness and unpredictability. Walton, Frankenstein, and the nameless monster all see their worlds from a position of helplessness. Desperately, if irrationally, they want both to join and to escape. As frame figure, Walton leaps from a "land of angels" in the West to a town called Archangel in the northeast, from the "Paradise of my own creation" that he has dreamed to the "country of eternal light that he seeks" (11, 10). He cannot or will not cope with the Middle Earth of civil life and mature responsibility. Nor will the novel as a whole, in its actions, its narrative incongruities, the mishmash of its form. It shows us, rather, what the rest of us have escaped from in growing up.

There have always been children. But there has not always been childhood, at least not as a state of mind. Norbert Elias deduced from studying conduct books that adults in eras before the seventeenth and eighteenth centuries were no more "civilized" than children: "The degree of restraint and control over drives expected by adults of each other was not much greater than that imposed on children. The distance between adults and children, measured by that of today, was slight."²² Latin made do with three terms that approximate what we think of as childhood: *infans* for the helpless young; *liberi* for offspring; and most commonly *puer*, a son (or, by extension, child generally), connoting sonship as a social condition or legal status. The last equates with the normal Greek term, παῖς, which is set off against babyhood only by a neuter diminutive, παιδίον. Likewise in German, the neuter *Kind* covered the whole range of experiences and conditions through adolescence. In contemporary German *Kind* has been supplemented by a late English import, *das Baby*, a diminutive of "babe," which, according to the *OED*, was itself only gradually restricted to infancy. The situation is little different in the Romance languages. To be sure, it was possible to think of childhood as a class, as Philippe Aries has theorized.²³ Increasingly, too, and more in line with *Frankenstein*, is a sense of childhood as a separate race, implicated in all the utopian or colonialist feelings about "natives" throughout the world. (In the *Ode on a Distant Prospect of Eton College*, Thomas Gray calls children "a sprightly race," who should be sheltered in "their paradise," though condemned eventually to endure all the torments of "men.") The word "child" itself tended to shade off into the sense of a servant, slave, or primitive. But that usage gradually grew outmoded, as childhood increasingly came to be viewed as a state within rather than a condition outside adult humanity. Whatever its much-debated resonance, Wordsworth's "The child is father to the man" conveys an inherence: Wordsworthian childhood is not outgrown or left behind as we age. Romantic idealization dematerialized childhood, so that it was no longer a species but only an aura. Only then, in Mary Shelley's era, did the child become a vision. "Sometimes produced through retrospective reclamation of the self embalmed within, sometimes constructed as a sequestered pastoral solitary, the Romantic child serves as a buffer against the vicissitudes of the public sphere. By *growing down*, the adult can insulate himself as a child self from the shocks of history, and also ally himself in fellowship with true timeless childhood, thus blotting out the actual contemporary ugliness of child exploitation" (Plotz, *Romanticism*, 39).

We have become accustomed to regarding the romantic child as an image of unspoiled, untainted perfection. Rousseau above all promoted such an ideal. Its most recent and outspoken proponent has been James Kincaid, who would like to make children of us all by ridding us of our adult anxieties. Childhood for him is "a melancholy fix on a golden time that we all slip away from" and that we should hold onto (*Child-Loving*, 51). Kincaid's book aims to evacuate all cultural fears by ventilating them. "The standard narrative manages to package all the horror gothic-style, fashioning an Outsider as monster and thus protecting us from the more knowing shadow-stories of incest and the seduction of children by those who are loved and trusted." He wants to "tell the story of the story" by "speak[ing] what is marginal and unspeakable." "Deconstructing the story we love to tell and believe, the story of the monster does give us a glimpse of another tale to tell!" (357). Maybe in the long run he is right in thus reinstating the most ardently innocent kind of romanticism. But it cannot be done without confronting the sources of the stories of childhood terror.

Judith Plotz's recent book explores the rifts within the romantic idealization of childhood. She discusses Wordsworth, for instance, under the title "More Clouds Than Glories: Wordsworth and the Sequestered Child," moving from the projection of the child of nature to a glimpse of the triumph of children over parents. Her chapter "Charles Lamb and the Child Within" culminates in "innocent guilt"; "Little Mr. De Quincey and the Affliction of Childhood" moves from fraternal sadomasochism toward adult anorexia; and, finally, "The Case of Hartley Coleridge: The Designated Genius," portrays an adorable and adored, self-conscious and self-centered, irresponsible child who grows into a failed adult. The beautiful child never came without its costs.

Other studies, from other perspectives, touch more or less systematically on the dark sides of the little angels of the house, that is, on "corruption in paradise," as Reinhard Kuhn has it in the title of his plot-oriented literary survey.[24] The most surprisingly pertinent of these, perhaps, is Giorgio Agamben's *Infancy and History*, a mixture of Heideggerian philosophy and Lévi-Straussian ethnography that illuminates the position of children at the peripheries of acculturation.

Agamben meditates upon the destabilizing boundary between nature and culture, silence and speech, ritual play and historical development, hot and cold societies. Children are the uncanny shifters breaking through limits and thus permitting evolutions. Hence for him they are intrinsically gothic, like ghosts in the flesh:

> If the ghost is the living-dead or the half-dead person, the baby is a dead-living or a half-alive person. It too, as tangible proof of the discontinuity between the world of the living and the world of the dead, and between diachrony and synchrony, and as an unstable signifier which can, at any moment, be transformed into its own opposite, thereby represents both a threat to be neutralized and a means of enabling the passage from one sphere to the other without abolishing its signifying difference. . . . Ghosts have a corresponding function to that of children.
>
> (Agamben, *Infancy and History*, 83)

Something about childhood haunts all adult or civilized views of its unfettered joys. As if echoing Percy Shelley, Agamben calls that something the "alastor," or wanderer impulse, "the spectre of the unburied" (82).

For the most part, the nineteenth century papered over the unsettling nature of childhood. Kant's *Anthropology* has a strange, if typically interminable, sentence right at the start about children as little tyrants who compel adoration through torturing the sounds of the language, but the sentence eventually drifts into a paean to the unfettered joys of childhood games. Dickens notoriously portrays children in all flavors, from fallen to redeemed, but the latter are the true children, while the former appear modeled on adult exploiters. George Eliot's Tom and Maggie Tulliver incarnate the impulsive, heartless, refractory impulses besetting all humans in an oeuvre where only visionaries, saints, and martyrs are truly mature, but their roots are explored only beginning with preadolescence and not with the more repressed and incalculable drives of infancy. Only toward the end of the century did childhood terrors or the terrors of childish wildness come to dominate, in figures like Hardy's Father Time (the murderous child in *Jude the Obscure*) or the doomed innocents in James's "Turn of the Screw." And only in the next century, with the second essay in *Three Contributions to the Theory of Sex*, did Freud account systematically for what he calls the "polymorphous perversity" of childhood and state explicitly that "cruelty [*Grausamkeit*—a gothically-tinged word] is especially near the childish character" (*Three Contributions*, 53).

In the light of romantic-period accounts of childhood and their subsequent evolution, gothic plots take on a decisive importance. The issues are voiced throughout the genre: one may note, among countless examples, the story of the Prince's childhood in book 2 of Schiller's *Ghost-Seer*, or the womblike cave in which the persecuted son Vivaldi fears he will be buried alive in volume 1, chapter 7, of Radcliffe's *The Italian*. And wild children abound, such as Goethe's Mignon and Kleist's Käthchen von Heilbronn. But no work focuses so insistently yet so deviously as *Frankenstein* on the terrors of the unsocialized.[25] As this chapter has shown, the capriciousness of the novel and of all the characters in it is the core, not the frame, of its experience. The sublime threats from without—whether from magic, science, familial or social patriarchy, or from the natural, sexual, or supernatural sublime—are all reflexes of the uncomprehending instability and powerlessness of the child. Without introducing infants as characters and thus without thematizing childhood as one allegorical topic among others, Shelley expresses the perversity of childhood while disguising her insights as a silly "ghost story" or "hideous phantom." Only thus could *Frankenstein*'s bitter pill be swallowed.

16

Postscript

Faust and the Gothic

*F*AUST AS GOTHIC NOVEL IS, to say the least, an unfamiliar notion. So far as we know, the topic remains today nearly virgin, though Faust's vision of Gretchen appears for a moment at the start of Mario Praz's classic *The Romantic Agony*.[1] Since, after all, *Faust* is not a gothic novel, we are not inclined to call this neglect startling. Goethe's play lacks almost totally the sadistic terror that was the visible hallmark of the gothic, and what motifs it shares with the gothic novel are also Shakespearian or general romantic features. Yet while Goethe was cool toward the fashionable gothic, he was not ignorant of it.[2] Surely he knew, for instance, the work of the Jena professor of philosophy Justus Christian Hennings, since he attacks Hennings in the "Walpurgis Night's Dream," both by name and as the "quondam Spirit of the Age [Ci-devant *Genius der Zeit*]" (speech head to line 4310). Writing in the spirit of the Enlightenment about supernatural beliefs in his book of 1780, *Von Geistern und Geistersehern*, Hennings asks derisively, "Maybe you think the evil one spooks for mankind's benefit?" (368)—a possibility that the more imaginative *Faust* plays with. As Faust says in the last speech before his blinding, "We can't, I know, be rid of daemons easily [*Dämonen, weiß ich, wird man schwerlich los*]" (11491). Perhaps it isn't so foolish to wonder what the old men—Faust and his creator—thought about ghosts and those who see them.

Certainly, early readers of the play perceived its gothic tendencies or potential. Despite their differences, Faust's devilish wager is readily assimilated to demonic pacts in works like Maturin's *Melmoth the Wanderer*.[3] When Balzac's Raphael starts hallucinating in the old curiosity shop of *The Wild Ass's Skin*, it was, the narrator says, "a weird witches' sabbath worthy of the fantasies glimpsed by Dr Faust on the Brocken" (*Peau*, 30; *Skin*, 42). Immediately a typically gothic mixture of sublime emotionalism, romantic science, and Rousseauist anthropology infuses the atmosphere: "The terrors of life had no hold on a soul which had already become familiar with the terrors of death [gothic]. He even favoured with a sort of mocking complicity the bizarre elements in this moral galvanism [science] whose prodigious manifestations were coupled with the last thoughts which gave him the feeling that he still existed [Rousseau]" (30; 42). In opera, too, the Faustian witches' sabbath undoubtedly provided a stimulus for gothic creators. Indeed, *Der Freischütz*, *La Damnation de Faust*, and *Mefistofele* seem to outpace by far Goethe's more pedestrian world. So too does that quintessentially gothic concert piece, the *Symphonie fantastique*, where the hallucinatory witches' sabbath is accompanied by so many other representative features: the dream of an ideal beloved (with its ungrounded or immaterial consciousness evoked by unsupported treble melodies), primitive pastoralism, the dissolution of aristocratic society in a mad waltz that serves as a kind of "Walpurgis Night's Dream," and the concluding march to the scaffold. *Faust* seems a stepping stone to greater horrors realized by others.

Faust self-evidently does share many elements with gothic novels dating from before, during, and after its composition. These include the following. Supernatural figures: devils, angels, witches, hags. Excessively natural figures: the innocent maiden, fatherless and ultimately orphaned; the warrior; the tormented natural scientist and philosopher. Figures of exceptional authority in church and state: rulers and holy men. Plot motifs: dangerous and illicit sexuality (though with infanticide rather than the more common gothic incest), disguises and doppelgänger figures, spying on actions near and far, religious rites and mysteries, political despotism and usurpation, a last-minute deathbed struggle of good and evil. Elements of setting:

prison-like enclosures, gothic chambers, churches, and fortresses; vast, moonlit natural expanses through which the characters voyage in space and time. Psychodynamics: a feminine focus; regression to infantile states; haunted reverie; impending doom, with the clock either stopped or moving with unnatural swiftness; helpless unconsciousness. Formal characteristics: most obviously the inserted songs and ballads, but also the multitude of fictional frames, together with the combination of epic sweep and dramatic concentration that makes the gothic novel into its own peculiar kind of *Gesamtkunstwerk*.

In addition to all these familiar gothic features, *Faust* shares the important but less well recognized one that has been a focus of this book: an ambivalence of tone and a self-conscious playfulness. The gothic often reinforced its aura of play with themes of gambling, and so does Goethe when he departs from earlier versions of the legend by couching Faust's pact with the devil as a wager. Throughout the gothic, the sublime is often not even a step away from the ridiculous. If critics argue endlessly about how we are supposed to feel at different moments in Goethe's play, perhaps the moral is not that critical analysis is futile but rather that the play participates in a mode in which such things are generically, uncannily undecidable.[4] "Once more you hover close, elusive shapes [*Ihr naht euch wieder, schwankende Gestalten*]" (*Faust*, 1).

The wavering visions of the ridiculous Proktophantasmist (Proctovisionary, introduced at 4143), for example, lead directly to the gothic milieu. Although commentaries correctly identify him as the Enlightenment pundit Friedrich Nicolai, they do not mention the original report of the story (in which, as in *Faust*, Nicolai's name is not given) in 1797 by C. W. Hufeland, who at the time was court physician in Weimar and Goethe's family doctor. The brief anecdote demonstrates the power of gothic visions to threaten even the most secure mind: "This utterly enlightened and unprejudiced man at last truly begins to feel giddy; never to be alone, to see himself perpetually surrounded by strange and ever-changing figures, indeed addressed by them, this finally robs him of all peace of mind, of all thoughts, and it puts him into the most painful agitation" ("Sonderbare Geistererscheinung," *Kleine Schriften*, 2: 378). Hufeland is the delightfully prosaic vitalist, widely known for his lifelong preoccupation with the premature burial of the dead, who was discussed in "Kant and the Doctors" (Chapter 8 above). Faust, like his epigones in the various sections of *Melmoth*, is prone to falling asleep at moments of crisis, in order to revive refreshed. And at the end, when Mephisto is in too big a hurry to inter him, Faust rises like one of Hufeland's none-too-dead souls to complete the proof that you can't keep a good self down.[5] Flea-bitten rationalism proves to be the nightmare from which even Goethe's gothic is always trying to awaken.

For the most part, when *Faust* approaches the characteristic gothic mood of terror, it veers off into satire—for example in "Witch's Kitchen"; "Walpurgis Night," with its dissolve into "Walpurgis Night's Dream"; and the scene with the mysteriously named and unseen Mothers, "Interment." But then, this book has argued that the Burkean terror often identified as the defining characteristic of the gothic is in fact the least significant aspect of the genre. Rather, the romantic gothic naturally interrogates or ironizes its most fearsome imaginings. Faust's death remains within the gothic orbit by arriving abruptly and then, just as abruptly, finding a rapid and miraculous salvation.

Goethe's complex stance toward the gothic can be conveniently examined through his use of the typically gothic verb *schaudern* and the nouns *Schauer* and *Grauen* ("shudder" and "horror").[6] "Don't be afraid [*O schaudre nicht!*]" (3188) Faust tells Gretchen just after she has plucked the last petal from the daisy and discovered that Faust loves her. Both recognize in this shudder the doom just allegorically executed upon the flower that bears her name. Gretchen had already had a similar moment of premonitory terror in "Evening" (2757), right after Mephistopheles left the first casket of jewels in her cupboard; in "Cathedral" the evil spirit transforms her into an object of terror for others (3831). Faust also has his moments of terror: when the Earth Spirit appears (473) and when he enters the dungeon at the end of Part I (4405), where the phrase "long-forgotten [*längst entwöhnt*]" connects his *Schauer* to his response to his study and to the Earth Spirit.

The conventional gothic sensationalism manifested in such moments is at its height in the prison scene at the end of Part I. Yet the revision of "Prison" and the conduct of the entire final text of Part I manifestly temper the temptations to sensationalize. The early text of "Prison" in the "Urfaust" (probably mid-1770s) predates the gothic fad, which began in the 1780s, yet it contains the most explicit mention of terror, "inward terror of mankind [*Inneres Grauen der Menschheit*]" (my translation), which was altered in the final version to the more sentimental "all mankind's miseries [*Der Menschheit ganzer Jammer*]" (4406). And the gothic stage direction in the "Urfaust," "He hears the chains rattle and the straw rustle [*Er hört die Ketten klirren und das Stroh rauschen*]" (my translation), turns into a detached report: "She's unaware her lover's listening, / can hear the clanking chains, the rustling straw [*Sie ahnet nicht, daß der Geliebte lauscht, / Die Kettern klirren hört, das Stroh, das rauscht*]" (4421–22). Thus, even before the addition of Gretchen's abrupt salvation, Goethe distanced himself from gothic terror even as its popularity was spreading. And then, just a few lines before Faust terrifies Gretchen for the last time ("I fear and loathe you [*Mir graut's vor dir*]," she tells him; 4610), Mephistopheles' horses shudder because dawn arrives (4599). Thus suddenly the supernatural is subject to the natural, the opposite of the gothic norm. Indeed, natural and supernatural complement one another: for the archangels in the "Prologue in Heaven," night is "deep and awesome [*schauervoll*]" (254), but for the devil, day is.[7] The process of terror is reversible: it can be part of building up a consciousness as well as of reducing one to its core.

If Part I has its gothic moments, Part II moves toward gothic on a cosmic scale, though never without qualification. To be sure, Act I hardly evokes a full-scale gothic response, despite its episodes of uncanny terror, such as the arrival of Faust's anti-masque or Mephistopheles' eery-grotesque evocation of the Mothers. Indeed the gothic Mothers—regressive, infantilizing images that elicit shudders— prompt Faust to say, "Awe is the greatest boon we humans are allotted [*Das Schaudern ist der Menschheit bestes Teil*]" (6272). The self answers terror with an assertion of creation, as Faust had already done earlier in the exchange by boasting, "In your Nothingness I hope to find my All [*In deinem Nichts hoff' ich das All zu finden*]" (6255). Resistance or recovery is more explicit in Act II, where *Schauer* and its compounds occur nine times, out of the total of twenty-two occurrences in all of *Faust II*. First, terror is trivialized in a series of elaborate compounds from the beginning of the act: "Schauderfest" ("dread celebration," 7005), "Schaudergrauen" ("weird and spectral," 7041), "schauderhaft" ("horror," "horrifying," 7518, 7788), "schauern" ("the willies," "dismayed," 7798, 7968)—notice the progression away from absurd compounds once the point is made. The most specific moment of terror is the eruption of Seismos, who makes the earth itself shake. He unleashes human greed and violence, supernatural forces of destruction (the meteor that destroys the mountain), and dream (we finally learn that the entire affair was an illusion). Other gothic elements around this scene include descent, night, uncertainty, disorientation, and Mephistopheles' demonic encounters with the Lamiae and the Phorkyads, ambiguous creatures for whom sexuality is a constant threat to identity. But the great oddity of these gothic elements is that terror is felt by the supernatural figures who themselves ought to evoke terror: the witch Erichtho, the sirens, Mephistopheles, the dryads, and Homunculus all experience *Schauer*. Whose consciousness is actually being narrated in Act II? Whose dream is it? Stuart Atkins has long since argued that Act II is Faust's dream (*Goethe's "Faust,"* 142), but we might go even further. Somehow this is a dream Goethe dreams for the spectator, calling the very boundaries of the individual into question.

Act V is more traditionally gothic. The Three Mighty Men terrorize the world around them, especially Baucis and Philemon, who are also terrorized by the mysterious nighttime goings-on at Faust's castle. Here are the evil and violence we conventionally expect from the gothic. Faust himself has become part of this terrorizing mentality, so that the alien shadow of Baucis's and Philemon's trees makes him shudder. A "Schauerwindchen" ("damp breeze," 11380) brings four ghosts: Want, Debt, Care, and Distress. In a gesture of stripping down to core consciousness, Care blinds Faust, and as Faust dies, Mephistopheles calls for the clock to stop. Faust's last moments in *Mitternacht* are perhaps the only moments of full gothic horror in *Faust*. Yet they, too, are soon ironized as angels descend to the rescue. Even here terror is rapidly commuted into play, and with a confident mastery that sets the play apart from the nervous, degraded, or condescending ironies of Walpole, Radcliffe, and Shelley.

Crucial to Faust's death is the experience of time, for which Markus Herz's terms *Schwindel* ("vertigo") and *Langeweile* ("boredom") remain pertinent. Clearly Faust suffers at the beginning of the play from boredom: he is desperate first to speed time up, to experience *Schwindel* ("into the torrents of time, / into the whirl of eventful existence [*in das Rauschen der Zeit, / Ins Rollen der Begebenheit*]," 1754–55), and then, with the wager, to stop it completely. But the eventual outcome proves to be something altogether different, namely, a healthy, purified temporal *Weilen* ("whiling"). Although Care at the end claims the power to stop time just before she blinds Faust (11455–56), the night of his soul approaches gradually, without terrifying suddenness ("The darkness seems to press about me more and more [*Die Nacht scheint tiefer tief hereinzudringen*]," 11499). And though early in the play Care was associated with the shipwreck of hopes in the maelstrom of time (643–44), that is, with arrested time, even earlier the Earth Spirit had awakened in Faust the courage to overcome shipwrecks (467). It follows, then, that Care now only provokes a counterspirit ("as one [*ein Geist*]," 11510) into activity. Faust resists Care with a notable speech about slowing down to the pace of nature: "If spirits haunt him, let him not break stride [*Wenn Geister spuken, geh' er seinen Gang*]" (11450). Here his absolute striving yields to a relation to transcendence mediated by his own imaginative consciousness. Thus *Faust* confronts the gothic challenge differently from the gothic novels: in place of a reduction to pure consciousness and internal selfhood, Faust outlines a healthy relationship to time extending beyond the self dynamically into the future.

Such reversals are characteristic of *Faust*'s response to the gothic. Like most of Goethe's writings, *Faust* is predicated on a daemonic ground—and in this case a demonic ground as well—that it posits in order to rise above it.[8] In the first lines of "Dedication," wavering forms approach us with their madness (4) and their magic breath, "Zauberhauch" (translated by Atkins as "youthful strength of feeling"; 8). In their train they bring the temporal disorientation of the second and third stanzas, and then, in the second half of the last stanza, a moment of terror—"I feel a sense of dread [*Ein Schauer faßt mich*]" (29)—whose language is later echoed by the Earth Spirit ("A dread chill / flows down from the ceiling-vault / and has me in its hold [*Es weht / Ein Schauer vom Gewölb' herab / Und faßt mich an!*]," 472–74). Yet in "Dedication" the terror turns peaceful:

> I feel a sense of dread, tear after tear is falling,
> my rigid heart is tenderly unmanned—
> what I possess seems something far away
> and what had disappeared proves real.
>
> [*Ein Schauer faßt mich, Träne folgt den Tränen,*
> *Das strenge Herz, es fühlt sich mild und weich;*
> *Was ich besitze, seh' ich wie im Weiten,*
> *Und was verschwand, wird mir zu Wirklichkeiten.*]
>
> (29–32)

The heart softens, consciousness releases its hold, yet as a result the whole world that had been lost now returns. Gothic nothingness is nowhere to be found, let alone feared.

But if there is no nothingness, then there is no pressing need either for the unconditional selfhood explored so intensely by the gothic or for the Rousseauist nostalgia for purity that I illustrated earlier with reference to Balzac. Gothic novels usually reach their climax in a prison, but Faust begins in one, feeling imprisoned in his "high-vaulted, narrow Gothic room [*hochgewölbten, engen gotischen Zimmer*]" (stage direction to 354).

The play's proper first word remains unspoken: instead of "ich," the omitted subject of his first verb, Faust utters only a depressive and paranoid "ach." Friedrich Kittler, who has called attention to these words, sees in this opening a condition of "pure soul" preceding Faust's fall into writing, a change in mode vital to the action of the play.[9] Yet Faust's initial condition of "pure soul" is as much an unhappy limbo as the successor condition is: whatever "pure" means here, it does not include health or effectiveness. Suspended in its gothic chamber, "Wandering between two worlds, one dead, / The other powerless to be born," the continuity of the self is tested and, very often, assured.[10] The gothic novel is, generically, a thought experiment with premature burial, and Faust in his dark and narrow chamber, almost like a figure from Poe or Matthew Arnold, starts off already dead and waiting to be born. He passes out of the gothic, not into or even through it.

What normally symbolizes a late stage in the reduction to pure consciousness is here a starting point that Faust vigorously rejects. Consciousness of self does not rescue Faust in the prison; on the contrary, it is itself the very prison to be escaped.[11] Time and again the play unmasks self-consciousness as empty solipsism. Imprisoned Gretchen in her madness is a paradigm of gothic reduction to the essence of the self: her continuing love for an infant and family and her core of innocence are unchanged from her earlier, sane moments, and she desires only to return to the past. But in *Faust* this essential self represents the temptation to stasis articulated in the bet: "tarry, remain [*verweile doch*]" (1700). It must be rejected, and indeed, "A Pleasant Landscape," at the opening of Part II, brings growth and change through positive erasure of the past. As Wilhelm Emrich says, "Sleep and spontaneously organic 'forgetting' are functions of a nature that only 'softens,' reconciles, and 'heals' because it has led its 'darling' to the borders of existence, beyond which there can be only terror or—forgetting."[12] Faust's monologue once again contains all the themes of the post-Kantian gothic self. "Life's pulses beat with fresh vitality [*Des Lebens Pulse schlagen frisch lebendig*]" (4679): the life force is the first thing to impinge on the consciousness of the waking Faust. Next comes continuity in time: "You also, Earth, have lasted out this night [*Du, Erde, warst auch diese Nacht beständig*]" (4681). But as Faust's awakening consciousness gathers force, it focuses less and less on a unified self, and more and more on a world that comes into being through the words he utters, "All that surrounds me forms a paradise [*Ein Paradies wird um mich her die Runde*]" (4694). By the end of the monologue his consciousness extends beyond the earth to the rainbow, a sign that is anchored both in scientific objectivity and in a tradition that evokes not gothic shudders but pastoral showers (as "Schauer" must clearly be translated in 4726).

In such manner *Faust* adds layer after layer until consciousness of self disappears in consciousness of the world. The first three acts of Part II abandon self-absorption for a phantasmagoria of the history of our culture and bring Faust and Helena onto the stage only as literary figures in elaborate costumes, conscious at every moment of themselves as constructs from a long tradition (as when Helena says, "I now grow faint, become a shade to myself too [*Ich schwinde hin und werde selbst mir ein Idol*]," 8881). And what then of the apparent return to an authentic self when Faust resists Care? Faust grounds his satisfaction with time and his supposed identity in the labors of others who will do what he has done all through Part II, namely, be conscious not of themselves but of the need to re-create the world each day through their own labor (11575–76).

Faust's death provokes a mock-epic battle in which each side looks gothic to its opponents. "Interment" represents the devil's perspective. To Mephisto all the wavering rescuers[13] appear as demons; he calls them "that superdiabolic element [*ein überteuflisch Element*]," "love-illusion [*Liebesspuk*]," and the like (11754, 11814). But the final scene revives the perspective of "Dedication," in which wavering and swaying are associated with the uncertain, preconscious reawakening to life. The "Chorus" and "Echo" that open "Mountain Gorges" begin the last revival of the song whose "first response [*erste{r} Widerklang*]" resonated behind "Dedication" (20). Answering to the gothic interior of Faust's monologue, the stage now presents a gothic exterior, a mountainous region reminiscent of the landscapes of *The Mysteries of Udolpho*. Yet the setting sheds the contamination by individualized conflict that polarizes the gothic self. Release proceeds in stages, without the cathartic shudder that would memorialize what is to be left behind. Hence, responding to Mephisto's mistaken boast, "The parts essential to a devil are all rescued [*Gerettet sind die edlen Teufelsteile*]" (11813), Goethe produces the following sequence. First, angels "hovering in the upper sky [*schwebend in der höheren Atmosphäre*]" (stage direction to 11934) emit a counterboast, "This worthy member of the spirit world / is rescued from the devil [*Gerettet ist das edle Glied / Der Geisterwelt vom Bösen*]" (11934–35). Next the more perfect angels correct them, complaining,

The remainder of earth,
it's distasteful to bear it;
even cremated,
it would still be impure.

[Uns bleibt ein Erdenrest
Zu tragen peinlich,
Und wär er von Asbest,
Er ist nicht reinlich.]

(11954–57)

And then the purifying Doctor Marianus, "in the highest and neatest cell [*in der höchsten, reinlichsten Zelle*]" (stage direction to 11989), mediates the ultimate release: "The view here is vast, / the spirit exalted [*Hier ist die Aussicht frei, / Der Geist erhoben*]" (11989–90). This once more evokes "Dedication," which ends, "What I possess seems something far away / and what had disappeared [Faust's body, in the final instance] proves real [*Was ich besitze, seh ich wie im Weiten, / Und was verschwand, wird mir zu Wirklichkeiten*]" (31–32). Redeeming the blinded, haunted Faust (along with other sinning ghosts, such as the deluded, impercipient Lynkeus), the clarified vision into the distance lifts spirituality to a new and higher level.

At the end, gothic conflict gives up the ghost. The younger angels, who were present at Faust's death, appear to speak of victory: "When [those roses] fell, the wicked faltered, / when they hit, the devils fled [*Böse wichen, als wir streuten, / Teufel flohen, als wir trafen*]" (11947–48). But in truth their attack transformed the nature of the encounter: "Spirits used to hellish torment / felt the pangs of love instead [*Statt gewohnter Höllenstrafen / Fühlten Liebesqual die Geister*]" (11949–50). War has become passionate love, and the necessary lessons of human violence have forged bonds between individuals. "See how his early, youthful vigor / shows to advantage in ethereal raiment! [*Und aus ätherischem Gewande / Hervortritt erste Jugendkraft!*]" (12090–91).

Finally Faust is truly born—but not into a merely personal condition of separated consciousness: "But when he senses there is new life here, / he soon will be the peer of any angel [*Er ahnet kaum das frische Leben, / So gleicht er schon der heiligen Schar*]" (12086–87).

A powerfully active response replaces the spiritual essentialism typical of the gothic, as the blessed youths, circling Faust, declare, "Already he has grown / bigger than we [*Er überwächst uns schon / An mächtigen Gliedern*]" (12076–77). The professor has become a good learner, and hence a good teacher at last: "But this man has gained learning, / he'll be our teacher [*Doch dieser hat gelernt, / Er wird uns lehren*]" (12082–83). But he becomes a good teacher by confronting his lack of maturity. A powerful child rather than an independent adult, Goethe's countergothic personality does not free himself by force of will, for "how can they, desire's slaves, / burst their bonds unaided? [*Wer zerreißt aus eigner Kraft / Der Gelüste Ketten?*]" (12026–27). Rather, the gothic manacles lose their terror to become an ecstatic living union transcending any possible individualism. In the penultimate strophe of the play, Doctor Marianus describes the process thus: "So that you may gratefully / be reborn for heaven [*Euch zu seligem Geschick / Dankend umzuarten*]" (12098–99). In this pair of lines, the collective plural "you" is as essential as its perhaps unprecedented verb of communal response, *umzuarten*, here translated as "be reborn," but suggesting a transformation (*um*) of the species (*Art*).[14]

Faust, then, preserves the legacy of the gothic in the very process of transmuting it. There is, to be sure, no novelty in claiming that *Faust* in some sense transvalues evil and that it in some sense honors collectivities, even if not all readers would agree with these propositions. But it does make a difference if we stress the gothic tonalities that persist into the final scene, even as the play abandons a conventionally gothic vision. The gothic is the realm of the sublime, of the unspeakable and unperformable that the final *chorus mysticus* invokes. Consequently, the gothic bequeathes to the play's ideological convictions a sense of urgency and a restless energy beyond conceptual grasp.[15] Because it has passed through the gothic crucible, the world of *Faust* must always view love as passion—a better form of war and not a negation of it. It must always view maturity under the sign of power, breaking the bonds of earth, and not as settled conviction. And it must always view teaching as a stab in the dark. "Woman, eternally, shows us the way [*Das Ewig-Weibliche / Zieht uns hinan*]," as the famous last lines of the play say (12110–11). Even through the desperate straits of Care and her companions, men must risk the drawing and being drawn, the *Hinanziehen* and *Hinangezogensein* of and by the eternal feminine, formerly represented by the spinning Gretchen, whose rest is always and forever gone because she does not and cannot hold her beloved firmly on the spot.

Gretchen knows, as the blessed youths in their blissful ignorance do not, that Faust has not really learned and cannot really teach. She answers them with a reminder that their new teacher is blind, with a blindness that he carries over from his prior, gothic existence, into a new day that can never fully dawn for humans whose humanity lies in acceptance, not rejection, of their gothic fetters: "Grant me permission to instruct him— / he still is dazzled by the strange new light [*Vergönne mir, ihn zu belehren! / Noch blendet ihn der neue Tag*]" (12092–93). This is the sublime condition that we transcend exactly to the extent that we learn to submit to it.[16]

What *Faust* rejects, then, is not the gothic as such—not human limitation, not the confrontation with evil, not fatality—so much as the rebelliousness that the gothic novels inscribe into their portrayal of the gothic condition. Gothic rebellion is contaminated by the forces it opposes. As Act V shows, if you command the devil, it is only to become a stronger devil yourself. Resistance is always tainted, whether by the perpetual melancholy of *The Castle of Otranto*, Radcliffe's undercurrents of sexual indulgence, or the recalcitrant monstrousness of Mary Shelley's pure-hearted monster. Like his creators who appear in the metatheatrical "Prelude on the Stage," Faust begins angry. Unlike his fellows in confrontation with forces of evil—and most unlike the increasingly angry Mephisto—Faust wins by losing, swallowing his pride, and submitting. The gothic mode is divided against itself, and Goethe rectifies it by refusing to bring its dialectic to a standstill.

Amid all the differences, then, *Faust* shares with the gothic a radical dialectic.[17] Indeed, insofar as the gothic novels bring their dialectic to a terminus, *Faust* outdoes their radicalism. It is a dialectic because its values insistently come in competing pairs: good and evil, heaven and earth, man and woman. Its two-souledness is radical in the political sense that human structures will not satisfy its demands. It is radi-

cal in the moral sense that erring, sin, care, and hopeless blindness remain inevitable, and so, consequently, does the struggle against them.
It is radical in the epistemological sense that mediations are relentlessly excluded or satirized in a series of ever more astonishing dramatic confrontations. And it is radical in the aesthetic sense that this
is all a wondrous spectacle, of value precisely to the extent that it does
not touch real—ordinary, petty—life. *Faust* consummates the gothic
self-critique not by turning against the gothic but rather by pursuing
the gothic impulse to its logical, bittersweet end.

What Virgil Nemoianu has termed the taming of romanticism thus
looks, from the gothic perspective, like an ambiguous legacy. Magic is
banished, to be sure, but the forces that drove authors to imagine it
and their characters to succumb to it have been released into the world
at large. That is the end of the story, just as it was the end of the story's
beginning. The gothic awakens into the fairytale of eternal peace that
we otherwise know as the mad savagery of bourgeois society.

NOTES

Chapter 1

1. Morse, *Romanticism*, 13–103, is an honorable exception, though its thematic focus on hypocrites and artists remains distant from my concerns.

2. Castle, "The Gothic Novel," in *Boss Ladies*, 85. Anne Williams, similarly, claims that "despite Gothic predilection of the flagrantly exotic, this is a most English, a most indigenous phenomenon" (*Art of Darkness*, 13)—a prophecy that is self-fulfilling since no foreign authors are mentioned, but harmless since the book concerns gender, not nation.

3. Allison, *Virtue's Faults*, 148–87, is a fine account of *The Recess*, nominally as a gothic novel. Allison's discussion includes gothic topoi (imprisonment, doubles, nature) that play a part in most fiction in the period, though, on my reading, not a dominant role in this novel. She regards the gothic as a "mode of sentimental fiction" that is "characteristically English" (197) and as one of the "feminine modes and genres," alongside "romance, sensibility, and the . . . epistolary form" (234). Probably any genre definition entails some circularity; still, with no accepted gothic novelists in Allison's mix apart from Radcliffe, her characterization of the genre is inadequately grounded.

4. Anon., "Life and Writings of Mrs. Radcliffe," preface to Radcliffe's posthumous novel *Gaston de Blondeville*, cited from Novak, "Extended Moment," 147. Novak's desultory essay on "the proper sluggishness that we want in a work of fiction" (155) relates landscape descriptions to dream descriptions, as this book will also do, but bases its understand-

ing on accounts of dreaming in the immediate wake of Locke and hence treats both dream and description as forms of realism, yielding an anachronistic picture of both Radcliffe and Charles Brockden Brown.

5. Hence, in the same essay cited above, Castle—a more careful student of gender concerns than of nationalities—finds in gothic novels "a powerful cross-sex appeal" (*Boss Ladies*, 98). Sedgwick, similarly troubling boundaries and over-ready assumptions, calls the multiple identity disturbances in gothic novels "a cognitive mess" operating to disrupt social orders (*Between Men*, 106). The best study of the complexities of feminization (specifically in Radcliffe, but with broader import) is Claudia Johnson, *Equivocal Beings*, 73–137. Williams's *Art of Darkness* can again be instanced for the kinds of dubious generalization that beset even books that are grounded in acutely observed specifics. Williams identifies "female" gothic (always in scare quotes) with a limited point of view, explained supernatural, happy ending, and spiritually reborn protagonist (102–4). Williams has no intention of associating narrative with authorial gender. Indeed, none of the "female" gothic characteristics applies either to Dacre's *Zofloya* or to Mary Shelley's *Frankenstein* (Dacre is not mentioned in the book; *Frankenstein* is discussed), while at least the first three apply to several stories by Poe, such as "The Pit and the Pendulum." In a more general study, Felski sensibly points out that "all of literature is about gender" at least to some degree (*Literature after Feminism*, 11), yet later argues that the gothic "is a key genre" in defining "an alternative [i.e., feminist] history of aesthetic experience" (155; the discussion of the gothic occurs on 149–55). At best, "female" gothic is a normal type, sometimes but not always appearing in works by women, composed of dissociable features that (apart from the supernatural) appear in many genres of fiction. The same should be said of Perry's "gay male" gothic. Two recent books on the topic, Haggerty's *Men in Love* and Brinks's *Gothic Masculinity*, touch on gothic novels—if only very fleetingly in the case of the latter book—but conspicuously avoid tying gender issues to formal genre. I follow their example in dissociating genre from gender.

Chapter 2

1. Godwin, *Caleb Williams*, 334, from the original version of the conclusion.
2. The spirit's resistance is the topic of DeLamotte's *Perils of the Night*. As she writes: "Gothic romance, despite its despairing fixation on the 'littleness' of the individual, also asserts the triumph of the soul 'in its immensity'" (119).

3. See Foucault, "Preface to Transgression," in *Language, Counter-Memory, Practice*, 36–40, where he brings Kant's testing of limits into proximity with Sade.

4. Moritz, "Fragmente," 55–56. This remarkable characterization of Kant appears in Γνῶθι Σαυτόν oder Magazin zur Erfahrungsseelenkunde (Know Thyself; or Journal of Empirical Psychology), a journal founded by Karl Philipp Moritz in 1783 as the first periodical devoted to the field of psychology. Later the philosopher Salomon Maimon assumed the editorship, and a successor journal, *Psychologisches Magazin*, was published from 1796–98 by the most faithful of Kant's early disciples, Carl Christian Erhard Schmid.

5. Napier, in *Failure of Gothic*, regards antinomy as the problem rather than the method of the gothic. See also Carter's *Specter or Delusion?*, a more balanced though more modest book. For a suggestive inventory of the antinomies of madness, see Foucault, *Folie et déraison*, 538–40 (this inventory is not in the abridged English translation).

6. Voller quotes an earlier formulation of this thesis about the gothic (*Supernatural Sublime*, 34), but cautions that conservative gothic novels end with stabilization. More recently, James Watt has argued throughout his book *Contesting the Gothic* that gothic novels refuse to settle into defined positions.

7. See two works by Kavanagh, *Enlightenment* and "The Libertine's Bluff," for illuminating treatments of gambling in Enlightenment literature. Passages on gambling were just as thrilling but not so metaphysical in the Enlightenment as in the romantic period.

8. For a nice discussion of the mixed tone at the end of Pushkin's story and of some of its cultural ramifications, see Rosenshield, "Choosing the Right Card."

9. Doody honors the import of gothic dreaming in a rich survey reaching the conclusion: "It was the gothic, in all its implications, that saved men from being seen as the sex without full consciousness. The Gothic novel gave men the freedom to have—and to live in—nightmares" ("Deserts, Ruins," 572).

Chapter 3

1. Condillac, quoted in Derrida, *Archeology*, 61. Derrida paraphrases: "The addition of the new arises from the sole association or complication—analogical connection—of a finite number of simple givens" (62).

2. Homer O. Brown's essay "*Tom Jones*: The 'Bastard' of History" illuminates the problems of consistency and control in Fielding, while explic-

itly omitting discussion of the novel's closure. Much of his discussion applies even more completely to *Otranto*.

3. "Earthquake" is Walpole's comic euphemism, in one letter, for sexual climax (Walpole to his favorite correspondent, Horace Mann, *Corr.*, 20: 140). Surely it can never have been overlooked that *The Castle of Otranto* is a travesty of sexual encounter, ending in postcoital depression. As Walpole writes at a moment of Theodorean gloom, "My towers rise, my galleries and cloisters extend—for what? For me to leave, or to inhabit by myself, when I have survived my friends?" (also to Mann, *Corr.*, 21: 506).

4. Walpole's longest poem, "An Epistle from Florence" (1740), gives a history of the bad kings and queens of England (basically, all except Elizabeth), ending with a call to virtue: "Glorious is the plan, / To build the free, the sensible, GOD MAN" (*Works*, 1: 16). The poem envisions a restoration fostered by a nurturing Athenian philosophy, but seems already to be haunted by the gothic collapse later enacted in *The Castle of Otranto*:

> To woods and caves she never bade retreat
> Nor fix'd in cloister'd monkeries her seat:
> No lonely precepts to her sons enjoin'd,
> Nor taught them to be men, to shun mankind.
>
> (*Works*, 1: 5)

5. Strawberry Hill was, of course, a similarly crowded and diminutive creation. So Walpole describes it at length in a letter to the Manns: "Then my little hill, and diminutive enough it is. . . . Like a Lilliputian seaport. . . . You must turn the perspective, and look at this vision through the diminishing end of the telescope; for nothing is so small as the whole" (*Corr.*, 25: 532). See also *Corr.*, 28: 234: "Some American . . . will smile at the diminutive scenes on the little Thames when he is planting a forest on the banks of the Oroonoko. I love to skip into futurity and imagine what will be done on the giant scale of a new hemisphere; but I am in little London."

6. In an earlier letter to Mann, Walpole suggests the contrasting values of indoor and outdoor settings and the affinity of the gothic with the indoors, though not yet the reversal that makes the indoor scenes of the novel more stable than the outdoor ones: "Gothic is merely architecture; and as one has a satisfaction in imprinting the gloomth of abbeys and cathedrals on one's house, so one's garden on the contrary is to be nothing but *riant*, and the gaiety of nature" (*Corr.*, 20: 372).

7. Stone, *Family, Sex and Marriage*, 138–39. Campbell does not note the religious nuance in her generally thorough study of the topic, "I Am No Giant."

8. "Psycho-narration" is Cohn's term in *Transparent Minds*. On p. 22 she describes Fielding's "avoidance of inside views," missing the climactic

scene where the avoidance breaks down. Examples prior to Austen are not cited.

9. Walpole, *Corr.*, 29: 255. The passage continues with an inventory of failed epics, from Virgil on. The word "silly" in my preceding sentence is applied by Walpole to Virgil (contrasting him with the more gothic Lucan) in a letter to Zouch (*Corr.*, 16: 23).

10. Castle, "The Spectralization of the Other in *The Mysteries of Udolpho*," in *Female Thermometer*, 120–39. Also valuable on the relation of the gothic to Freud and the psychology of consciousness are Castle's sequel essays in the same volume, "Phantasmagoria and the Metaphorics of Modern Reverie" (140–67) and "Spectral Politics: Apparition Belief and the Romantic Imagination" (168–89).

11. Hence Stevenson persuasively traces the psychic origin of the novel to a funeral Walpole witnessed as a small child (*British Novel*, 103–9).

12. Finding initially in the gothic novel the romantic-era roots of Freudian subjectivity, Belsey writes of "the powerlessness of the fragmented human animal which precedes subjectivity" ("Romantic Construction of the Unconscious," 73). Sensing less nervousness than I do in Walpole's tone, she finds the fragmentation comically redeemed in *The Castle of Otranto* and manifest in its full tragic extent only in Lewis's *The Monk*.

Chapter 4

1. The citations I will give in the text refer first to the French edition of La Fayette, then to the English edition, separated by a semicolon. However, translations are my own, since the widely used translation I am citing for reference is too free to be of use. This passage is found in La Fayette, *Romans*, 352; *Princess*, 116.

2. In *Form of Victorian Fiction*, 1–27, Miller identifies intersubjectivity, characterized by interpenetrating minds, as the characteristic mode of Victorian fiction. He is right about its prevalence and sensitivity, but should not be understood to imply that the narration of minds reading other minds originated in the nineteenth century.

3. On the suppressed violence of feeling in Mme de La Fayette, see Poulet, *Studies*, 131–38. For my reasons for claiming a gulf between thinking and feeling in Descartes, see my essay "Kant's Misreading of Descartes," especially the endnotes on p. 297.

Chapter 5

1. Whitmore, *Supernatural in Tragedy*, and Stroup, "Supernatural Beings." Clemens, in *Return of the Repressed*, has a brief section (20–24) comparing gothic novels with Jacobean tragedy. On supernatural drama of

the romantic period, see Evans, *Gothic Drama from Walpole to Shelley*; Reno, "James Boaden's *Fountainville Forest*"; and the chapter "Baillie, Germany, and the Gothic Drama" in Gamer's *Romanticism and the Gothic* (127–62), which is excellent despite its egregiously mistaken assertion, "Before *The Castle Spectre* [1797], even the most spectacular of gothic dramas had avoided representing ghosts on stage" (131). Ranger, *"Terror and Pity,"* is concerned exclusively with staging. Ghost plays (from the romantic period) are discussed only briefly (75–78) and dismissed as "not a formula for success" (78)—a judgment not fortified by the misidentification of Schiller's unfinished novel *Der Geisterseher* as a "drama" (78).

2. Greenblatt's chapter "Staging Ghosts" (*Hamlet in Purgatory*, 151–204) subdivides spirits into four figures: "false surmise, . . . history's nightmare, . . . deep psychic disturbance, . . . [and] a figure of theater" (157).

3. The distinction between the rhetorical and the psychological sublime forms the basis of Monk's *The Sublime*. In his chapter "The Sublime in Transition," Monk conflates the Shakespearian and the gothic sublime (68).

4. About Walpole and Hill I can report the following information, from the Lewis-Walpole Library in Farmington, Connecticut, where about a quarter of Walpole's library has been reassembled. The collection includes a copy of Hill's *Merope* bound with other plays. I was told by one of the librarians that Walpole purchased most of the books himself, and the catalog suggests that the volume was bound before 1760. This copy of *Merope* has no marginalia, but not many of the plays owned by Walpole do. A different collection of books from Walpole's library does contain a later play of Hill's, *Roman Revenge* (1753), in which a number of passages are marked, notably a whole speech by Cassius (act 5, scene 2) about the evil posterity of tyrants. There are also occasional marks in a 1753 edition of Hill's *Works*, with the following gothic lines from "The Actor's Epitome" heavily highlighted:

> WONDER is curious fear—Suppose, by night,
> Some pale, met *spectre* cross'd the *moon's* dim light!
> Sudden, the *back'ning* [*sic*] *blood*, retreating swift,
> Swells the *press'd heart*:—Each *fibre* fails, to *lift*;
> *Lost*, in short *pause*, arrested *motion* lies,
> And *sense* climbs *doubtful*, to the straining *eyes*.
>
> (4: 80)

And a hyperbolic manuscript note on the topic of mistakes in Voltaire's preface to *Zaire* (a play that Hill adapted) reads, in part, "He says . . . that Aaron Hill translated it to introduce a new kind of tragedy, he who translated anything to get a dinner." Overall, one gets the impression that Walpole had a moderate interest in Hill, and particularly in his gothic dimensions.

5. "Quand j'aurai dit un mot, la terre est à ses pieds. . . . / Je l'épouse, et pour dot je lui donne le monde. / Enfin ma gloire est pure, et je puis la goûter." Voltaire, *Sémiramis* 3.3, in *Théâtre*, 498.

6. In den bestgedeuteten Träumen muß man oft eine Stelle im Dunkel lassen, weil man bei der Deutung merkt, daß dort ein Knäuel von Traumgedanken anhebt, der sich nicht entwirren will, aber auch zum Trauminhalt keine weiteren Beiträge geliefert hat. Dies ist dann der Nabel des Traums, die Stelle, an der er dem Unerkannten aufsitzt. Die Traumgedanken, auf die man bei der Deutung gerät, müssen ganz allgemein ohne Abschluß bleiben. . . . Aus einer dichteren Stelle dieses Geflechts erhebt sich dann der Traumwunsch wie der Pilz aus seinem Mycelium.

(Freud, *Die Traumdeutung*, in *Studienausgabe*, 2: 503)

Jeder Traum hat mindestens eine Stelle, an welcher er unergründlich ist, gleichsam einen Nabel, durch den er mit dem Unerkannten zusammenhängt. (Ibid., 130)

The first translation is my own; the second comes from *Interpretation of Dreams*, trans. Strachey, 111. Strachey's translation of the first passage (525) contains misleading nuances that I italicize in the following excerpts: (A) "There is often a passage in *even* the most thoroughly interpreted dream which has to be left obscure." With the added "even," Strachey suggests that the aim of interpretation is to smooth out the irregularity. To my mind, on the contrary, Freud appears to mean that only the most productive interpretations arrive at the navel of the dream; the uninterpretability is a mark of success not of failure. (B) "The dreamthoughts to which *we are led* by interpretation *cannot, from the nature of things*, have any definite endings." By introducing a passive and negating the main verb, Strachey makes the English sound like the helpless interpreter's admission of defeat at the hand of circumstance. (C) "It is at *some* point where this meshwork is particularly close that the dreamwish *grows up*, like a mushroom out of its mycelium." Freud's mushroom is a bit more assertive than Strachey's. No randomizing "some" occurs in the German, and the important verb *erhebt sich* is more emphatic.

7. A related example, from the earliest years of the Restoration, would be Sir Aston Cokayne's play *The Tragedy of Ovid* (1662). Here a hanged criminal returns as a ghost and invites the wicked Roman Capt. Hannibal and his servant Cacala to a dinner, where the ghost stages a masque

then drags Hannibal down to hell. These characters form the lowest (and sometimes comic) stratum of the multiplotted play, and the specter (an unfunny Don Juan travesty) is quarantined from whatever serious meaning the play aspires to.

8. For an inventory without much analysis, see Stroup, "Supernatural Beings."

9. Prologue by Luke Gardiner, lines 15–16, in Robert Jephson, *The Count of Narbonne*. A prologue by the author replaced Gardiner's. A note explains that Gardiner's prologue arrived too late, which is a common formula in eighteenth-century publications; I wonder here if it might have been a polite pretext for replacing too clear a statement of why the play couldn't succeed.

10. Conrad is "sickly, and of no promising disposition" (Walpole, *Otranto*, 51), and Matilda begins in "melancholy" on account of "the solitude in which our father keeps us" (76). The debility spreads to Theodore (77, 108) and Jerome (96); distempers Isabella (138), who had started out being "of a cheerful disposition" (76); and ultimately spreads to the whole "disconsolate company," becoming the eternal melancholy of the new ruler in the final sentence (148). A fine discussion of the *Otranto* melancholy is Moglen's "Walpole and the Nightmare of History."

11. In Jephson's *Count of Narbonne*, Alfonso is the father of the villain (here named Raymond), not the grandfather—one of the play's subtler yet more revealing rationalizations.

Chapter 6

1. The separation of the dreamer from the waking consciousness seems to have remained standard doctrine in France, even among theorists of abnormal states: see James, *Dreams*, 14–66, esp. 35, where James summarizes a theory propounded by the romantic-period *idéologue* Maine de Biran: "The somnambulistic self knows the other person and judges her, as it would judge a stranger, whereas the waking self has no idea about the somnambulistic self, which remains completely unknown." In 1778 Horace Walpole's Strawberry Hill Press published *The Sleep-Walker*, translated by Lady Craven from a French play by Antoine de Ferriol, in which somnambulism appears like a comic, if somewhat risqué, "masquerade at a wedding" (Craven, *Sleep-Walker*, 50).

2. In "La Théorie kantienne de la conscience," Piclin skillfully marshals the relevant passages to argue that the notion of consciousness in the *Critique of Pure Reason* presupposes a certain degree of indeterminacy and that Kant departed from his original conception as he edged toward an empirical specification of pure consciousness. Even Piclin, however, concludes in the gothic mode: "considered in isolation, the I would be

temporality, originally finite [but then] haunted by the transcendental Ideal of Reason." Representative of the cautious interpretation of Kant in his own day is Jakob, *Grundriß der Erfahrungs-Seelen-Lehre*; see esp. secs. 508–19 (pp. 277–82), arguing that the causes of consciousness cannot be known and that consciousness comes in varying degrees of illumination—of which self-consciousness is the clearest—but is never completely dark. While the book is dedicated to Reil, the main authorities cited in the interpretation of Kant are Platner, Schmid, and, on dreams, Mauchart and Nudow. Platner was a philosopher (and eventually professor of medicine in Leipzig) who promoted the idea of the unconscious; see, e.g., *Philosophische Aphorismen*, sec. 49 (1: 15): "Underneath the least possible clarity, ideas are still possible, but only ideas without consciousness." The other figures are discussed in text or notes below.

3. C. B. Brown, *Edgar Huntly*, 152. The passage (in chap. 16) continues for some pages, and the novel as a whole is an inventory of gothic devices.

4. Porter discusses Battie's Locke-inspired "new formulation of the nature of insanity itself," in *Mind-Forg'd Manacles*, 206–7. In Porter's extensive bibliography, Battie's *Treatise* is the earliest book with "madness," "insanity," or "mental derangement" in the title (it followed *Treatise on Phrenzy*, by P. Frings, dated 1746), and I have not come across anything comparable that was published earlier. Porter's book contests Foucault's *Folie et déraison* on many points, but the books do not so much conflict as diverge in focus: Porter studies the treatment and the experience of mental disorders in England; Foucault examines most successfully the conception of mental disorders in France; and the two foundational books come together in romantic psychiatric understanding, with (as Porter says in conclusion) its "new sense of self as something inner, private and potent" (282). Hence, despite their vast historiographical and political disagreements, both books, when used with discrimination, are invaluable background for the present chapter. Also useful for English literary and medical contexts are Byrd, *Visits to Bedlam*; De Porte, *Nightmares and Hobbyhorses*; and Feder, *Madness in Literature*, 147–202. My discussion seeks to resolve the seeming paradox that, in the late eighteenth century, "madness becomes slowly explicable" (Byrd, *Visits*, 132) while becoming associated with a sublime, hidden self (ibid., 136–44). For German theories of treatment of the insane, see Osinski, *Über Vernunft und Wahnsinn*, an ill-written but well-researched book, more useful on Moritz (164–73) and on Reil and his times (221–29) than on the literary works that are summarized at length.

5. Lorry, *De Melancholia*, 1: 365, 366.

6. On reverie as the result of the association of ideas see also Crichton, *Mental Derangement*, 2: 3–6.

7. Both quotations are by Richerz, in Muratori, *Einbildungskraft*, 1: 49, 247, the first from the introduction, the second from Richerz's response to Muratori.

8. Dufour, *L'Entendement humain*, 60–61, my italics. See also Darwin, *Zoonomia*, 1: 99: "In respect to consciousness, we are only conscious of our own existence, when we think about it; as we only perceive the lapse of time, when we attend to it; when we are busied about other objects, neither the lapse of time nor the consciousness of our own existence can occupy our attention. Hence, when we think of our own existence, we only excite abstracted or reflex ideas, (as they are termed), of our principal pleasures or pains, or our desires or aversions, or of the figure, solidity, colour, or other properties of our bodies, and call that act of the sensorium a consciousness of our existence. Some philosopher, I believe it is Des Cartes, has said 'I think, therefore I exist.' But this is not right reasoning, because thinking is a mode of existence, and it is thence only saying, 'I exist, therefore I exist.'"

9. Kant, *Critique of Pure Reason* A155 = B194. The section "On the Paralogisms of Pure Reason" warns against imputing empirical existence to "a transcendental subject of thoughts . . . = X" (A346 = B404), but the first edition contains two other, more positive references to this "third thing" that were subsequently deleted: "etwas anderes (X)" at A8, and "Etwas = X" at A250. Dutoit, "Ghost Stories," does an excellent job of relating "Geist" and the "third thing" in a range of Kant's writings to supernatural fiction, specifically Heinrich von Kleist's story "Das Bettelweib von Locarno."

10. Rush, *Medical Inquiries*. The book contains noteworthy passages on booksellers' fever, a product of the "sudden transitions . . . felt after reading a volume of reviews or magazines" (37); on "the tory rot, and the protection fever," among other forms of "political hypochondriasm" (114–15); and on poor spelling and feminine indelicacy as symptoms of mental illness (253). Not at all as eccentric as his writing sometimes sounds, Rush was one of the great physicians of his day and founded what later became Philadelphia General Hospital.

11. Cullen, *Kurzer Inbegriff der medicinischen Nosologie*, 1: 340. Also translated in this period were Cullen's 1766 lectures, *Nervenkrankheiten*, another partly symptomatic, partly behavioral nosology. Pargeter, in his 1792 treatise on madness (*Theoretisch-praktische Abhandlung über den Wahnsinn*), praises Cullen for abolishing the mania-melancholia distinction and proposing a single insania universalis; however, given Cullen's emphasis on the hysteria-hypochondria distinction and Pargeter's judgment that madness is "a secret, and will remain altogether inexplicable for human reason" (13), the conceptual unity of

madness remains a pipe-dream. The German translation is interesting for using "Lebenskraft" to render "nervous power" (13).

12. As if in involuntary demonstration of these involuntary spasms of the brain, the grammar of the German here is even more incoherent than is normal in Kant, though the sense is adequately clear. My interpolated "that" rationalizes the English but doesn't work in German. An emendation reported in Kant's *Werke*, 6: 390, constructs a feasible sentence only by moving the verb *bewirkt* a line and a half and supplying four additional words. Should we perhaps read at the end "the unity of consciousness of [the brain] itself" (*desselben*) rather than "of [the representations] themselves" (*derselben*)?

13. Here are some examples of pre-Kantian discussions of dreams. I quote at length because the books are hard to find. The influential midcentury naturalist Charles Bonnet writes, "the greater or lesser intensity in the movements [of the soul] appears to differentiate these two states," i.e., waking and sleeping (*Essai de psychologie*, 362). The flip side of the doctrine that dreams are periods of deficient wakefulness can be found around the same time, in the *Physiologie* of the physician and poet Albrecht von Haller: "I consider dreams to be a kind of sickliness and a kind of irritant cause that interrupts the perfect repose of the sensorium. Therefore dreamless sleep refreshes us the most" (448). Among Kant's contemporaries, the empiricist view was promulgated in the treatise *Von den Träumen und Nachtwanderern* by the Jena philosophy professor Justus Hennings: "A complete sleep is thus the lack of all consciousness" (188); "The cause of sleep thus lies in the body" (i.e., in physical or external rather than mental or internal factors) (192); "A dream is the beginning of awakening" (239). Hennings had earlier written two equally large books against visions, *Von den Ahndungen und Visionen* and *Visionen vorzüglich neuerer und neuester Zeit*, and a vast book against belief in ghosts, *Von Geistern und Geistersehern*. His principle was, "Natural causes must be presumed until the opposite is sufficiently proved," which, of course, can never happen (*Von Geistern*, 420). The book concludes with a section on ghosts in dreams (835–44). Written in the same spirit are Kinderling's *Der Somnambulismus*, and letters 7, 8, and 12 of May's *Vermischte Schriften*, 1: 73–119, 119–53, 207–17. "Heil der Aufklärung!" as May's typesetter quaintly allows himself to insert (1: 338).

14. Indeed, even a rationalist, taking his cue from Kant, might write in praise of dreams: see Rupp, "Versuch einer psychologisch-teleologischen Beurtheilung." There are some fine passages on the theme of dreaming in Kant in Clark, "Kant's Aliens," 210–26.

15. Here Kant's text points toward a romantic view that in sleep we know more and can do more than in the categorically restricted waking world.

See in particular the medical dissertation on sleepwalking by the author of "The Vampire," John Polidori, in Polydorus, *Disputatio*. Using extremely selective evidence to establish his thesis (only two instances of sleepwalking are actually cited), Polidori claims first that sleepwalkers not only can engage in all forms of human activity but can even walk safely along precipices from which they would fall to their deaths if they were awake (5–6; for a fictional exemplification see the opening episode in Balzac's *Séraphita*), and second that sleepwalkers remember what they have done both awake and asleep, whereas in their waking moments they do not remember their fits of sleepwalking (20–21). In sum, "the intellect [of the sleepwalker] seems to have been enlarged" (21). In the German realm, see K. E. Schelling, "Ideen und Erfahrungen": "somnambulism is nothing more than a completely idealized or internalized sensibility, whereas conversely the latter [i.e., sensibility] is a completely externalized, and outwardly self-reflecting somnambulism, while a single fundamental law is present in both. . . . For we only see, hear, and touch everything that we see, hear, and touch because it magnetizes us, whence in each moment force (or whatever one might name it) flows through all our senses and limbs out into the world, and from the world back into us" (11).

16. For incisive readings of these Kant essays, see Müller-Sievers, *Desorientierung*, 21–50.

17. The impulse toward an applied Kantianism (a practical idealism)—which, I am arguing, is also the impulse behind the gothic—is explicitly acknowledged in a review by Reil of a book on the life force by David Veit: "The concept of *force* is . . . perfected and presented discursively in the *Critique of Pure Reason*," and though "its real use in experience is nonetheless subject to great difficulties," Veit largely overcomes them (Reil, Review, 507).

Chapter 7

1. The distinction between *Kraft* and *Vermögen* had been made earlier, in Christian Wolff's *Deutsche Metaphysik*. Wolff, however, does not oppose the terms but relates them as genus to species: the soul has one *Kraft* that activates many different *Vermögen* (Latin: *facultates* or *potentiae*). On Wolff, see Grau, *Die Entwicklung des Bewußtseinsbegriffes*, 189–90.

2. Schmid here is mouthing straight empiricist dogma. Dufour invokes the Berlin philosophe Formey to the same effect a few pages after denying that the soul can know itself: "M. *Formey* says: that an impenetrable obscurity remains and will always remain for us in the essence of each simple being, which however does not entail an obscurity in the properties"

("Essai," 67). In the course of a long afterword on hypochondria in the German translation of Dufour, Platner writes: "In every thinking moment of wakefulness [the soul has] a clear, but confused feeling of the condition of the entire machine, which is composed of thousands upon thousands of . . . nerve impulses, and collects into a single animal consciousness; although the soul has no distinct representation either of these nerve impulses singly or of the activity with which it reacts against them" (Dufour, *Versuch*, 305–6).

3. On epigenesis see Müller-Sievers, *Self-Generation*, esp. 46–47.

4. Letter from Herder to Jean Paul, Nov. 1798, *Briefe*, 388; also quoted in my *Preromanticism*, 75.

5. This chapter must observe some limits of its own. Otherwise it might look beyond Kant's dry understanding, the genius of his shore, to the sublime and treacherous ocean beyond, strange seas of thought that he shares with Locke and Hume (*Critique of Pure Reason* A236–37 = B294–95 and A297 = B353–54; *Critique of Judgment* A77 = B77; *Prolegomena* A8 and 27), and then proceed to the stormy ocean journey that launched the career of Kant's greatest and least faithful student, Johann Gottfried Herder.

6. Section 33 of the *Prolegomena*, which might be called Kant's philosophy in the annex, helps to explain the link that Lacan propounds between Kant and Sade's *Philosophie dans le boudoir*. Pure consciousness / pure pleasure must be sought outside the realm of ordinary, law-abiding thought / action constrained by the force of time. See Lacan, "Kant avec Sade." Related issues are discussed in Chaouli, "Van Gogh's Ear."

7. Another revealing early response to Kant is Abel's long *Einleitung in die Seelenlehre*. Explicitly pitting his own empirical psychology against Kant's metaphysical psychology (vii), Abel argues that all ideas come from the senses, or if not, that innate impressions are too early and deeply buried to be relevant to empirical psychology (12), that ideas continue active even in sleep (60), that consciousness is in no sense original but rather the "picture of an impression" (122), that space and time are inductive abstractions (hence the opposite of Kant's "pure forms of sensible intuition," 155–57), that "all thought rests on a Thing that we think" (164), so that finally we know only being (*Dasein*), not essence (*Wesen*, 169). In denial, Abel is more clearheaded about Kant's innovations than Kant's subsequent commentators.

Chapter 8

1. For a full discussion of Kant and the Cartesian cogito see my essay "Kant's Misreading of Descartes."

2. For a good factual history see Young, *Mind*.

3. Schmid, "Über das Gehirn als Seelenorgan." Mauchart had written an overview of the controversies, entitled "Über den Sitz der Seele."

4. A fine discussion of Sömmerring's essay and Kant's response is given in Müller-Sievers, *Desorientierung*, 64–66.

5. Platner, "Ridiculum," 349. The essay ends with praise of Sömmerring (351).

6. Trăn-Dúc-Tháo, *Phénoménologie*, 243. Even more impressive, yet equally inert on account of attending only to the disciplinary, philosophical responses, is Beiser's *Fate of Reason*.

7. A different literary resonance of Herz is explored in Weder, "Der Schwindel des Phantastischen," which relates Herz's ideas to a number of moments in Hoffmann's fiction. Weder identifies these affinities without having, as she says, any direct evidence of Hoffmann's familiarity with Herz's book. For a (perhaps overly compartmentalized) subsequent history of "Schwindel," see Hagner, "Psychophysiologie und Selbsterfahrung."

8. Hufeland, "Mein Begriff von der Lebenskraft" (1798), in his *Kleine medizinische Schriften*, 2: 344–54. Schmid had earlier drawn the same conclusion about the unlocatability of life, in section 40 of his *Empirische Psychologie*, headed "Lebenskraft," 445. In Hufeland's wake the life force became the single most widely debated issue in Reil's periodical. Also rather interesting, and drawing on Moritz but apparently not on Hufeland, is Brandis's *Versuch über die Lebenskraft*, a book aiming to steer a middle ground, welcoming speculation but rejecting enthusiasm, and hence uncertain about the limits of knowledge and the boundary between the material and the spiritual.

9. Hufeland, *Kleine medizinische Schriften*, 1: 272–324. Two additional essays followed in the same year: "Öffentlicher Unterricht über die gewissen und ungewissen Kennzeichen des Todes, über die Zeichen des wiederkehrenden Lebens und wie man überhaupt mit Leichen zu verfahren habe" (Public Inquiry into the Certain and Uncertain Indications of Death, into the Signs of Returning Life and How Corpses Should be Handled, ibid., 1: 325–35) and "Neuere Beispiele von wiedererwachten Todten" (New Examples of Revived Corpses, ibid., 1: 336–42). And 1808 brought a 346-page book, *Der Scheintod* (Sham Death), which, after quoting Herz's *Über die frühe Beerdigung der Juden* (On Early Burial Among the Jews, 1788), goes on to claim that more people are buried alive than commit suicide, and to recommend that victims who have drowned in water, wine, or beer—though not those drowned in fermenting beer—be wrapped in cold, wet sheets and have tobacco smoke blown over them through a tube. Hufeland's work counters, for in-

stance, the theory of Marcard, "Fragment einer medicinischen Abhandlung vom Tode" (Fragment of a Medical Treatise on Death), which argues that even though the causes of death are often invisible and inscrutable, they must nevertheless be physical.

10. Yet more extreme is an essay by Christian Friedrich Nasse, "Beobachtungen über den Somnambulismus von seiner psychischen Seite" (Observations on Somnambulism from the Psychical Side): "Should not then the life of the psyche appear at its freest and most splendid precisely in death, when all bodily organs are shut?" (313); "A higher psychic life appears in somnambulism. . . . Thus somnambulism arises, like the enthusiasm of a poet, transfiguring ordinary life" (336).

11. Formey, "Essai," 129. Formey (1711–1797), who was more than a decade older than Kant, continued active until late in life, with relatively constant views, so far as I can tell.

12. Wizenmann, "An den Herrn Professor Kant." The term *Schwärmerei* appears on pp. 136, 137, and 141–42, and the accusation that Kant's basic argument is "both enthusiastic and groundless" ("gleich schwärmerisch und grundlos") on p. 124. The curious thing is that Kant's disease seems to have infected Wizenmann: his quite reasonable essay ends abruptly in indecision, with the author's confession that he is unable to proceed or even to add a line of positive insight to his fragmentary critique (156). Studying Kant evidently did him in.

13. Mauchart, "Ueber den eigentlichen Siz des Wahnsinnes," 10. Mauchart attacks Kant more vigorously (in favor of a "practical doctrine of the soul [*praktische Seelenlehre*]") in the unpaginated preface to his *Anhang zu den sechs ersten Bänden des Magazins zur Erfahrungsseelenkunde.* Mauchart was another author who attacked superstitious belief in ghosts, in his *Phänomene der menschlichen Seele,* a book dedicated, curiously, to Moritz and, less curiously, to Abel.

14. Hufeland, "Über den Wahnsinn, seine Erkenntniß, Ursachen, und Heilung," in his *Schriften,* 4: 16.

15. Selle, *Grundsätze,* 3. Also see his "Versuch eines Beweises."

16. Weikard, *Der philosophische Arzt,* 3: iv. Weikard was a resolutely retrograde Lockean who believed that dreams are caused by indigestion (1: 23) and that daydreams are tantamount to madness (1: 41).

17. In addition to the spectrum of "gothic" post-Kantianisms reported in my main text, there was also a devout religious line that "dare[s] . . . to go beyond the bounds of experience" in search of the transcendental "reality of [God] in the supersensual," as Johannes Kern put it in his intelligent book, *Die Lehre von Gott,* 21. Friedrich Schelling writes similarly, but with more sensationalism: "We know nothing but what is in experi-

ence, says *Kant*. Quite true; but the existent in experience is precisely that which is alive, eternal, or God. God's existence is an empirical truth. It is the ground of experience" ("Kritische Fragmente," 283).

18. Reil, "Das Zerfallen," 551–52. The essay continues with remarkable cases of dissolving consciousness, both from Reil's own practice and from the literature (including a lengthy account of a case reported by Herz in the *Magazin zur Erfahrungsseelenkunde*). They include one report of a man who "saw his brain, his nerves, senses, intestines, in short all his limbs and organs separated and lying around him in disorderly confusion, [while] in the midst of them sat his I like a spider at the focus of its web and busied itself with each individual part" (571). Ultimately, for Reil, madness becomes the theater of self-consciousness: "In madness and in dreams the I dissects itself, dramatizes its powers, is actor and spectator at once" (583). More empirical in its vocabulary but similar in its stance is Nudow's *Versuch einer Theorie des Schlafs*, which is of interest because it was issued by Kant's publisher. Dreams, says Nudow, reflect an indistinct consciousness or inner feeling ("innere Empfindung, —oder das Bewußtseyn unserer selbst," 18); sleep is initiated by a confusion of ideas and "a kind of madness" (23); "sleep lays the actual foundation for waking" (51); dreams are continuous with waking (111–49), as death is with life (285).

19. For a vitalist—meaning anyone who had read with any sympathy Kant's "Critique of Teleological Judgment" or even the essay on negative quantities—it was only an apparent paradox that a pathology can also be a norm. Hoffbauer (a collaborator of Reil's), for instance, writes that all illness is a disproportion of forces ("Ueber den Begriff des Lebens," "Ideen zu einer Classification der Seelenkrankheiten"), and Reil's last work elaborates the thesis that disease is never a negation but rather a struggle for life that typically brings into conflict the norms of the individual and the norms of the species: *Entwurf einer allgemeinen Pathologie*, chap. 4 ("Die Natur der Krankheit"), 278–348. (Thus, 331: "Disease is a condition of the *living* animal body.") Also see Canguilhem, "Le Normal et le pathologique."

Chapter 9

1. Zimmermann and Radcliffe are briefly juxtaposed in Brissenden, *Virtue in Distress*, 70–72. Lepenies, *Melancholy*, 63–65, discusses Zimmermann as a bourgeois sensibility, another affinity with Radcliffe.
2. Clara Reeve's *Old English Baron* (1777) is a major exception to the internalization of quest. *The Castle of Otranto* had originally been welcomed as a historical novel. In her novel Reeve emphasizes the historical milieu

and reduces the supernatural to the minimum compatible with reasonable sales prospects. The book is also significant in attaching the restored estate to the paternal, or exogamous, line. It is symptomatic that the couple in the novel have six children. Radcliffe's *Sicilian Romance* still concludes in the fashion of a social novel by glancing ahead to the continuation of the line, but *Udolpho* and *The Italian* make no reference to future generations, even though *Udolpho* ends with a temporal prospect where mention of children would readily find a place. A noteworthy sublimation of the "female gothic" may be found in *Godwi, or the Stone Image of the Mother* (1798–1802), by Clemens Brentano, a landmark novel of German romanticism, where the principle of selfhood is located in a mysterious statue rather than a mysterious dungeon: the substitution of the artist's mother-figure for the sadist's corresponds roughly to a substitution of Sternean for Kantian self-consciousness.

Chapter 10

1. Balzac, *Peau de chagrin*, 16; *Wild Ass's Skin*, 27. (Below in my text I will cite these editions by page numbers only, the French page first, followed by a semicolon and the page in Herbert Hunt's English translation.) Historically *Wild Ass's Skin* was the novel that initiated the whole series of the *Comédie humaine*; in Balzac's systematic arrangement it opens the collection of gothic tales grouped as "Etudes philosophiques."

2. My reading of *The Wild Ass's Skin* approaches Samuel Weber's *Unwrapping Balzac* most closely in recognizing the centrality of antithesis. See his chapter 12 (73–83), "The Matrix." In general, Weber's psychoanalytic Freudianism, like Peter Brooks's interpretation (*Reading*, 48–61), privileges the material dimensions of the novel as a study of character. I look more toward ideal dimensions and plot.

Chapter 11

1. Webber presents a thoughtful phenomenology of doubling in *Doppelgänger*, 1–55, and is particularly good on Fichte (23–32). In his analysis of *The Devil's Elixirs* itself (184–94), Webber adopts the perspective of the characters and their experience, without the more distanced irony of author and reader. Webber calls the protagonist an "automaton," yet says he "finds a talking-cure for his pathological speech disorder. . . . The stammering and giggling double is transformed, after his last uncanny visitation at Medardus's death-bed, into the figure of the painter as master raconteur of Medardus's life-story, the creator of true-to-life portraits" (192). In a study obsessed with the double as a Narcissus figure, the notion of truth to life is, it seems to me, both over-earnest and suspect.

2. Kierkegaard, *Concept of Irony*, 274. The end of the paragraph (and of the chapter) makes the link to the gothic explicit: "Finally, the ironic nothingness is that deathly stillness which irony returns to 'haunt and jest'" (275). "Haunt" and "jest" are the two meanings of Kierkegaard's single Danish word *spøger*: in this conclusion, irony gets spooked.

Chapter 12

1. The native home of the soul is an indistinct realm where white and black, desert and world of water meet. This is the credo of *Frankenstein* and of romantic Mont Blanc poetry, but also, transposed out of the gothic key, of Swiss nationalist writing. See "Briefe über ein Schweizerisches Hirtenland," by the Swiss philosopher Karl Victor von Bonstetten: "Come! Here Nature and Man are free and great. These deserts, these cliffs, these ice-valleys, these roaring Alpine waters, these high black woods will please you more than the soulless beauties of the plain" (*Schriften*, 11). The Swiss landscape is the realm of the soul, and soul is self-consciousness: "The consciousness of our own selfhood is the true reality of the soul, without which each soul ceases to be a soul" ("Ueber Tod und Unsterblichkeit," ibid., 271). Soul, self-consciousness, life, are then a pulse or an energy emerging from a realm of indistinctness (as will also appear in *Melmoth*): "Life is the swell that is lifted by a breath and that subsides with it back into the sea of eternity" ("Ueber Tod und Unsterblichkeit," ibid., 257).
2. "*Discordant unison*," italicized by Maturin, specifically describes the terrifying monks who accompany the Superior in his visitations on Monçada, but also appropriately characterizes all the more shadowy evils toward which the persecutions are ultimately directed.
3. Thomas Penrose's quite interesting poem "Madness" comes from his 1755 volume *Flights of Fancy*; I found it in Anderson, *British Poets*, 11: 614–15.

Chapter 13

1. That *Caleb Williams* is fundamentally "an account of mental phenomena" (212) is the guiding thesis of the penetrating reading in Rothstein's *Systems of Order and Inquiry*, 208–42.
2. In *Confinement and Flight*, 127–32, the best discussion of *Caleb Williams* I have seen from a metaphysical perspective, W. B. Carnochan speaks of Caleb's impulsiveness as a kind of suspended animation, a "permanent mode of feeling to be represented now in flight and futility" (131).
3. See the sections "Babil" and "Bords" in Barthes's *Le Plaisir du texte*, 11–24. Barthes's *S/Z*, however, stands together with Algirdon Greimas's

Maupassant and Stanley Fish's *Surprised by Sin* as a monument to the intolerability of a totally punctual reading.

4. Byron, "The Prisoner of Chillon," secs. 9 and 14.

Chapter 14

1. The term "literariness" is fundamental to Russian formalist aesthetics. Thus, Riffaterre opens his formalist work *Text Production* with the statement: "The essential problem confronting linguists in a verbal work of art is its *literariness*" (1). In the title essay of his book *Resistance to Theory*, Paul de Man defines literariness as "a rhetorical rather than an aesthetic function of language . . . that . . . contains no responsible pronouncement on the nature of the world," combining "negative knowledge about the reliability of linguistic utterance" with "a strong illusion of aesthetic seduction" (10). His usage (recently well elucidated in Redfield, *Politics of Aesthetics*, 7–9, 26–29) remains, however, merely skeptical, without proceeding to disclosures such as I try to identify in Radcliffe's clichés. Pinch discusses the "literariness" (66) and "echo chamber" quality (60) of the leading woman poet of the decade in "Sentimentality and Experience in Charlotte Smith's Sonnets" (*Strange Fits of Passion*, 51–71). Also pertinent are the philosophical reflection in Fenves, "*Chatter*," especially the title section, pp. 14–18; and the sociological approach in the section "Shorthand and the Unity of Design" in Christensen's *Lord Byron's Strength*, 201–7.

2. The 1860s was also the period when the term "kitsch" came into use, initially among German artists. As a more global term that typically characterizes a whole work rather than an aspect or portion of it, "kitsch" suggests pervasive degradation or pandering and thus inflicts damage that is less recuperable than that inflicted by the label "cliché." See Calinescu, *Five Faces of Modernity*, 225–62.

3. Hoeveler notices the pervasiveness of music in Radcliffe generally—and specifically here, where, as she points out, "the singing voice of Ellena Rosalbo [*sic*] first attracts her noble lover in *The Italian*" (*Gothic Feminism*, 86). Wolstenholme discusses the voices in relation to ineffability, in *Gothic (Re)visions*, 32. The theme of voice is missed by one of the sharpest-eyed readings of *The Italian* when Sedgwick uses the opening of Radcliffe's tale to support the generalization that "characters in Gothic novels fall in love as much with women's veils as with women" ("Character in the Veil," 256).

4. Here I follow Sedgwick's conclusion: "A truly dynamic or economic reading of these novels would discern the rules of circulation of conventional 'material.' It would, I think, have to discuss sexual desire and,

more generally, the will or motivation of individual characters—the illusion of individuality, in fact, and the wracking, dominant struggle between that illusion and the fascination of the hieroglyphic" ("Character in the Veil," 266–67). My two types of reading should be compared to the two kinds of vision described in Dutoit's clever and subtle essay "Epiphanic Reading."

5. Another sharp-eyed reader, Adela Pinch, in her chapter on *The Mysteries of Udolpho* (*Strange Fits of Passion*, 111–36), focuses on repetition, in an arc leading from "clichés" (117) through nostalgia toward "primal fantasies" (131).

6. *The Mysteries of Udolpho*, however, does approach the verbal formula in its opening chapter, where, following an encounter with Valancourt's voice, Emily hears the wind, "like the spirit of some supernatural being—the voice of the spirit of the woods" (15).

7. Claudia Johnson begins a nuanced account of gender and class tensions in the novel with the spurious consolations offered by the landscapes and with the anxieties of narration (*Equivocal Beings*, 117–37). Cottom's chapter entitled "The Figure in the Landscape" (*Civilized Imagination*, 35–50) regards the landscapes as a "redemptive topography" (45) expressing aesthetic transcendence. While recognizing that "one can only assert a vision of nature as art through a contradiction in terms" (45), Cottom does not analyze passages or probe the contradiction in any detail. Ware notes the silence characteristic of Radcliffe's landscapes ("The Telescope Reversed," 174–76), which he relates to the distancing and softening intention of the depictions, without acknowledging the dialectic that makes every cure also imply the threat to which it responds.

8. See, notably, this linkage of "scenery" with painting: "he found the scenery [the adjacent country] exhibited infinitely surpassing all that his glowing imagination had painted; he saw it with the eye of a painter, and felt it with the rapture of a poet" (Radcliffe, *Romance of the Forest*, 326). The *OED* cites Cowper's *Task* (1784) as the earliest locus for "scenery" in reference to the natural landscape, preceded slightly by the more theatrical-sounding "sceneries" (1777). There are two older citations in Johnson's spelling, "scenary," but they both have a theatrical ring to them. "Scene" in the sense of "A view or picture of a place, concourse, incident, . . . etc." is dated back to the mid-seventeenth century, but the earlier citations all carry specific qualifiers that make them more or less allegorical or denotative, as in Gibbon's "scene of peace and plenty" from 1787. As the earliest absolute, hence aesthetic, use of "scene," the *OED* cites a sentence from *The Italian*—"The travellers stopped to admire the scene" (158).

9. See, in particular, the fine account of scenic nostalgia in Duncan, *Modern Romance*, 40–44.

10. The fairyland topos also appears in the last chapter of *The Mysteries of Udolpho*, as well as at some other moments in that novel and at least once in *Romance of the Forest* (in chap. 18). It always evokes the perfected assimilation of individual, society, and nature, dream and waking, desire and fulfillment.

11. The principal passages by Freud synthesized in this paragraph are the opening pages of the essay "Die Verdrängung" and the opening of chapter 4 of the essay "Das Unbewußte" (*Studienausgabe*, 3: 109 and 139–40). See also Freud's analysis of Schreber, "Psychoanalytische Bemerkungen über einen autobiographisch beschriebenen Fall von Paranoia (Dementia Paranoides)," ibid., 7: 190–91, and, for the location of language within the preconscious, chap. 2 of "Das Ich und das Es," ibid., 3: 289.

12. To be sure, some recent discussions have verged on the topic of cliché by stressing the superficiality of gothic renderings of personality. Henderson, for instance, has written about "relational identity" as opposed to a depth model of identity (*Romantic Identities*, 38–58), and Hogle has written eloquently of gothic ghosts as "counterfeits" and "simulacra" ("Gothic Ghost," "'Frankenstein' as Neo-Gothic"). Hogle's terms are another way of labeling what I have called the literariness of the gothic as it reflects reading experience rather than lived experiences. Yet as finely as Henderson and Hogle argue, they ignore the production of these products and the specificity of the narrative employment of superficiality. Freud shows us what motivates cliché, both as "breakdown" and as "probe" (to invoke the terms from the suggestive discussions in McLuhan, *From Cliché to Archetype*, 48–61). For a formalist approach to cliché as either the ground or the parody of expression, see Riffaterre, "Fonction du cliché." A book-length study that does not get much beyond classification is Amossy and Rosen, *Les Discours du cliché*.

13. Freud, *Studienausgabe*, 2: 470. The quoted phrases refer to a specific dream strategy: the notation "This is just a dream." However, the passage opens the section on secondary elaboration and clearly is intended as an instance for this aspect of dream-work in general.

14. in his analysis of Schreber, Freud provides the following footnote: "Those who would shake their heads in rejection of these leaps of neurotic fantasy should remind themselves of similar caprices in which artists sometimes indulge their fantasy, e.g. the *Diableries érotiques* of Le Potevin" (*Studienausgabe*, 7: 190–91). There are now many treatments of realist fiction as a sublimation of gothic fiction; classics are Wilt, *Ghosts of the Gothic*; Levine, *Realist Imagination*; and Sedgwick, "Jane Austen and the Masturbating Girl."

15. Kilgour singles out the episode as a narrative that seems "straight from the subconscious" and that is "typical of the gothic's general self-

consciousness about the ways in which stories get told" (*Rise of the Gothic Novel*, 182), though she seems more interested in its disjointed relation to its lower-class origin.

16. Polk, writing about Jason in Faulkner's *Sound and the Fury* ("Trying Not to Say," 157).

17. Richter's essay, published in *Progress of Romance*, 86–90, explains incoherence in terms of incompatible generic expectations. This explanation facilitates a plausible literary-historical account of the gothic as a transitional mode but deflects consideration of its distinctive manner and success.

18. See Poovey, "Ideology," for a successful "realist" reading (focusing on *The Mysteries of Udolpho*) of Radcliffe as a social novelist.

19. Where revelation is so fragile, to be sure, there remains a fine line between communicative insinuation and voluble concealment, creating, in Cottom's words, a "radical uncertainty even to judgments that would seem unquestionable" (*Civilized Imagination*, 58). (Cottom proceeds, however, to argue for the real basis of her imagined worlds, citing Marc Bloch on feudal society as evidence that castles really had *oubliettes*.) The "fairyland" catharsis remains as uncertain an outcome as in most of Freud's case studies. Hence, where I see psychic revelation of the characters, Claudia Johnson, in *Equivocal Beings*, sees political inconsistency in the author, leading her to mistrust the endings of both *The Italian* (136) and *The Mysteries of Udolpho* (116). Halfheartedness is a besetting vice of gothic criticism, as when Howells writes, "She cannot stop herself making positive claims for imagination and feeling, even if she has to hide behind a mask to do it" (*Love, Mystery and Misery*, 61). Miall calls the ending a sterile "freeze frame" ("Preceptor as Fiend," 41) and says that the animistic hallucinations of Radcliffe's novels "correspond to the actual forces that shaped the lives of women and sought to confine them to a state of perpetual adolescence" (40). The questions are whether the correspondence points toward submission or detection, and whether "actual forces"—ideological or psychological—are buried or conscious.

Chapter 15

1. Here I follow Lipking's spirited and original essay in resisting any clear or settled message. Lipking identifies Rousseau's pedagogical novel *Emile* as a crucial source for *Frankenstein* but does not connect the source with the topic of childhood on which the present chapter focuses.

2. They were reading *Fantasmagoriana*, a mélange of eight long narratives translated from German with no sources indicated. These are typical *histoires galantes*, replete with remarkable incidents, deceptions, and

explained and unexplained supernatural episodes. The collection begins with a long, bantering tale from the popular *Volksmärchen der Deutschen*, by Johann Karl August Musäus; the general tone of the volumes is close to Jane Austen's in *Northanger Abbey*. Two passages that discuss the problems of explanation and evidence (1: 126–27 and 2: 264) give the overall impression that both a modern ruse ("Le Revenant," *Fantasmagoriana*, 2: 163–224) and an ancient curse ("Les Portraits de famille," ibid., 1: 117–225) make equally improbable stories. This was a model that Shelley and the others could have wished only to depart from, not to imitate.

3. "Tale of superstition" is Percy's phrase. Mary originally wrote "ghost story," pointing up even more glaringly the contrast between Frankenstein and *Frankenstein*. See Shelley, *Frankenstein Notebooks*, 75 (henceforth cited as *Notebooks*).

4. See, however, Hogle, "'Frankenstein' as Neo-Gothic," for a lively, Baudrillard-inspired argument that Shelley's novel, typical of romantic gothic, updates *The Castle of Otranto* by featuring a counterfeit ghost.

5. "Why is it a he?" asks Homans (*Bearing the Word*, 106). Eventually she suggests that the monster is androgynous. I propose that Walton's and Frankenstein's "he" tries to humanize a phenomenon they cannot face in its full alienness. Regarding them both as unreliable narrators, I use the neuter, the pronoun that Frankenstein uses in the first moment of creation ("It breathed hard," Shelley, *Frankenstein*, 16) and that Walton seems unable to resist following William's murder: "A flash of lightning . . . discovered its shape plainly to me; its gigantic stature, and the deformity of its aspect, more hideous than belongs to humanity, instantly informed me that it was the wretch, the filthy dæmon, to whom I had given life. What did he there? Could he be . . . the murderer of my brother? . . . The figure passed me quickly, and I lost it in the gloom. Nothing in human shape could have destroyed that fair child. *He* was the murderer! I could not doubt it" (54–55).

6. A striking gothic example of existence that is unearthly yet within the world, natural yet seemingly supernatural, is the disembodied voice of the ventriloquist. In speaking without being seen, Charles Brockden Brown's Carwin resembles Frankenstein's monster: "I was studious of seclusion: I was satiated with the intercourse of mankind, and discretion required me to shun their intercourse. For these reasons I long avoided the observation of your family, and chiefly visited these precincts at night" (*Wieland*, 224–25). Another instance—interesting because notably incidental—is Brother Nicola in Radcliffe's *Italian*.

7. A related discursive account of will may be found in the report of the

Treatise on the Will attributed to Raphael in Balzac's *Wild Ass's Skin*, but then subsequently reattributed to another Balzac character, Louis Lambert, in whose novel the contents are summarized (*Louis Lambert, Comédie humaine*, 10: 389–97). Especially pertinent is the narrator's response, which replaces "will" with its synonym "thought": "Thus THOUGHT appeared to me like a wholly physical power, accompanied by its incommensurable generations. It was a new Humanity in another form" (10: 397).

8. On the gothic conversion of quantity into sublime quality, see Foucault, "Language to Infinity," in *Language, Counter-Memory, Practice*, 53–67; and Liu, "Toward a Theory of Common Sense," 184–200. The topic derives from the discussions of repetition and infinity in Burke's *Enquiry.*

9. Cf. Mary Shelley's letter to Percy Shelley, May 29, 1817: "Why is not life a continued moment where hours and days are not counted—but as it is a succession of events happen—the moment of enjoyment lives only in memory and when we die where we are?" (*sic*, as if the counting problem even causes the grammatical stumbling). Shelley, *Selected Letters*, 25.

10. The designation "being" (*Frankenstein*, 16, 107) may be chiefly Percy's. On one manuscript page (Mary Shelley, *Notebooks*, 175) he twice inserted the word "being," substituting it first for "wretch," then for "creature," where Mary's original ("A creature whom I myself had created") suggests the derivation of the latter name from one perspective on the monster. The published text gives "being" once again, following the monster's long narrative, where "creature" stands uncorrected in the manuscript (*Notebooks*, 401).

11. The *OED* does not record "creature" in the sense of "monster"—Hollywood's "creature from outer space"—but one might conjecture that it derives directly from *Frankenstein*'s onomastic confusion.

12. The concern with causality pervades Dacre's *Zofloya*, in numerous allusions to the "resistless influence" of a dream (223), to the "original cause" (251, in the last chapter), and the like. (*Zofloya* was a major source for the young Percy Shelley's gothic novels.) Critics of the gothic rarely focus on the topic, a major exception being Todorov, *The Fantastic*, 109–13.

13. The problem of seemingly coincidental secondary causes in the gothic has already been glanced at in connection with *The Wild Ass's Skin* above in Chapter 10. See Andropoulos, "Invisible Hand," for a particularly illuminating study. Fielding had already struggled with the problem in the last of the *Tom Jones* prefaces: "We will lend [our hero] none of that supernatural assistance with which we are entrusted. . . . If he doth not, therefore, find some natural means of extricating himself from all his distresses, we will do no violence to the truth and dignity of history

for his sake" (*Tom Jones*, 781). This passage is cited in Kayman's essay "New Sort of Specialty" (634), in which he argues that Fielding represents a series of transitions between older and more modern social constitutions.

14. "It is only this factor of involuntary repetition which surrounds with an uncanny atmosphere what would otherwise be innocent enough, and forces upon us the idea of something fateful and unescapable where otherwise we should have spoken of 'chance' only." Freud, "The Uncanny," 144.

15. The problem of a monster story is the focus of the *Frankenstein* chapter of Garrett's new book, *Gothic Reflections*, 83–102. Garrett naturalizes the monster by psychologizing the problem and thereby understating the uncanniness of its form. For instance: "we are urged to respond as Frankenstein does . . . [bringing] him closer to us and mak[ing] it possible to feel with him, to recognize ourselves in his monstrousness" (95).

16. Speaking French, the Irish magistrate Mr. Kirwin offers kindness to the imprisoned and delirious Frankenstein, calling his country a "shore, renowned for its hospitality" (*Frankenstein*, 138). However, Frankenstein had heard a different tune when he landed there. "Surely it is not the custom of Englishmen to receive strangers so inhospitably," he complains, but is rudely answered: "I do not know . . . what the custom of the English may be; but it is the custom of the Irish to hate villains" (134).

17. "How strange, I thought, that the same cause should produce such opposite effects!" And, later in the same paragraph, "I reflected on this; and, by touching the various branches, I discovered the cause" (*Frankenstein*, 78–79). Contrast the monster's lucidity here (beginning just above: "My sensations had, by this time, become distinct") with Frankenstein's delirium after the monster murders his bride: "all this time no distinct idea presented itself to my mind; but my thoughts rambled to various subjects, reflecting confusedly on my misfortunes and their cause" (225 and 131; the first clause and the word "confusedly" were added in 1831). Condillac was evidently the philosopher who most forcefully asserted that thought depends upon language, but for Locke, too, thought cannot be clear if words are misused; see Aarsleff, *Study of Language*, 13–43.

18. Kant also resorts to qualifying parentheses in the following passages, among others: "the subject of this determination (man)" and "the subject of this will (man)" (*Critique of Practical Reason* A15 and A87).

19. Brooks, "What Is a Monster?" 217; and Veeder, *Mary Shelley*, 212. Brooks's discussion (unlike Veeder's) makes clear that the presumption of sexual desire is Frankenstein's mistake; Brooks sees that the issue lies

in a deeper, primal narcissism, and he goes on to discuss gender ambiguity: "the Monster never is given the chance to function sexually, and we are never given a glimpse of those parts of the body that would assure us that he is male" (219). While demonstrating aspects of infantilism in the monster, Brooks does not proceed to the converse claim I make in this chapter, that the novel represents infancy as monstrous.

20. Mellor, *Mary Shelley*, 38–51, illuminates the novel's portrayal of children's feelings and its stance toward education, but bypasses the novel's representation of the immature childish understanding of the world.

21. Even so peripheral a figure as the Irish magistrate Kirwin exemplifies the inscrutable instability of character. At his introduction he appears "calm and mild," yet "with some degree of severity" (*Frankenstein*, 135). He proceeds to torment Frankenstein with the abrupt sight of Clerval's corpse, knocking the scientist into two months of helpless delirium. When Frankenstein starts to recover, Kirwin reemerges with "sympathy and compassion" (138), but when Frankenstein shies, he again trifles with Frankenstein's feelings, offering an unnamed "friend" and reacting with summary judgment—"a troubled countenance . . . a presumption of my guilt, . . . rather a severe tone" (139). Frankenstein covers his eyes as if Kirwin or the unknown friend (who will turn out to be Frankenstein's father) were the monster, and Kirwin accuses him of rejecting his father before Frankenstein has had a chance to learn who is there. (Indeed Frankenstein could hardly expect the arrival of his father, who had earlier been spared from attending to Frankenstein's even longer illness in Ingolstadt on account of his "advanced age, and unfitness for so long a journey" [43].) So much for the "renowned . . . hospitality" (138) of the Irish!

22. Elias, *Civilizing Process*, 120. Elias's theoretical generalization on the topic comes on pp. 153–54: "The problems relating to the child's consciousness and drive economy vary with the nature of the relations of children to adults" (153). He determined that the word "civilisation," which distinguishes adults from children, emerged in France only in the 1760s (and, according to the *OED*, in the following decade in England); see *Civilizing Process*, 33–34 and the associated note on 519.

23. "The concept of the separate nature of childhood, of its difference from the world of adults, began with the elementary concept of its weakness, which brought it down to the level of the lowest social strata" (Aries, *Centuries of Childhood*, 262). Throughout his text, Aries traces the development of this concept to its climax in the eighteenth century.

24. See Kuhn, *Corruption in Paradise*. Other examples of such studies include Knoepflmacher, "Mutations of the Wordsworthian Child of Na-

ture," which beautifully outlines Victorian literary disquietude with the Wordsworthian child; Walvin, *A Child's World*, a social history of children in nineteenth-century Britain that contrasts the glorious ideals with the hard Victorian realities of early death, punishment, poverty, and crime; and Dieter Richter, *Das fremde Kind*, an elegant anthropological study of "the wild child" throughout history that acknowledges the lawlessness attaching to fairytale and utopian images.

25. Perhaps the wild, asocial character of *Frankenstein* explains why Steedman pointedly omits it from her study *Strange Dislocations* despite acknowledging it in her preface (p. ix) as a crucial provocation for her work. Despite its span from Goethe's Mignon to Freud, her book is a medley of the physiology, dramaturgy, and sociology of childhood, deflecting psychology onto "the point where Wilhelm sees a real child and recognises her, in the social world of the novel" (158) and climaxing in a critique of Kincaid for omitting "evidence" that pedophilia is abusive (167). There is indeed no place for Frankenstein in work oriented toward "the search for the child" Mignon, "as she really was" (158).

Chapter 16

1. Praz, *Romantic Agony*, 26. The nod to Gretchen opens the book, following only a long Percy Shelley quote. Other bits of *Faust*, Part I, figure very sporadically later as analogies to Maturin's *Melmoth the Wanderer* and to victimized females.

2. See Goethe, *Werke*, Pt. I, vol. 42.2, pp. 86–88 (Goethe's treatments of Scott and Hoffmann). Goethe repeatedly refers to Walpole's *Castle of Otranto* (*Werke*, Pt. III, 2: 224; Pt. IV, 13: 91, 343, 361; 14: 54, and 15: 50), also to Walpole's *Mysterious Mother* (Pt. I, 35: 86). He even translated a bit of Maturin's *Bertram* (Pt. I, 11: 353–58) and was aware of Monk Lewis. Closer to home, Goethe knew both Tieck's "romantic" writings, as he refers to them (Pt. III, 2: 259), and Schiller's *Geisterseher* (Pt. III, 3: 124). Of the romantic psychiatrists discussed below, Hufeland was his family physician, Reil a good friend. On Kant as an ironist, see Pt. II, 11: 54–55 and 13: 448. Redfield, *Phantom Formations*, 81–94, analyzes themes of ghostliness in *Wilhelm Meister*.

3. The most detailed comparison of *Faust* and *Melmoth* can be found in Conger, *Matthew G. Lewis*, 12–42.

4. See, for instance, the "quite astonishing" claim by Jane K. Brown that the final moments of Part I derive from the comic-opera tradition, in her *Goethe's "Faust,"* 111–14 (quoted words on p. 111). The more conventional reading can be illustrated with Stuart Atkins's emphasis on the "tragic defeat," "horror," and "tragic dignity" of Gretchen's "secular-sentimental apotheosis," in his *Goethe's "Faust,"* 99–100.

5. Staiger mentions Hufeland in connection with Faust's resurrection, in *Goethe*, 3: 451.

6. As part of his demonstration of the thematic unity of *Faust*, Joachim Müller surveys representative occurrences of *schauern* and *schaudern* in the play, without discussing their significance. See his *Zur Motivstruktur*, 9–11.

7. Note that Atkins's translation, much the most scrupulously literal available, scrupulously skirts the gothic resonances of the vocabulary in this and some of the subsequent passages. For line 11380, as will be seen below, he even takes *Schauer* most improbably in the homonymic sense of "shower"; in line 11510 *Geist* is omitted altogether, and in line 8 *Zauber*.

8. Matthew Arnold's lines on Goethe in "Memorial Verses: April, 1850," note the gothic ground of Goethe's detachment:

> And he was happy, if to know
> Causes of things, and far below
> His feet to see the lurid flow
> Of terror, and insane distress,
> And headlong fate, be happiness.

Emrich builds his passing mention of madness (*Symbolik von Faust II*, 73–74) on a line from *Egmont*, "wrapped in amiable madness, we sink and cease to exist [*eingehüllt in gefälligen Wahnsinn versinken wir und hören auf zu sein*]." But Emrich's Hegelian bias toward redemptive *Gefälligkeit* leads him to slight the significance of *Wahnsinn*, a word that is absent from his index of concepts.

9. Kittler, *Discourse Networks*, 3.

10. The verses are from Matthew Arnold, "Stanzas from the Grande Chartreuse."

11. See the groundbreaking general discussion of this phenomenon by Geoffrey H. Hartman, "Romanticism and Anti-Self-Consciousness."

12. Emrich, *Symbolik von Faust II*, 71. Also see Michelsen's "Fausts Schlaf und Erwachen," a nice analysis of "Pleasant Landscape" in relation to Faust's opening monologue. Michelsen identifies cathartic forgetting as the new motif at this point in the play, and compares the action here to the procedures "of scientific experimentation" (38). For his theory of sleep, Michelsen draws on the *Aphorismen aus der Physiologie der Pflanzen* (1808) by Goethe's friend and admirer Dietrich Georg Kieser. The passages Michelsen quotes (40–41) were, however, commonplace, both among mystics and, in variants, among rationalists like Heinrich Nudow. For a more powerful account of the power of forgetting in the play, see Adorno, "Zur Schlußszene des Faust." Schanze, "Szenen, Schema, Schwammfamilie," presents the final scene as a theatrum mem-

oriae; however, Schanze's thesis differs less from ours than might appear, since he emphasizes collective memory and transcendence of individual perspective.

13. Mephisto characterizes the wavering rescuers in these lines: "drifts towards us [*Schon schwebts heran*]," line 11723; "fighting off the roses that drift about him [*Sich mit den schwebenden Rosen herumschlagend*]," line 11740 stage direction; "You're hovering without direction [*Ihr schwanket hin und her*]," line 11787.

14. Grimm's *Deutsches Wörterbuch* cites only this passage to illustrate a transitive use of *umarten*. Its two prior instances of intransitive *umarten* do not appear to constitute a precedent. In a subsection of his essay "Theatrum Mundi" (145–52), Kunisch transmutes the reflexive into a passive, "ein Umgeartetwerden in dem gnadevollen Sichmitteilen der Liebe [a being transformed in the merciful self-communication of love]" (46).

15. We argue here against the type of idealizing reading canonized by Kommerell in "Faust II: Letzte Szene." "Put into prose" (116)—which is to say, substituting doctrinal pieties for human feeling—Goethe's conclusion seems to Kommerell a "mystery" that preaches "a seraphic sociability and collegiality" (121) and that portrays "the geniality of the condition of love in that generality which the style of the second part confers" (129). "All at once," as one critic writes in Kommerell's vein, "the scenes of black magic, the second part's interminable promenades through ancient and modern deviltry, pale before this ending of a blinding, visionary centenarian" (Grappin, "Faust aveugle," 146).

16. Lyotard has provided the most apposite analyses of the sublime as a darkness that wrings morality out of disintegration. See in particular his "L'Intérêt du sublime." In the more concise formulation of another of his essays, "the sublime is the affective paradox, the paradox of feeling (of feeling publicly) in common a formlessness for which there is no image or sensory intuition" ("Sign of History," 176).

17. Valuable comments about *Faust* as a dialectic *in extremis* are offered in Jochen Schmidt, "Die 'katholische Mythologie.'" See particularly the essay's last sentence: "So the spectrum of demythologization expands into totality, since not merely an old world of figurally stamped representations of beliefs and figured meanings, but altogether the representation of an all-encompassing figure of sense—the representation of a totally ordered cosmos as a mythic form of representation—is sublated in a beyond that, as the sphere of that which has grown unreal, turns at once into nothingness" (256). Having let the genie out of the bottle, however, Schmidt tries to nail it to the wall, claiming that Dionysius the Areopagite is the secret source that explains all. "Only then does the sense of the

hitherto unexplained famous lines [of the final chorus] become exactly
graspable" (245)—a claim that would be more persuasive if the "exact"
meaning that he finds were more than a conventionally hermetic approximation: "Therefore God is not to be known in His particularity, but
rather through approximation or simile" (246).

WORKS CITED

Aarsleff, Hans. *The Study of Language in England, 1780–1860*. Minneapolis: University of Minnesota Press, 1983.

Abel, Jacob Friedrich. *Einleitung in die Seelenlehre*. Stuttgart: Johann Benedikt Meyer, 1786.

Adorno, Theodor. "Zur Schlußszene des Faust." In *Noten zur Literatur*, 129–38. Frankfurt am Main: Suhrkamp, 1981.

Agamben, Giorgio. *Infancy and History: The Destruction of Experience*. Trans. Liz Heron. London: Verso, 1993.

Allison, April. *Virtue's Faults: Correspondences in Eighteenth-Century British and French Women's Fiction*. Stanford, Calif.: Stanford University Press, 1996.

Alter, Robert. *Fielding and the Nature of the Novel*. Cambridge, Mass.: Harvard University Press, 1968.

Amis, Martin. *The War Against Cliché: Essays and Reviews, 1971–2000*. New York: Talk Miramax Books/Hyperion, 2001.

Amossy, Ruth, and Elisheva Rosen. *Les Discours du cliché*. Paris: Société d'édition d'enseignement supérieur, 1982.

Anderson, Robert, ed. *The Works of the British Poets*. 13 vols. London: Arch, 1795.

Andropoulos, Stefan. "The Invisible Hand: Supernatural Agency in Political Economy and the Gothic Novel." *ELH* 66 (1999): 739–58.

Aries, Philippe. *Centuries of Childhood: A Social History of Family Life*. Trans. Robert Baldick. New York: Knopf, 1962.

Arnold, Thomas. *Observations on the Nature, Kinds, Causes, and Prevention of Insanity*. 2 vols. New York: Arno, 1976.

Atkins, Stuart. *Goethe's "Faust": A Literary Analysis*. Cambridge, Mass.: Harvard University Press, 1964.

Balzac, Honoré de. *La Comédie humaine*. 10 vols. Paris: Bibliothèque de la Pléïade, Gallimard, 1950–56.

———. *La Peau de chagrin*. In Balzac, *La Comédie humaine*, 9: 11–249.

———. *The Wild Ass's Skin*. Trans. Herbert H. Hunt. Harmondsworth, Eng.: Penguin, 1977.

Barthes, Roland. *Le Plaisir du texte*. Paris: Seuil, 1973.

Battie, William, M.D. *Treatise on Madness*. London: J. Whiston and B. White, 1758. Reprinted together with John Monro, *Remarks on Dr. Battie's "Treatise on Madness,"* ed. Richard Hunter and Ida Macalpine. London: Dawsons of Pall Mall, 1962.

Beck, Lewis White. "Did the Sage of Königsberg Have No Dreams?" In *Essays on Kant and Hume*, 38–60. New Haven, Conn.: Yale University Press, 1978.

Beiser, Frederick. *The Fate of Reason: German Philosophy from Kant to Fichte*. Cambridge, Mass.: Harvard University Press, 1987.

Belsey, Catherine. "The Romantic Construction of the Unconscious." In *1789: Reading Writing Revolution*, ed. Francis Barker et al., 67–80. N.p.: University of Essex, 1982.

Berkeley, George. *"A New Theory of Vision" and Other Select Philosophical Writings*. London: Dent, 1910.

Bonnet, Charles. *Essai de psychologie; ou, Considérations sur les opérations de l'âme, sur l'habitude et sur l'éducation*. London, 1755.

Bonstetten, Karl Victor von. *Schriften*. Ed. Friedrich Matthisson. Zurich: Orell, Füßli and Compagnie, 1824.

Botting, Fred. "The Gothic Production of the Unconscious." In *Spectral Readings: Towards a Gothic Geography*, ed. Glennis Byron and David Punter, 11–36. New York: St. Martin's, 1999.

Brandis, J. D., M.D. *Versuch über die Lebenskraft*. Hannover: Hahn, 1795.

Brinks, Ellen. *Gothic Masculinity: Effeminacy and the Supernatural in English and German Romanticism*. Lewisburg, Penn.: Bucknell University Press, 2003.

Brissenden, R. F. *Virtue in Distress: Studies in the Novel of Sentiment from Richardson to Sade*. New York: Barnes and Noble, 1974.

Brooks, Peter. *The Melodramatic Imagination: Balzac, Henry James, Melodrama, and the Mode of Excess*. New Haven, Conn.: Yale University Press, 1995.

———. *Reading for the Plot: Design and Intention in Narrative*. New York: Knopf, 1984.

———. "What Is a Monster? (According to *Frankenstein*)." In *Body Work:*

Objects of Desire in Modern Narrative, 199–220. Cambridge, Mass.: Harvard University Press, 1993.

Brown, Charles Brockden. *Edgar Huntly: or, Memoirs of a Sleep-Walker*. Ed. Norman S. Grabo. New York: Viking Penguin, 1988.

———. *Wieland, or The Transformation*. Ed. Fred Lewis Pattee. New York: Harcourt, Brace Jovanovich, 1958.

Brown, Homer O. "*Tom Jones*: The 'Bastard' of History." *Boundary* 2 7 (1979): 201–32.

Brown, Jane K. *Goethe's "Faust": The German Tragedy*. Ithaca, N.Y.: Cornell University Press, 1986.

Brown, Marshall. "Kant's Misreading of Descartes." In *Turning Points: Essays in the History of Cultural Expressions*, 156–72. Stanford, Calif.: Stanford University Press, 1997.

———. "Philosophy and the Gothic." In *Approaches to Teaching Gothic Fiction: The British and American Traditions*, ed. Diane Long Hoeveler and Tamar Heller, 46–57. New York: Modern Language Association, 2003.

———. *Preromanticism*. Stanford, Calif.: Stanford University Press, 1991.

———. "Romanticism and Enlightenment." In *Turning Points: Essays in the History of Cultural Expressions*, 195–219. Stanford, Calif.: Stanford University Press, 1997.

Byrd, Max. *Visits to Bedlam: Madness and Literature in the Eighteenth Century*. Columbia: University of South Carolina Press, 1974.

Calinescu, Matei. *Five Faces of Modernity*. Durham, N.C.: Duke University Press, 1987.

Campbell, Jill. "'I Am No Giant': Horace Walpole, Heterosexual Incest, and Love Among Men." *The Eighteenth Century: Theory and Interpretation* 39 (1998): 238–60.

Canguilhem, Georges. "Le Normal et le pathologique." In *La Connaissance de la vie*, 155–70. Paris: J. Vrin, 1971.

Carnochan, W. B. *Confinement and Flight*. Berkeley: University of California Press, 1977.

Carter, Margaret L. *Specter or Delusion? The Supernatural in Gothic Fiction*. Ann Arbor: UMI Research Press, 1986.

Castle, Terry. *Boss Ladies, Watch Out: Essays on Women, Sex, and Writing*. New York: Routledge, 2002.

———. *The Female Thermometer: Eighteenth-Century Culture and the Invention of the Uncanny*. New York: Oxford University Press, 1995.

Chaouli, Michel. "Van Gogh's Ear." In *Modern Art and the Grotesque*, ed. Frances S. Connelly, 47–62. Cambridge, Eng.: Cambridge University Press, 2003.

Chiarugi, Vincenzo. *Abhandlung über den Wahnsinn überhaupt und insbe-*

sondere, nebst einer Centurie von Bemerkungen. 3 vols. Leipzig: David Meyer, 1795.

Christensen, Jerome C. *Lord Byron's Strength: Romantic Writing and Commercial Society.* Baltimore: Johns Hopkins University Press, 1993.

Clark, David. "Kant's Aliens: The *Anthropology* and Its Others." *The New Centennial Review* 1 (2001): 201–89.

Clemens, Valdine. *The Return of the Repressed: Gothic Horror from "The Castle of Otranto" to "Alien."* Albany: State University of New York Press, 1999.

Clery, E. J. *The Rise of Supernatural Fiction, 1762–1800.* Cambridge, Eng.: Cambridge University Press, 1995.

Cohn, Dorrit. *Transparent Minds: Narrative Modes for Presenting Consciousness in Fiction.* Princeton, N.J.: Princeton University Press, 1978.

Conger, Syndy M. *Matthew G. Lewis, Charles Robert Maturin and the Germans: An Interpretative Study of the Influence of German Literature on Two Gothic Novels.* Salzburg: Institut für englische Sprache und Literatur, Universität Salzburg, 1977.

Cottom, Daniel. *The Civilized Imagination: A Study of Ann Radcliffe, Jane Austen, and Sir Walter Scott.* Cambridge, Eng.: Cambridge University Press, 1985.

Craven, Lady. *The Sleep-Walker.* Strawberry-Hill: T. Kirgate, printer, 1778.

Crébillon, Claude. "Tanzaï et Néadarné: Histoire japonaise." In *Oeuvres complètes,* ed. Jean Sgard, 1: 235–439. Paris: Garnier, 1999.

Crichton, Alexander, M.D. *An Inquiry into the Nature and Origin of Mental Derangement.* 1798. Ed. Robert Ellenbogen. New York: AMS, 1976.

Cullen, William. *Klinische Vorlesungen über die Nervenkrankheiten.* Trans. N. B. G. Schreger. Leipzig: Köhler, 1794.

————. *Kurzer Inbegriff der medicinischen Nosologie.* 2 vols. Leipzig: Caspar Fritsch, 1786.

Dacre, Charlotte. *Zofloya; or, The Moor: A Romance of the Fifteenth Century.* Ed. Adriana Craciun. Peterborough, Ont.: Broadview, 1997.

Darwin, Erasmus. *Zoonomia.* 1794. 2 vols. Boston: Thomas and Andres, 1809.

DeLamotte, Eugenia. *Perils of the Night: A Feminist Study of Nineteenth-Century Gothic.* New York: Oxford University Press, 1990.

de Man, Paul. *The Resistance to Theory.* Minneapolis: University of Minnesota Press, 1986.

De Porte, Michael. *Nightmares and Hobbyhorses: Swift, Sterne, and Augustan Ideas of Madness.* San Marino, Calif.: Huntington Library, 1974.

Derrida, Jacques. *The Archeology of the Frivolous: Reading Condillac.* Trans. John P. Leavey, Jr. Pittsburgh: Duquesne University Press, 1980.

Descartes, René. *Oeuvres*. Ed. Charles Adam and Paul Tannery. 13 vols. Paris: Cerf, 1897–1913.

Doody, Margaret Anne. "Deserts, Ruins, and Troubled Waters: Female Dreams in Fiction and the Development of the Gothic Novel." *Genre* 10 (1977): 529–72.

Dryden, John [and Nathaniel Lee]. *Oedipus*. In *Works*, ed. Sir Walter Scott, 18 vols., 6: 117–225. London: William Miller, 1808.

Dufour, Jean-François. *Essai sur les opérations de l'entendement humain et sur les maladies qui les dérangent*. Amsterdam: Merlin, 1770.

———. *Johann Friedrich Düfours Versuch über die Verrichtungen und Krankheiten des menschlichen Verstandes*. Leipzig: Weygand, 1786.

Duncan, Ian. *Modern Romance and Transformations of the Novel: The Gothic, Scott, Dickens*. Cambridge, Eng.: Cambridge University Press, 1992.

Dutoit, Thomas. "Epiphanic Reading in Ann Radcliffe's *The Mysteries of Udolpho*." In *Moments of Moment: Aspects of the Literary Epiphany*, ed. Wim Tigges, 85–100. Amsterdam: Rodopi, 1999.

———. "Ghost Stories, the Sublime and Fantastic Thirds in Kant and Kleist." *Colloquia Germanica* 27 (1994): 225–54.

Elias, Norbert. *The Civilizing Process: Sociogenetic and Psychogenetic Investigations*. Ed. Eric Dunning, Johan Goudsblom, and Stephen Mennell. Trans. Edmund Jephcott. London: Blackwell, 1994.

Emrich, Wilhelm. *Die Symbolik von Faust II: Sinn und Vorformen*. Frankfurt am Main: Athenäum, 1964.

Evans, Bertrand. *Gothic Drama from Walpole to Shelley*. Berkeley: University of California Press, 1947.

Fairer, David. "'Sweet Native Stream!': Wordsworth and the School of Warton." In *Tradition in Transition: Women Writers, Marginal Texts, and the Eighteenth-Century Canon*, ed. Alvaro Ribeiro, SJ, and James G. Basker, 314–38. Oxford: Clarendon, 1996.

Falconer, William. *Dissertation on the Influence of the Passions upon Disorders of the Body*. London: C. Ditty, Poultry, 1796.

Fantasmagoriana, ou Recueil d'histoires d'apparitions de spectres, revenants, fantômes, etc. 2 vols. Paris: F. Schoell, 1812.

Fearn, John. *An Essay on Human Consciousness*. London: Longman, 1811.

Feder, Lillian. *Madness in Literature*. Princeton, N.J.: Princeton University Press, 1980.

Felski, Rita. *Literature After Feminism*. Chicago: University of Chicago Press, 2003.

Fenves, Peter. *"Chatter": Language and History in Kierkegaard*. Stanford, Calif.: Stanford University Press, 1993.

Ferguson, Frances. *Solitude and the Sublime: Romanticism and the Aesthetics of Individuation.* New York: Routledge, 1992.

Fielding, Henry. *Tom Jones.* New York: Random House, 1950.

Formey, Johann Heinrich Samuel. "Essai sur le sommeil." In *Mélanges philosophiques,* 2 vols., 1: 127–73. Leiden: Elie Luzac, 1754.

Foucault, Michel. *Folie et déraison: Histoire de la folie à l'âge classique.* Paris: Gallimard, 1972.

———. *Language, Counter-Memory, Practice,* ed. Donald F. Bouchard, trans. Donald F. Bouchard and Sherry Simon. Ithaca, N.Y.: Cornell University Press, 1977.

———. *Madness and Civiliation: A History of Insanity in the Age of Reason.* Abridged translation of *Folie et déraison.* Trans. Richard Howard. New York: Vintage, 1988.

Franci, Giovanna. *La Messa in Scena del Terrore: Il Romanzo Gotico Inglese (Walpole, Beckford, Lewis).* Ravenna: Longo, 1982.

Freud, Sigmund. *The Complete Introductory Lectures on Psychoanalysis.* Trans. James Strachey. New York: Norton, 1966.

———. *The Interpretation of Dreams.* Trans. James Strachey. New York: Wiley, 1961.

———. *Studienausgabe.* Ed. Alexander Mitscherlich et al. 11 vols. Frankfurt: Suhrkamp, 1982.

———. *Three Contributions to the Theory of Sex.* Trans. A. A. Brill. New York: Dutton, 1962.

———. "The Uncanny." In *On Creativity and the Unconscious,* ed. Benjamin Nelson, 122–61. New York: Harper, 1958.

Gamer, Michael. *Romanticism and the Gothic: Genre, Reception, and Canon Formation.* Cambridge, Eng.: Cambridge University Press, 2000.

Garrett, Peter K. *Gothic Reflections: Narrative Force in Nineteenth-Century Fiction.* Ithaca, N.Y.: Cornell University Press, 2003.

Godwin, William. *Caleb Williams.* Ed. David McCracken. New York: Norton, 1977.

———. *St Leon.* Ed. Pamela Clemit. Oxford: Oxford University Press, 1994.

Goethe, Johann Wolfgang. *Faust I & II.* Trans. Stuart Atkins. Boston: Suhrkamp/Insel, 1984.

———. *Werke.* 143 vols. Weimar: Böhlau, 1887–1919.

Grappin, Pierre. "Faust aveugle." *Etudes germaniques* 38 (1983): 138–46.

Grau, Kurt Joachim. *Die Entwicklung des Bewußtseinsbegriffes im XVII. und XVIII. Jahrhundert.* Halle: Niemeyer, 1916.

Greenblatt, Stephen. *Hamlet in Purgatory.* Princeton, N.J.: Princeton University Press, 2001.

Haggerty, George. *Men in Love: Masculinity and Sexuality in the Eighteenth Century.* New York: Columbia University Press, 1999.

Hagner, Michael. "Psychophysiologie und Selbsterfahrung: Metamorphose des Schwindels und der Selbsterfahrung im 19. Jahrhundert." In *Aufmerksamkeiten: Archäologie der literarischen Kommunikation VII*, ed. Aleida Assmann and Jan Assmann, 241–63. Munich: Fink, 2001.

Haller, Albert von. *Grundriß der Physiologie für Vorlesungen*. Trans. Samuel Thomas von Sömmerring. Berlin: Haude and Spener, 1788.

Hart, Francis Russell. "The Experience of Character in the English Gothic Novel." In *Experience in the Novel*, ed. Roy Harvey Pearce, 83–105. New York: Columbia University Press, 1968.

Hartman, Geoffrey H. "Romanticism and Anti-Self-Consciousness." In *Beyond Formalism*, 298–310. New Haven, Conn.: Yale University Press, 1970.

Haslam, John. *Observations on Madness and Melancholy*. London: J. Callow, 1809. Originally published in 1798 as *Observations on Insanity*.

Haywood, Eliza. *Love in Excess*. Ed. David Oakleaf. Peterborough, Ont.: Broadview, 2000.

Hegel, Georg Wilhelm Friedrich. *Hegel's Phenomenology of Spirit*. Trans. A. V. Miller. Oxford: Oxford University Press, 1977.

———. *Phänomenologie des Geistes*. Ed. Johannes Hoffmeister. Hamburg: Felix Meiner, 1952.

———. *Schriften*. Ed. Eva Moldenhauer and Karl Markus Michel. 20 vols. Frankfurt: Suhrkamp, 1969–79.

Henderson, Andrea. *Romantic Identities: Varieties of Subjectivity 1774–1830*. Cambridge, Eng.: Cambridge University Press, 1996.

Hennings, Justus Christian. *Visionen vorzüglich neuerer und neuester Zeit*. Altenburg: Richter, 1781.

———. *Von den Träumen und Nachtwanderern*. Weimar: Erben, 1784.

———. *Von Geistern und Geistersehern*. Leipzig: Weygand, 1780.

Herder, Johann Gottfried. *Briefe*. Ed. Wilhelm Dobbek. Weimar: Volksverlag Weimar, 1959.

Herz, Markus. *Versuch über den Schwindel*. 1786. Expanded 2nd ed. Berlin: Vossische Buchhandlung, 1791.

Hill, Aaron. *Dramatic Works*. 2 vols. London: T. Lownds, 1760.

———. *Works*. 4 vols. London: privately printed, 1753.

Hoeveler, Diane Long. *Gothic Feminism: The Professionalization of Gender from Charlotte Smith to the Brontës*. University Park: Pennsylvania State University Press, 1995.

Hoffbauer, Johann Christian. "Ideen zu einer Classification der Seelenkrankheiten aus dem Begriffe derselben, nebst beyläufigen Bemerkungen über den Wahnsinn." *Archiv für die Physiologie* 5 (1802): 448–87.

———. "Ueber den Begriff des Lebens, und der Gesundheit und Krankheit, als Zustände desselben; an den Herrn Professor *Reil*." *Archiv für die Physiologie* 3 (1799): 465–76.

Hoffmann, E. T. A. *The Devil's Elixirs*. Trans. Ronald Taylor. London: John Caler, 1963.

———. *"Die Elixiere des Teufels." "Die Lebensansichten des Katers Murr."* Ed. Walter Müller-Seidel. Darmstadt: Wissenschaftliche Buchgesellschaft, 1970.

———. *The Life and Opinions of the Tomcat Murr.* Trans. Anthea Bell. London: Penguin, 1999.

Hogg, James. *The Private Memoirs and Confessions of a Justified Sinner.* Ed. Robert M. Adams. New York: Norton, 1970.

Hogle, Jerrold E. "'Frankenstein' as Neo-Gothic: From the Ghost of the Counterfeit to the Monster of Abjection." In *Romanticism, History, and the Possibilities of Genre: Re-Forming Literature 1789–1837*, ed. Tilottama Rajan and Julia M. Wright, 176–210. Cambridge, Eng.: Cambridge University Press, 1998.

———. "The Gothic Ghost as Counterfeit and Its Haunting of Romanticism: The Case of 'Frost at Midnight.'" *European Romantic Review* 9 (1998): 283–92.

Homans, Margaret. *Bearing the Word: Language and Female Experience in Nineteenth-Century Women's Writing.* Chicago: University of Chicago Press, 1986.

Home, John. *Douglas.* In *Plays of the Restoration and Eighteenth Century*, ed. Dougald MacMillan and Howard Mumford Jones, 646–72. New York: Henry Holt, 1931.

Howard, Jacqueline. *Reading Gothic Fiction: A Bakhtinian Approach.* Oxford: Clarendon, 1994.

Howells, Coral Ann. *Love, Mystery and Misery: Feeling in Gothic Fiction.* London: Athlone, 1978.

Hufeland, C. W. *Kleine medizinische Schriften.* 4 vols. Berlin: Reimer, 1822–28.

———. *Der Scheintod, oder Sammlung der wichtigsten Thatsachen und Bemerkungen darüber, in alphabetischer Ordnung.* Berlin: Matzdorff, 1808.

Hume, David. *Treatise of Human Nature.* Garden City, N.Y.: Doubleday, 1961.

Jakob, Ludwig Heinrich. *Grundriß der Erfahrungs-Seelen-Lehre.* 1791. 2nd ed. Halle: Hammerde und Schwetschke, 1795.

James, Tony. *Dreams, Creativity, and Madness in Nineteenth-Century France.* Oxford: Clarendon, 1995.

Jephson, Robert. *The Count of Narbonne.* 1781. In *The Plays of Robert Jephson*, ed. Temple James Maynard. New York: Garland, 1980.

Johnson, Anthony. "Gaps and Gothic Sensibility: Walpole, Lewis, Mary Shelley, and Maturin." In *Exhibited by Candlelight: Sources and Developments in the Gothic Tradition*, ed. Valeria Tinkler-Villani and Peter Davidson, with Jane Stevenson, 7–24. Amsterdam: Rodopi, 1995.

Johnson, Claudia. *Equivocal Beings: Politics, Gender, and Sentimentality in the 1790s: Wollstonecraft, Radcliffe, Burney, Austen.* Chicago: University of Chicago Press, 1995.

Kant, Immanuel. *Werke.* Ed. Wilhelm Weischedel. 6 vols. Frankfurt: Insel, 1956–64.

Kaufmann, David. *The Business of Common Life: Novels and Classical Economics Between Revolution and Reform.* Baltimore: Johns Hopkins University Press, 1995.

Kavanagh, Thomas M. *Enlightenment and the Shadows of Chance: The Novel and the Culture of Gambling in Eighteenth-Century France.* Baltimore: Johns Hopkins University Press, 1993.

———. "The Libertine's Bluff: Cards and Culture in Eighteenth-Century France." *Eighteenth-Century Studies* 33 (2000): 505–22.

Kayman, Martin A. "The 'New Sort of Specialty' and the 'New Province of Writing': Bank Notes, Fiction, and the Law in *Tom Jones.*" *ELH* 68 (2001): 633–64.

Kelly, Gary. *English Fiction of the Romantic Period.* London: Longman, 1989.

Kern, Johannes. *Die Lehre von Gott, nach den Grandsätzen der kritischen Philosophie, zum Behuf für angehende Theologen.* Ulm: Wohler, 1796.

Kiely, Robert. *The Romantic Novel in England.* Cambridge, Mass.: Harvard University Press, 1972.

Kierkegaard, Søren. *The Concept of Irony.* Trans. Lee M. Capel. Bloomington: Indiana University Press, 1968.

Kilgour, Maggie. *The Rise of the Gothic Novel.* London: Routledge, 1995.

Kincaid, James R. *Child-Loving: The Erotic Child and Victorian Culture.* New York: Routledge, 1992.

Kinderling, Johann Friedrich August. *Der Somnambulismus unserer Zeit, mit der Incubation oder dem Tempelschlaf und Weissagungstraum der alten Heiden in Vergleichung gestellt.* Dresden: Breitkopf, 1788.

Kittler, Friedrich. *Discourse Networks 1800/1900.* Trans. Michael Metteer. Stanford, Calif.: Stanford University Press, 1990.

Knoepflmacher, U. C. "Mutations of the Wordsworthian Child of Nature." In *Nature and the Victorian Imagination,* ed. U. C. Knoepflmacher and G. B. Tennyson, 391–425. Berkeley: University of California Press, 1977.

Kommerell, Max. "Faust II: Letzte Szene." In *Geist und Buchstabe der Dichtung,* 112–31. Frankfurt am Main: Klostermann, 1956.

Kuhn, Reinhard. *Corruption in Paradise: The Child in Western Literature.* Hanover, N.H.: Brown University Press, 1982.

Kunisch, Hermann. "Theatrum Mundi: Anfang und Schluß von Goethes 'Faust.'" In *Goethe-Studien,* ed. Franz Link, 131–58. Berlin: Duncker und Humblot, 1991.

Lacan, Jacques. *The Four Fundamental Concepts of Psycho-Analysis*. Ed. Jacques-Alain Miller. Trans. Alan Sheridan. New York: Norton, 1981.

———. "Kant avec Sade." In *Ecrits II*, 119–48. Paris: Seuil, 1971.

———. *Speech and Language in Psychoanalysis*. Ed. and trans. Anthony Wilden. Baltimore: Johns Hopkins University Press, 1984.

La Fayette, Mme de. *The Princess of Clèves*. Trans. Walter J. Cobb. New York: Penguin, 1989.

———. *Romans et nouvelles*. Ed. Emile Magne. Paris: Garnier, 1961.

Lepenies, Wolf. *Melancholy and Society*. Trans. Jeremy Gaines and Doris Jones. Cambridge, Mass.: Harvard University Press, 1992.

Levine, George. *The Realist Imagination: English Fiction from Frankenstein to Lady Chatterley*. Chicago: University of Chicago Press, 1981.

Lewis, Matthew G. *The Monk*. Ed. Louis F. Peck. New York: Grove, 1952.

Lipking, Lawrence. "*Frankenstein*, the True Story; or, Rousseau Judges Jean-Jacques." In Mary Shelley, *Frankenstein*, ed. J. Paul Hunter, 313–31. New York: Norton, 1996.

Liu, Alan. "Toward a Theory of Common Sense: Beckford's *Vathek* and Johnson's *Rasselas*." *Texas Studies in Literature and Language* 26 (1984): 183–217.

Lorry, Annaeus-Carolus. *De Melancholia et Morbis Melancholicis*. 2 vols. Lutetiae Parisiorum: Apud P. Guillelmum Cavelier, 1765.

Lyotard, Jean-François. *The Inhuman: Reflections on Time*. Trans. Geoffrey Bennington and Rachel Bowlby [and others]. Stanford, Calif.: Stanford University Press, 1991.

———. "L'Intérêt du sublime." In J. F. Courtine, M. Deguy, J.-F. Lyotard, et al., *Du sublime*, 149–77. Paris: Belin, 1988.

———. "The Sign of History." Trans. Geoff Bennington. In *Post-Structuralism and the Question of History*, ed. Derek Attridge et al., 162–80. Cambridge, Eng.: Cambridge University Press, 1987.

MacAndrew, Elizabeth. *The Gothic Tradition in Fiction*. New York: Columbia University Press, 1979.

"Magnetische Desorganisation in Paris, Straßburg, und Zürch, nebst zwei Schreiben vom Herrn Diakonus Lavater und Herrn Hofmedikus Marcard." *Berlinische Monatsschrift* 6 (1785): 430–49.

Maimon, Salomon. "Einleitung." Γνῶθι Σαυτόν *oder Magazin zur Erfahrungsseelenkunde* 9 (1792): 8–9.

Manley, Delarivier. *The New Atalantis*. Ed. Rosalind Ballaster. New York: New York University Press, 1992.

Marcard, Heinrich Matthias. "Fragment einer medicinischen Abhandlung vom Tode." In *Medicinische Versuche*, 2 vols., 2: 230–44. Leipzig: Weidmanns Erben und Reich, 1778.

Maturin, Charles. *Melmoth the Wanderer*. Ed. Douglas Grant. London: Oxford University Press, 1972.

Mauchart, J. D. *Anhang zu den sechs ersten Bänden des Magazins zur Erfahrungsseelenkunde.* Stuttgart: Erhard und Löflund, 1789.

———. *Phänomene der menschlichen Seele: Eine Materialien-Sammlung zur künftigen Aufklärung in der Erfahrungs-Seelenlehre.* Stuttgart: Erhard und Löflund, 1789.

———. "Über den Sitz der Seele." *Allgemeines Repertorium für empirische Psychologie und verwandte Wissenschaften* 3 (1793): 289–316.

———. "Ueber den eigentlichen Siz des Wahnsinnes." *Allgemeines Repertorium* 2 (1792): 3–51.

May, Franz. *Vermischte Schriften.* Mannheim, 1786.

McLuhan, Marshall, with Wilfred Watson. *From Cliché to Archetype.* New York: Viking, 1970.

Mehrotra, K. K. *Horace Walpole and the English Novel: A Study of the Influence of "The Castle of Otranto," 1764–1820.* Oxford: Blackwell, 1934.

Mellor, Anne K. *Mary Shelley: Her Life, Her Fiction, Her Monsters.* New York: Methuen, 1988.

Miall, David S. "The Preceptor as Fiend: Radcliffe's Psychology of the Gothic." In *Jane Austen and Mary Shelley and Their Sisters,* ed. Laura Dabundon, 31–43. Lanham, Mass.: University Press of America, 2000.

Michelsen, Peter. "Fausts Schlaf und Erwachen." *Jahrbuch des freien deutschen Hochstifts* (1983): 21–61.

Miles, Robert. *Ann Radcliffe: The Great Enchantress.* Manchester: Manchester University Press, 1995.

Miller, J. Hillis. *The Form of Victorian Fiction.* New York: University of Notre Dame Press, 1968.

Mishra, Vijay. *The Gothic Sublime.* Albany: State University of New York Press, 1994.

Modiano, Raimonda. "Words and 'Languageless' Meanings: Limits of Expression in 'The Rime of the Ancient Mariner.'" *Modern Language Quarterly* 38 (1977): 40–61.

Moglen, Helene. "Walpole and the Nightmare of History." In *The Trauma of Gender: A Feminist Theory of the English Novel,* 109–38. Berkeley: University of California Press, 2001.

Monk, Samuel Holt. *The Sublime: A Study of Critical Theories in XVIII-Century England.* Ann Arbor: University of Michigan Press, 1960.

Moritz, Karl Philipp. "Fragmente aus dem Tagebuch eines Beobachters Seinselbst." Γνῶθι Σαυτόν *oder Magazin zur Erfahrungsseelenkunde* 6 (1788): 55–61.

Morris, David A. "Gothic Sublimity." *New Literary History* 16 (1985): 299–319.

Morse, David. *Romanticism: A Structural Analysis.* Totowa, N.J.: Barnes and Noble, 1982.

Müller, Joachim. *Zur Motivstruktur von Goethes "Faust."* Berlin: Akademie, 1972.

Müller-Sievers, Helmut. *Desorientierung: Anatomie und Dichtung bei Georg Büchner.* Göttingen: Wallstein, 2003.

———. *Self-Generation: Biology, Philosophy, and Literature Around 1800.* Stanford, Calif.: Stanford University Press, 1997.

Muratori, Ludwig Anton. *Über die Einbildungsksaft des Menschen,* mit vielen Zusätzen herausgegeben von Georg Hermann Richerz ["edited with copious additions by Georg Hermann Richerz"]. Leipzig: Weygand, 1785.

Nancy, Jean-Luc. *Logodaedalus.* Vol. 1 of *Discours de la syncope.* Paris: Flammarion, 1976.

Napier, Elizabeth. *The Failure of Gothic: Problems of Disjunction in an Eighteenth-Century Literary Form.* Oxford: Clarendon, 1987.

Nasse, [Christian Friedrich]. "Beobachtungen über den Somnambulismus von seiner psychischen Seite." *Beyträge zur Beförderung einer Kurmethode auf psychischem Wege* 2 (1809): 317–36.

Nemoianu, Virgil. *The Taming of Romanticism: European Literature and the Age of Biedermeier.* Cambridge, Mass.: Harvard University Press, 1984.

Nodier, Charles. *"Smarra," "Trilby" et autres contes.* Ed. Jean-Luc Steinmetz. Paris: Garnier, 1980.

Novak, Maximillian. "The Extended Moment: Time, Dream, History, and Perspective in Eighteenth-Century Fiction." In *Probability, Time, and Space in Eighteenth-Century Literature,* ed. Paula R. Backscheider, 141–66. New York: AMS, 1979.

Nudow, Heinrich. *Versuch einer Theorie des Schlafs.* Königsberg: Nicolovius, 1791.

Osinski, Jutta. *Über Vernunft und Wahnsinn: Studien zur literarischen Aufklärung in der Gegenwart und im 18. Jhdt.* Bonn: Bouvier, 1983.

Otway, Thomas. *Venice Preserved; or, A Plot Discovered.* In *Restoration Plays,* ed. Sir Edmund Gosse. London: Dent, 1974.

Pargeter, William. *Theoretisch-praktische Abhandlung über den Wahnsinn.* Leipzig: Johann Friedrich Junius, 1793.

Peacock, Thomas Love. *"Headlong Hall" and "Nightmare Abbey."* Ed. P. M. Yarker. London: Dutton, 1965.

Perry, Ruth. "Incest as the Meaning of the Gothic Novel." *The Eighteenth Century: Theory and Interpretation* 39 (1998): 261–77.

Piclin, Michel. "La Théorie kantienne de la conscience." *Les Etudes philosophiques* 4 (1981): 457–68.

Pinch, Adela. *Strange Fits of Passion: Epistemologies of Emotion, Hume to Austen.* Stanford, Calif.: Stanford University Press, 1996.

Platner, Ernst. "An ridiculum sit, animi sedem inquirere?" In *Opuscula academica,* ed. C. G. Neumann, 341–52. Berlin: Flittner, 1824.

————. *Philosophische Aphorismen.* 2 vols. Leipzig: Schwickert, 1776, 1782.

Plotz, Judith. *Romanticism and the Vocation of Childhood.* New York: Palgrave, 2001.

Polk, Noel. "Trying Not to Say: A Primer on the Language of *The Sound and the Fury.*" In *New Essays on "The Sound and the Fury,"* ed. Noel Polk, 139–75. Cambridge, Eng.: Cambridge University Press, 1993.

Polydorus, Joannes Gulielmus [John Polidori]. *Disputatio medica inauguralis, quaedam de morbo, oneirodynia dicto, complectens.* Edinburg: Robertus Allan, 1815.

Poovey, Mary. "Ideology and 'The Mysteries of Udolpho.'" *Criticism* 21 (1979): 307–30.

Porter, Roy. *Mind-Forg'd Manacles: A History of Madness in England from the Restoration to the Regency.* London: Athlone, 1987.

Poulet, Georges. *Studies in Human Time.* Trans. Elliott Coleman. New York: Harper, 1956.

Praz, Mario. *The Romantic Agony.* Trans. Angus Davidson. London: Oxford University Press, 1970.

Punter, David. *The Literature of Terror: A History of Gothic Fiction from 1765 to the Present Day.* London: Longman, 1980.

Pushkin, A. C. *Sochineniya v trekh Tomakh.* Moscow: Khudozhestvennaia Literatura, 1960.

Radcliffe, Ann. *The Italian.* Ed. Frederick Garber. London: Oxford University Press, 1971.

————. *The Mysteries of Udolpho.* Ed. Bonamy Dobrée. Oxford: Oxford University Press, 1980.

————. *The Romance of the Forest.* London: Routledge, n.d.

Ranger, Paul. *"Terror and Pity Reign in Every Breast": Gothic Drama in the London Patent Theatres, 1750–1820.* London: Society for Theatre Research, 1991.

Redfield, Marc. *Phantom Formations: Aesthetic Ideology and the* Bildungsroman. Ithaca, N.Y.: Cornell University Press, 1996.

————. *The Politics of Aesthetics: Nationalism, Gender, Romanticism.* Stanford, Calif.: Stanford University Press, 2003.

Reil, Johann Christian. *Entwurf einer allgemeinen Pathologie.* Halle: Curt, 1816.

————. "Nachschrift des Herausgebers." *Beyträge zur Beförderung einer Kurmethode auf psychischem Wege* 1 (1808): 592–93.

————. Review of Dav. Veit, *Dissertatio medica. . . . Archiv für die Physiologie* 2 (1797): 505–24.

————. *Rhapsodien über die Anwendung der psychischen Curmethode auf Geisteszerrüttungen.* Halle: Curt, 1803.

————. "Über den Begriff der Medicin und ihre Verzweigungen, besonders in Beziehung auf die Berichtigung der Topik der Psychiaterie [*sic*]." *Beyträge zur Beförderung einer Kurmethode auf psychischem Wege* 1 (1808): 161–279.

———. "Ueber die Lebenskraft." *Archiv für die Physiologie* 1 (1795): 8–162.

———. "Das Zerfallen der Einheit unsers Körpers im Selbstbewusstseyn." *Beyträge zur Beförderung einer Kurmethode auf psychischem Wege* 1 (1808): 550–85.

Reinhold, Karl Leonhard. *Versuch einer neuen Theorie des menschlichen Vorstellungsvermögens.* Darmstadt: Wissenchaftliche Buchgesellschaft, 1963.

Reno, Robert P. "James Boaden's *Fountainville Forest* and Matthew G. Lewis' *The Castle Spectre*: Challenges of the Supernatural Ghost on the Late Eighteenth-Century Stage." *Eighteenth-Century Life*, n.s. 9, no. 1 (Oct. 1984): 95–106.

Richter, David H. *The Progress of Romance: Literary Historiography and the Gothic Novel.* Columbus: Ohio State University Press, 1996.

Richter, Dieter. *Das fremde Kind: Zur Entstehung der Kindheitsbilder des bürgerlichen Zeitalters.* Frankfurt: Fischer, 1987.

Riffaterre, Michael. "Fonction du cliché dans la prose littéraire." In *Essais de stylistique structurale,* trans. Daniel Delas, 161–81. Paris: Flammarion, 1971.

———. *Text Production.* Trans. Terese Lyons. New York: Columbia University Press, 1983.

Robbins, Bruce. *The Servant's Hand: English Fiction from Below.* New York: Columbia University Press, 1986.

Rosenshield, Gary. "Choosing the Right Card: Madness, Gambling, and the Imagination in Pushkin's 'The Queen of Spades.'" *PMLA* 109 (1994): 995–1008.

Rothstein, Eric. *Systems of Order and Inquiry in Later Eighteenth-Century Fiction.* Berkeley: University of California Press, 1975.

Rowe, Nicholas. *The Fair Penitent.* Ed. Malcolm Goldstein. Lincoln: University of Nebraska Press, 1969.

Rupp, G. Ch. "Versuch einer psychologisch-teleologischen Beurtheilung des Träumens." *Allgemeines Repertorium* 1 (1792): 3–13.

Rush, Benjamin, M.D. *Medical Inquiries and Observations of the Mind.* Philadelphia: Kimber and Richardson, 1812.

Schanze, Helmut. "Szenen, Schema, Schwammfamilie: Goethes Arbeitsweise und die Frage der Struktureinheit von *Faust* I und II." *Euphorion* 78 (1984): 383–400.

Schelling, Friedrich. "Kritische Fragmente." *Jahrbücher der Medicin als Wissenschaft* 2 (1807): 283–304.

Schelling, K. E. "Ideen und Erfahrungen über den thierischen Magnetismus." *Jahrbücher der Medicin als Wissenschaft* 2 (1806): 3–46.

Schleiermacher, F. E. D. *Hermeneutik und Kritik*. Ed. Manfred Frank. Frankfurt: Suhrkamp, 1977.

Schmid, Carl Christian Erhard. "Abriß der Metaphysik der innern Natur." *Psychologisches Magazin* 3 (1798): 294–353.

———. *Empirische Psychologie*. Jena: Cröker, 1791.

———. "Über das Gehirn als Seelenorgan." *Psychologisches Magazin* 3 (1798): 102–11.

———. *Wörterbuch zum leichteren Gebrauch der Kantischen Schriften*. Jena: Cröker, 1788.

Schmidt, Jochen. "Die 'katholische Mythologie' und ihre mystische Entmythologisierung in der Schlußszene des *Faust II*." *Jahrbuch der deutschen Schillergesellschaft* 34 (1990): 230–56.

Sedgwick, Eve Kosofsky. *Between Men: English Literature and Male Homosocial Desire*. New York: Columbia University Press, 1985.

———. "The Character in the Veil: Imagery of the Surface in the Gothic Novel." *PMLA* 96 (1981): 255–70.

———. "Jane Austen and the Masturbating Girl." In *Tendencies* 109–29. Durham, N.C.: Duke University Press, 1993.

Selle, D. Christian Gottlob. *Grundsätze der reinen Philosophie*. Berlin: Himburg, 1788.

———. "Versuch eines Beweises, daß es keine reine von der Erfahrung unabhängige Vernunftbegriffe gebe." *Berlinische Monatsschrift* 4 (1784): 565–75.

Serres, Michel. "Turner Translates Carnot." Trans. Marilyn Sides. In *Hermes: Literature, Science, Philosophy*, ed. Josué V. Harari and David F. Bell, 54–62. Baltimore: Johns Hopkins University Press, 1982.

Shelley, Mary Wollstonecraft. *Frankenstein*. Vol. 1 of *Novels and Selected Works*, ed. Nora Crook. London: Pickering, 1996.

———. *Frankenstein*. New York: Airmont, 1963.

———. *The Frankenstein Notebooks*. Ed. Charles E. Robinson. New York: Garland, 1996. 2 vols., continuously paginated.

———. *Selected Letters*. Ed. Betty T. Bennett. Baltimore: Johns Hopkins University Press, 1995.

———. *Valperga; or, The Life and Adventures of Castruccio, Prince of Lucca*. Ed. Stuart Curran. New York: Oxford University Press, 1977.

Sherwin, Paul. "*Frankenstein*: Creation as Catastrophe." *PMLA* 96 (1981): 883–903.

Sömmerring, Samuel Thomas von. *Über das Organ der Seele*. Königsberg: Nicolovius, 1796.

Spurzheim, J. G., M.D. *Observations on the Deranged Manifestations of the Mind, or Insanity*. London: Baldwin, Cradock, and Joy, 1817.

Staiger, Emil. *Goethe*. 3 vols. Zurich: Atlantis, 1957–59.

Starr, G. Gabrielle. *Lyric Generations: Poetry and the Novel in the Long Eighteenth Century.* Baltimore: Johns Hopkins University Press, 2004.

Steedman, Carolyn. *Strange Dislocations: Childhood and the Idea of Human Interiority 1780–1930.* London: Virago, 1995.

Stevenson, John. *The British Novel, Defoe to Austen: A Critical History.* Boston: Twayne, 1990.

Stone, Lawrence. *The Family, Sex and Marriage in England 1500–1800.* New York: Harper, 1977.

Stroup, Thomas B. "Supernatural Beings in Restoration Drama." *Anglia* 61 (1937): 186–92.

Todorov, Tzvetan. *The Fantastic: A Structural Approach to a Literary Genre.* Trans. Richard Howard. Cleveland: Case Western Reserve University Press, 1973.

Trăn-Dúc-Tháo. *Phénoménologie et matérialisme dialectique.* Paris: Minh-Tân, 1951.

Veeder, William. *Mary Shelley and Frankenstein: The Fate of Androgyny.* Chicago: University of Chicago Press, 1986.

Voller, Jack G. *The Supernatural Sublime: The Metaphysics of Terror in Anglo-American Romanticism.* DeKalb: Northern Illinois University Press, 1994.

Voltaire. *Théâtre.* Paris: Garnier, n.d.

Walpole, Horace. *The Castle of Otranto.* New York: Cromwell-Collier, 1968.

———. *The Castle of Otranto.* In *Three Gothic Novels*, ed. Peter Fairclough, 37–148. Harmondsworth, Eng.: Penguin, 1968.

———. *Correspondence.* 48 vols. Ed. Wilmarth Sheldon Lewis et al. New Haven, Conn.: Yale University Press, 1937–83.

———. *Works.* 5 vols. London: G. G. and J. Robinson and J. Edwards, 1798.

Walvin, James. *A Child's World: A Social History of English Childhood 1800–1914.* New York: Penguin, 1982.

Ware, Malcolm. "The Telescope Reversed: Ann Radcliffe and Natural Scenery." In *A Provision of Human Nature: Essays on Fielding and Others in Honor of Miriam Austin Locke*, ed. Donald Kay, 169–89. University: University of Alabama Press, 1977.

Watt, Ian. *The Rise of the Novel: Studies in Defoe, Richardson and Fielding.* Berkeley: University of California Press, 1967.

Watt, James. *Contesting the Gothic: Fiction, Genre and Cultural Conflict, 1764–1832.* Cambridge, Eng.: Cambridge University Press, 1999.

Webber, Andrew J. *The Doppelgänger: Double Visions in German Literature.* Oxford: Clarendon, 1996.

Weber, Samuel. *Unwrapping Balzac: A Reading of "La Peau de Chagrin."* Toronto: University of Toronto Press, 1979.

Weder, Christine. "Der Schwindel des Phantastischen. Zu einer Chiffre der

Überforderung bei E. T. A. Hoffmann—im Vergleich mit der medizinischen Theorie von Marcus Herz." *Colloquium Helveticum*, no. 33 (2002): 195–215.

Weikard, Melchior Adam. *Der philosophische Arzt.* 3 vols. Frankfurt am Main: Andreä, 1790–99.

Weissberg, Liliane. *Geistersprache: Philosophischer und literarischer Diskurs im späten achtzehnten Jahrhundert.* Würzberg: Königshausen und Neumann, 1990.

Whitmore, Charles. *The Supernatural in Tragedy.* Cambridge, Mass.: Harvard University Press, 1915.

Williams, Anne. *Art of Darkness: A Poetics of Gothic.* Chicago: University of Chicago Press, 1995.

Wilt, Judith. *Ghosts of the Gothic: Austen, Eliot, and Lawrence.* Princeton, N.J.: Princeton University Press, 1981.

Wizenmann, Thomas. "An den Herrn Professor Kant von dem Verfasser der Resultate Jakobischer und Mendelssohnscher Philosophie." *Deutsches Museum*, Feb. 1787: 116–56.

Wolstenholme, Susan. *Gothic (Re)visions: Writing Women as Readers.* Albany: State University of New York Press, 1993.

Young, Robert M. *Mind, Brain, and Adaptation in the Nineteenth Century: Cerebral Localization and Its Biological Context from Gall to Ferrier.* New York: Oxford University Press, 1970.

Zimmermann, Johann Georg. *Ueber die Einsamkeit.* 4 vols. Leipzig: Weidmann, 1784–85.

Žižek, Slavoj. *The Sublime Object of Ideology.* London: Verso, 1989.

INDEX